THE EMPIRE'S OLD CLOTHES

WHAT THE LONE RANGER,
BABAR, AND OTHER INNOCENT
HEROES DO TO OUR MINDS

ARIEL DORFMAN

PENGUIN BOOKS

PENGUIN BOOKS
Published by the Penguin Group
Penguin Books USA Inc., 375 Hudson Street, New York, New York 10014, U.S.A.
Penguin Books Ltd, 27 Wrights Lane, London W8 5TZ, England
Penguin Books Australia Ltd, Ringwood, Victoria, Australia
Penguin Books Canada Ltd, 10 Alcorn Avenue, Toronto, Ontario, Canada M4V 3B2
Penguin Books (N.Z.) Ltd, 182–190 Wairau Road, Auckland 10, New Zealand

Penguin Books Ltd, Registered Offices: Harmondsworth, Middlesex, England

First published in the United States of America by Pantheon Books,
a division of Random House, Inc. 1983
Published in Penguin Books 1996

10 9 8 7 6 5 4 3 2 1

"Of Elephants and Ducks," "The Lone Ranger's Last Ride," and "The Infantilization
of the Adult Reader" are translated by Clark Hansen.

THE LIBRARY OF CONGRESS HAS CATALOGUED THE HARDCOVER AS FOLLOWS:
Dorfman, Ariel.
The empire's old clothes.
Includes bibliographical references.
1. Popular literature.   2. Literature—Psychology.
I. Title.
PN56.P55D66   1983   801´.92   82–48954
ISBN 0-394-52723-2 (hc.)
ISBN 0 14 02.5637 7 (pbk.)

Printed in the United States of America
Set in New Caledonia

For Rodrigo and Joaquín

CONTENTS

PREFACE

INDUSTRIALLY PRODUCED FICTION has become one of the primary shapers of our emotions and our intellect in the twentieth century. Although these stories are supposed merely to entertain us, they constantly give us a secret education. We are not only taught certain styles of violence, the latest fashions, and sex roles by TV, movies, magazines, and comic strips; we are also taught how to succeed, how to love, how to buy, how to conquer, how to forget the past and suppress the future. We are taught, more than anything else, how not to rebel.

The overriding influence of this kind of fiction has been increasingly recognized, and yet there has also been a tendency to avoid scrutinizing these mass media products too closely, to avoid asking the sort of hard questions that can yield disquieting answers. It is not strange that this should be so. The industry itself has declared time and again with great forcefulness that it is innocent, that no hidden motives or implications are lurking behind the cheerful faces it generates.

This book starts from another sort of assumption. It explores some of the major cultural myths of our time as they have been expressed in popular comic books and magazines, and tries to map out their concealed social and political messages. This can be a painful process. To get rid of old clothes, clothes that are comfortable, that wear well, that hold pleasant memories, is not easy. All too often our bodies have adapted to these clothes and taken on their form, their color, their smell. It is as if they had become our skin and we had been born with them. People have grown accustomed, in the Western world, to consider as absolutely natural and beyond reproach the ways in which reality is interpreted and conflicts are neutralized by figures and institutions like Babar the Elephant, Donald Duck, the *Reader's Digest*, and the Lone Ranger. By asking readers to take another long—and mischievous—look at these cultural products, I am in fact challenging them to look at their own selves and their society with eyes newer than their clothing. I can only hope that their old clothes, and their old lives, will never feel quite the same.

Ariel Dorfman
Washington, D.C.
October 1982

ONE

Childhood as Under-development

THESE ESSAYS WERE originally written for someone whose name and face I cannot remember. She was a slum dweller, a woman whom I only met twice, years ago, in Chile.

Even then, I didn't notice anything special about her. Misery has a way of leveling individual nuances. In recollection, therefore, she turns into a blurred picture. She was very poor, and lived in one of the numerous shantytowns that mushroom around all big cities in Latin America. They brim with migrant workers and their families. She, like them, had built a small shack out of any stray sort of material that life had washed within her reach. I vaguely recall that she had children, and there must have been many of them. The rest is conjecture, almost a sociological construct, valid for her as for so many other women living in those subhuman conditions. Filth, disease, hunger, and a husband who was unemployed, alcoholic, or plagued by worse demons. Or maybe no husband at all. I just don't remember.

But what she said to me on the two separate occasions when we talked still rings clear. An intellectual, I suppose, remembers words better than people.

She came up to me and asked quite frankly if it was true that I thought people shouldn't read photo novels. Photo novels are just like comics, but instead of using drawings, they convey their romantic love stories through photographs peopled by handsome actors. When she asked me the question, I was digging a ditch. I had come to that shanty town with my students in order to help after a severe thunderstorm had left everything a sea of mud. They had been talking to the slum dwellers and had informed this particular woman of my crusade against the industrial products of fiction. Comics, soap operas, westerns, radio and TV sitcoms, love songs, films of violence—you name it—I had it under scrutiny.

So I stopped digging and answered her. It was true. I thought that photo novels were a hazard to her health and her future.

She did not seem to feel any special need for purification. "Don't do that to us, *compañerito*," she said in a familiar, almost tender way. "Don't take my dreams away from me."

We were unable—and now I suspect I understand the reasons— to convince each other. She wanted, she needed, to dream. I wanted to dissect those dreams, the ones that had nourished my childhood and adolescence, that continued to infect so many of my adult habits and simply would not disappear. I wanted to discover the underlying principles of the buried behavioral models which simmered inside me. But there were other, more significant, reasons for what I was doing. I believed that these models and illusions clashed head-on with the immediate needs of their consumers. This was especially so in a land like Chile, which imported most of these forms of entertainment or simply imitated them in bastardized local versions. We imported our weapons, our machinery, our banking techniques, our freeways, our technology. We also imported much of our popular culture. But this was of little importance to the woman in front of me. She required those illusions in order to survive. She had to make up somehow for what was missing in her life, and she didn't mind—or care—if she was being manipulated. So what sort of conversation could we hold, if I couldn't offer her any concrete alternative or substitute for those myths? Between the nakedness of her urgent, practical needs and my own psychological and intellectual needs there was not much room, or chance, for a fruitful dialogue.

Some months later, as will happen from time to time, history stepped into our lives, and that dialogue became possible—indeed, imperative: In September 1970, Salvador Allende was elected president of Chile.

Her attitude, and mine, were about to be modified.

A few years went by—that would make it 1972 or the beginning of 1973—and I returned to that same part of town for some sort of inauguration. It might have been a neighborhood clinic or an alphabetization center. (There were many buildings and events in those days.) By chance, I ran into that woman again. I didn't recognize her at first, but she remembered me. She came up to me, just like that, and announced that I was right, that she didn't read "trash" anymore. Then she added a phrase which still haunts me. "Now, *compañero*, we are dreaming reality."

She had experienced, in those years, something truly different. She had outdistanced her old self, and was no longer entertained by those images which had been her own true love. She could now oppose her experience of liberation, and that of her community, to the fraudulent visions of the media, run and owned by the same people who ran and owned Chile's economy and political system. She no longer perceived those media experiences as real, as eternal, as natural.

Of course, what had happened to her was happening to everybody. When a people attempts to liquidate centuries' worth of economic and social injustice, when they begin to gain a sense of their dignity as a nation, what is really at stake, what really inspires them, is an alternate vision of humanity, a different way of feeling and thinking and projecting and loving and keeping faith. And a different future. Allende's government nationalized our natural resources and minerals, reallocated the land to those who tilled it, allowed workers to participate in the management of their own factories, and democratized most of society's institutions. But that was not enough. Simultaneously we had to democratize and control a territory more difficult to split up and expropriate, a territory called communication.

That woman from the slums was being shoved, poked, awakened. And while she was in that turbulent, searching stage, what she needed was a parallel interpretation at all levels of what her situation, of what the world, was. Not just a political explanation of why things were one way and how they might be transformed, but channels for expressing the joys, the doubts, the anxieties that come when people who were previously powerless begin to have some say in their existence. What she needed was a new language.

The Chilean people and its intellectuals tried to produce that new language, or at least fragments, intimations of it. We had always proclaimed that here was one task the dispossessed could not postpone. They had to take control of the production of their own ideas and gain access to the means and methods which would help them

5

communicate with one another. The task could not be postponed, and yet it was, time and again. Without effective outlets, resources, industries, what else could be done but patiently fabricate with the scantest of means an extended, almost subterranean network of cultural visions?

Allende's victory gave this enterprise a real grounding, and a vaster dimension. At least, what had previously been declared by generations of politicians and intellectuals to be urgent and unavoidable could now be put into practice. The economic transformations had placed in the hands of the government and the workers the industrial tools and human resources necessary to attempt a profound alteration of mass culture's fictional outgrowths. There were printing presses, record companies, television and radio programs available. For the first time, it was within our means to conceive and explore far-reaching creative alternatives to existing mass-market fictions. I was personally involved in producing new comic books, in inexpensive paperback literature sold on newsstands, a series of TV programs, a magazine for adolescents.

The problems the people involved in this undertaking had to solve were gigantic. How to subtly use and change publications, programs, and formats which already had a following; how to create new messages without making them into propaganda; how to find new ways of distribution and getting feedback; how to stimulate contributions from a generally passive audience. And how to do all this without losing money.

Among all these pressing matters, one in particular attracted me. In order to change a structure, it became necessary to understand it, to examine the manner in which these prevailing fantasies functioned. Why did these widespread myths enjoy such an immense success among the very people whose daily practices should have called them into question?

These essays were conceived as one of many responses to that need. So, during their first incarnation, they were born for eminently practical reasons. The purpose of investigations such as these, and books like *How to Read Donald Duck* (which I co-authored with the Belgian sociologist Matelart), was to expose the mechanisms behind those industrialized works of fiction, strip them of their mystery, or lay bare their secret structures. To do so, we felt, would assist in the elaboration of another sort of communications system which would reject authoritarian and competitive models and provoke doubts, questions, dialogue, real participation, and, eventually, a breakthrough in popular art.

But the essays transcended their utilitarian ends. If this were not so, it wouldn't make much sense to present them ten years later to foreign readers. I believe that those irreverent views still retain their relevance. Once you have penetrated the invisible network of everyday domination which lurks behind the genres and characters analyzed here (children's mass literature of assorted varieties, superheroes, the infantilization of knowledge in magazines such as *Reader's Digest*), you are left with something far more valuable than a mere guidebook on how to read popular culture. What unfolds before us is a veritable black-and-blueprint of the ways in which men and women repress themselves in contemporary society, the way they transform reality's unsettling questions into docile, comforting, bland answers.

It is this inadvertent process of self-censorship that is meant to be revealed by a book like this one. And such a process does not happen only in Chile. On the contrary, if people in the so-called Third World are expected to swallow these deformed versions of reality (along with heavier goods and foreign technology), it is because those messages have been produced by the "developed" countries in the first place and injected into their populace in hardly more sophisticated forms. The same methods which the cultural industry uses to narrate, observe, transmit problems in Europe and especially in the U.S. are those which, with minor modifications and at times adaptations, are imported into our miserable and twisted zones.

Their point of view is supposed to be accepted as the universally valid means of human measurement, definition, and perspective, the only one by which we can see ourselves in the global mirror. I'll go deeper into this subject as the book progresses, but it is worth noting here that this imposition is possible, among other reasons, because within their own borders the industrial nations have already colonized their own conflicting social strata—their minorities, their

7

women, their working classes, their immigrants, their unruly and rebellious elements. The Third World of humanity is just a filthy, undesirable, oversized, underdeveloped brother to the fourth, fifth, sixth, and infinite contradictory worlds which teem within the frontiers of the "advanced" nations.

Among all these subordinate worlds there is one, however, which might be more important than all the rest, which might be the only universal world, and which constitutes the axis of all processes of domination: namely, the world of children. No matter whether a country is oozing with opulence or on the path to pauperdom, the new generation is always required to accept the status quo of their parents, comfortably, devoutly, and without interruption, at the same time learning to judge and pre-interpret every rupture and rift in reality with the same indisputable assumptions used by their forefathers.

Since those communities, classes, races, continents, and individuals who don't fit the official mold tend to be viewed as "children," as incomplete beings who haven't yet reached the age of maturity, it is children's literature, or the infantilization of mass market adult literature, which forms the basis for the entire process of cultural domination. Henry Kissinger, the whiz kid of international politics, put it in those terms when he justified the intervention of the CIA in the overthrow of my country's legitimate president by saying, "I don't see why we need to stand by and watch a country go Communist due to the irresponsibility of its own people."

Obviously, irresponsible people and "children"—begging Kissinger's pardon—have at times been known to contribute something besides their raw materials or overworked muscles to our heritage. Sometimes we manage to come up with original ways of viewing a world hardened, stratified, overweened by its own power, a world which believes itself as omnipotent as its technological achievements might seem to imply. It is possible that a society undergoing rebirth, that is painfully casting off the habits of domination and tradition which before went unquestioned, could be able, with more rigor, more rage, more insight, to criticize the patterns and structures which, as their own champions victoriously proclaim, have been standardized and uniformly spread throughout the planet. It is possible that the way to look at these patterns is to try to remove them like a layer of clothing which you had all along thought to be your own skin. Indeed, there may be no better way for a country to know itself than to examine the myths and popular symbols that it exports to its economic and military dominions.

This is an insolent point of view, an underdog, ironic, proud point of view. It drifts through the essays. It can be attributed to many causes. I felt absolutely certain, when I first wrote these essays, that our victory was just around the corner, and that our language should anticipate the glorious command we expected to have over our own existence. Or maybe that insolence derives from the sheer, almost animal pleasure of defiantly reinterpreting reality, after centuries—or at least decades, as far as I was concerned—of submission. An outsider who suddenly ceases to be a passive producer and consumer and finds himself thrust into active participation in history tends to feel as if he could battle and deride the gods themselves.

When I began to rewrite these essays, therefore, along with preserving the essence of their revelations about the mass media, I was even more interested in keeping, and in fact prolonging, the stubborn, blasphemous tone with which these ideas first glowed.

Indeed, I believed that they might be published for the foreign-language reader with only some minor retouching. After all, working on something you wrote years ago can be a harrowing experience. It can become a double assassination: First you kill the father you once were, that work which is older and more venerable than we are, which paved the way for your contemporary outlook; and then you kill your own son, the ideas you had when you were younger, a part of yourself which you should not be tampering with. In short—since this is a book which abounds in family metaphors— an act of both patricide and fratricide.

So if I have decided to revise these essays thoroughly, it was because it could not be avoided. In some cases it was merely a matter of updating the material or taking into consideration the latest bibliography. Instead of examining the 1971 *Reader's Digest*, for example, I reviewed the twelve issues that came out in 1981, ten years later, plus an extra one from 1980.

But more than an update was necessary.

Originally, the essays were written under stress, amidst the pressures of everyday life in Chile. We wrote, when we did write, at a furious, infuriating pace, at life's intersections and in its crannies, amidst emergencies, diapers, and routine work. We wrote when we returned at two or three in the morning from a *rayado mural* (painting the town's walls with artistic and political slogans). We wrote in the early morning hours before giving a class or planning a program for television. We wrote during those few moments when we felt we could—sweating with guilt—steal some time from other activities.

If during that era they bore with honor the stamp of their hasty gestation, it is important, now that I have the misfortune of living in a situation where most of what I then undertook is impossible and faraway, to calmly construct, with the care they deserve, a more cohesive whole, searching out the interrelations between the different subjects and pursuing each point to its ultimate conclusion.

But there are other changes.

The first edition of this book came out before General Pinochet, with the blessing of such responsible adults as Henry Kissinger, turned my country into a laboratory where multinational corporations could conduct experiments on the solution to the international economic crisis. Those essays, by meticulously inspecting the messages we devour daily, anticipated all the hidden weight of domination which would finally come out into the savage open as soon as the military decided to remodel the nation and put the "house" in order. But I don't think that my analyses were able to fully appreciate how deeply rooted our myths are in the mind of the common man and woman, how tenaciously they cling to their dreams when someone tries to shatter them, or how easy it is for those in power, once they feel threatened, to make use of that arsenal of ready-made ideas to convince and mobilize potential followers.

In a crisis situation there is a decisive tendency, as my people discovered against their will, to embrace and promote the most irrational and authoritarian solutions, searching for salvation through the deification of that which is supposed to be the eternal human condition and which in point of fact is a constellation of traditional values which have been handed down and drilled into us over the years. These are the values of a social class: Its members impose their views on their subordinates. The fear of the unknown, of losing your identity, of having to undergo changes in your familiar landscape, encourages the repression of everyone else as well as the repression of your own doubts. The propositions of the neoconservative crusade, which appears to be gaining momentum as we enter the decade of the eighties, have been fertilized in advance by industrial culture and the unconscious conduct which it prescribes. The added political importance and influence of the fictional experiences I was reanalyzing had, therefore, to be taken into account.

But it wasn't only the world that had changed. Once I got down to the arduous task of rewriting the essays, they forced me to admit that I had changed as well.

When I originally worked on them, I felt I had all the answers. In a sense, for that historical moment, I did. We did. Even when we didn't, the fact that we were sure enough about our intentions and what we were fighting for, the fact that the ruling groups had made such a mess of everything and were such a failure at providing the basics of life for the great majority, helped us to take a stand and rebel against the way things were. When attempting to modify society and injustice so radically, there may be no other way of proceeding initially, if one wants massive support, than to seek some clear and clean answers, some guidelines. We constructed our social movement, and our intellect, with the materials we had at hand.

But these years of exile and defeat have taught me some new things. It is essential, above all, to go beyond the sphere of those who are already convinced. Not because you want to entice them into a trap, sweeten them up so they don't know they're secretly being radicalized, but because if you are right, they can be convinced. And without them you really can't change the world. And, more important for a writer, to take their obstinate point of view into account is to ensure permanent criticism and revision of your own position. Their resistance requires the use of a language more refined, perhaps less abrupt, a language which distrusts formulas and dogmas, which avoids the dictionary of the absolute, which has to justify itself with those who do not nod in instant agreement.

I have also been discovering and exploring, through my poetry and fiction, that jungle which each of us can become. These violent undergrowths of imaginary characters are successful because in our own inner provinces and sewers, they match and accompany certain deep-seated tendencies and fears. These internal contradictions will not disappear with a simple change in the ownership of the means of production. Naturally, I continue to believe that the external and material circumstances in which this kind of behavior is produced have a tremendous impact on the way we act, and that it is cardinal to have the majority control the process and all the links in the chain whereby they can communicate. But I am also certain now that Superman and his buddies will stubbornly try to persist in all the errors and recrimination, the envy and the sloganeering, the fears and pettiness, the prejudices against sex, race, and age which are repeated like a broken record from generation to generation.

When we sum up all these changes, they mean that my style and my emphasis have shifted, my attitudes and perceptions are not the same as ten years ago.

But there is a limit to such alterations. No matter how far removed these essays seem from their native land, no matter how removed from the people and the historical moment which forced me to rethink the way I habitually looked at the world, I would not want them to forget their origins. I refuse to eliminate from these pages the disturbing presence of that woman, that slum dweller, for whom, after all, they were really intended.

What has become of her?

It is better not to ask that question. I would rather not wonder about her, about her children, about what happened to her newfound dignity, about what she could be pondering now, once again surrounded by filth and disease—that person who one day announced to me that she was tired of living on trash and another day heard the sound of military boots in her neighborhood and realized that she was no longer allowed to think—let alone live or work—for herself.

What has become of her?

It is unlikely that she got out of Chile, as I was able to do. It is usually difficult for the poor, lost deep within the caverns of their age-old exile from power and knowledge, even to consider that more visible and physical exile which is the body's emigration to a less hostile climate.

I remember neither her face nor her name.

But I would hope that her image and her demand for a new kind of fiction, a new kind of world, would invade and possess every opinion I have poured into this volume. I would hope that these remodeled essays continue to be faithful to her and to the interests of her descendants. Because in contrast to the characters tarred and feathered on the following pages, people like her remind people like us that we have the obligation to change the course of history (as well as that of stories) if we are to survive and grow.

At this point authors usually beg their reader's indulgence.

Instead, the only thing I ask of my new readers—those of you who cast a glance at these words written a decade ago so that women like her would one day be as ubiquitous as Superman—all I ask, as you read these words in a language she would not understand is simply this: Please bear in mind, while you read, that illiterate woman who had the courage to dream reality.

TWO

Of Elephants and Ducks

ONCE UPON A TIME, there were two children in a faraway land. One day their mother made up a story, as mothers sometimes do, about a little elephant.

This particular character, however, was not destined to be forgotten like so many other clumsy and adorable animals that inhabit the stories spun at the edge of the bed before the lights go out. This elephant would make a greater name for himself and attract a much more significant audience.

It just so happens that the children's father was a painter, and once he had baptized the elephant with the name Babar, he proceeded to illustrate his life in a series of children's books which would one day achieve worldwide acclaim.[1] Babar, owing to his peculiar education and ties to the world of men, would become king of the elephants and redeem and transform his country. On the other hand, even though the painter would not be crowned a king among men, he would, because of his tender, sensual, and simple style, come to be regarded as one of the princes of children's literature.

When the story is told like that—as the triumphant march of a character and his author—and recreated like a legend or a fairy tale, it could not seem more innocent and less worthy of critical analysis.

Babar is born like any average pachyderm. He grows up and plays in an idyllic world, along with the other little animals. Nonetheless, this primitive paradise must come to an end once a "wicked hunter" kills Babar's mother. But even though this initial contact with human adults and their civilization is negative—leaving Babar an orphan—the end result of such destructive activity turns out to be highly beneficial: Babar escapes to the bedazzling city, where fate rewards him with something even greater than what it had taken from him. He comes upon an "Old Lady," a female figure who takes his mother's place and eventually adopts him.

From that moment on, Babar is going to "progress." His initial desire is to be "well-dressed," and the Old Lady gives him all the money he needs. In the first few pictures he walks on four feet, but no sooner has he lost his horizontal nakedness and seen his clothed twin in a mirror, than he becomes aware of his stature, his skin, his clothes. Babar rises up on two feet. He mimics men and begins to adopt biped mannerisms. That is when his education begins. Somehow, without losing his animal appearance, Babar will be transformed into a polite and decent human being. He uses a napkin, sleeps in a bed, does exercises, has his picture taken, bathes in a tub with a sponge, drives his own car, and dresses in the latest fashions. He's a pampered elephant, because the Old Lady "gives him whatever he wants." Babar responds by leaving behind the ignorance of his instincts, following the teachings and examples of the world that has given him refuge, and learning how to behave in the proper manner. He also picks up some practical skills: A learned professor comes to teach him how to read and write, add and subtract, and interpret history and geography.

Could there be anything less pernicious?

Young readers are encouraged to conduct themselves in a similar manner: They should be obedient and intelligent, have good manners, get dressed by themselves, and eat with a knife and fork. Supposedly the child starts from the same point as Babar, free from social influences, and only gradually begins to lose his savage and ignorant ways in order to become a responsible member of society. He crawls on all fours and then, still babbling, begins to walk. One innocent identifies with another, and together they grow up. But be careful: There's more to this process than mere socialization. In a corner of the picture in which the learned professor teaches Babar 4 + 3, there is a map of the world where one can distinguish the continent known by its Greek name: Africa.

At this point in the story it is necessary to furnish the reader with a few uncomfortable historical facts. The year in which this charming tale was written was not once upon a time but 1931. And in case the reader did not already know, it should be added that fifty years ago the countries of Africa—the supposed land of the elephants—had not yet achieved their independence. They were still colonies.

This is why Babar is something more than a child growing up. In contrast to his tiny admirers—first they were French, then British, then North American—he is dealing with a native country that has not evolved along with him and continues to be primitive, tribal, and naked. It is out of that reality—or more precisely, out of those areas of his personality which can never be suppressed or erased, out of that ever present animality—that emissaries come to seek him out. There appear before him two totally naked little elephants. And although it may seem indecent in this childlike atmosphere, let us emphasize the word "naked."

That first contact between the now civilized (we might even say adult) Babar and the other elephants, who are like reflections of the way he once was, prophetically synthesizes the future of the country in which they all were born, for his cousins are immediately absorbed into the Old Lady's sphere of influence. She dresses them, and as a reward for having taken their first wobbly steps, they all go and have some cake. As Mary Poppins sings in the Walt Disney film, "Just a spoonful of sugar helps the medicine go down."

The time has now come for that medicine, with its domesticating sweetness, to be sent back to the jungle. There's no danger that Babar will revert to his primitive ways. As demonstrated by the rapid conversion of his cousins, this type of education is contagious. From now on, every inferior place or person will either follow Babar's example or remain condemned to immobility, regression, and ridicule.

Such is the case when they leave Paris, all dressed up and perched victoriously with their suitcases on top of a car. Horns blaring and people cheering, they seem like tourists off to some out-of-the-way place. But who could that be behind them, running on all fours, choking on the dust churned up by the automobile? Could it be two big elephants?

Sure enough, it's . . . the mothers of the two rascals who, it seems, had escaped from the jungle without asking permission. Their mothers have been looking for them. In a pedagogical book such as this, in which the virtues of submission and respect for one's elders are extolled, such disobedience cannot go unpunished. So, during their first confrontation with their unruly children, (in a previous scene) the irate mothers scold the two little elephants, who show themselves to be repentant and contrite. However, once this elevated ethical function has been performed, things change. The youngsters are now fully clothed and upright, while the good ladies who supposedly brought them into the world still look at the horizon horizontally—and in the buff, to boot. They must run behind the vehicle that carries their progeny farther in the direction of progress.

This is the last time we shall see them. Whereas Babar's mother was eliminated by a depraved hunter, the mothers of Celeste and Arthur will be exterminated with more kindness and less trauma. They will be forgotten like so many others who did not know how to respond fast enough to the modern artifacts offered them by history. The painter's brush will simply omit them.

In contrast, the narrator tells us as Babar leaves that "he would never forget the Old Lady."

He's going to need her. For the king of the elephants has died accidentally. He's eaten a poisonous mushroom, proving himself stupid and ineffectual by doing something even the youngest readers would be careful not to do. The three oldest elephants get together to choose a new king. They are "extremely upset"; it is an "ill-fated day"; "what a calamity." Such are the circumstances of Babar's arrival like some kind of Messiah who will solve their problems.

Actually, the only difference between the previous king of the elephants and everyone else was the crown he wore on his head; but if he (presumably the very best of the elephants) behaves so irresponsibly, what are we to expect from the rest of them? The new ruler must come from the outside, a native instructed in the ways of men.

While the older elephants frantically deliberate, Babar has just left that prestigious town (complete with houses, a plaza, airplanes, a church, cars, monuments, and neatly planted fields in the background), bearing all the illustrious signs of his ties to that world. His reception in Elephantland is overwhelming. "What beautiful clothes you're wearing! What a lovely car!" Compared to the large undifferentiated mass of gray which greets them, Babar, Celeste, and Arthur stand out because of their defined personalities. They've got color, movement, and savoir faire—the upright, external signs of their assimilation of the values, objects, and concepts of the fascinating and unknown universe of Homo sapiens. In a barbaric world such as this, where everyone is naive and defenseless, Babar's proximity to the Western cosmos (the adult cosmos), to the illustrious center, now and in future episodes will become the foundation of his investiture, the fount of his regency. And that's just how Cornelius, the oldest and wisest of the elephants, sees it when he suggests that they crown Babar: "He's learned so much in the city." The other elephants agree because Cornelius has spoken like a book—in other words, like a cultural object laden with authority and wisdom, which men control and elephants do not.[2] At the outset, Cornelius is distinguished from his colleagues by a pair of spectacles. This small sign of urbanity singles him out for his function as interpreter or mediator, making him similar to the first blacks or Indians who had to learn the language of their conquerors.

Cornelius's reward isn't far behind. "You have good ideas," Babar tells him, even though the only one he's had was to proclaim the new arrival king. "I will therefore make you general, and when I get my crown, I will give you my hat." Whoever helps to place him in power is rewarded with the distinguishing features of civilization and the privileges that pertain to it. Babar imitates men. Cornelius imitates Babar. Eventually everyone will imitate Cornelius. The entire country will have to elevate itself. So the first thing Babar does to legitimize his pretension to the throne isn't surprising. He tells "the dromedary to go to the town and buy some beautiful wedding clothes." During the celebration that follows—which is also a wedding reception, since Babar is marrying the only female to equal him in hierarchy or status, his cousin Celeste—all the invited animals (mouse, lizard, hippopotamus, leopard, lion, rhinoceros, giraffe, and, naturally, the elephants) get up on two legs for the first time and dance. Although they are still naked, they are already transfigured. They are already beginning to raise their condition, seeking the elevation that is Babar's obsession. Gradually, they will shed their animal condition.

And on this dancing note, the first book of Babar ends.[3]

One might think that we are confronted with a structure that has its antecedents in children's literature and folklore; one which, from the dawn of time, has nourished the incessant dream of running away from home, on the condition that the prodigal or reluctant son not forget his homeland. One day he must return, having matured and acquired some device or special magic that aids him in saving his family or country.[4]

But this child's dream—the need to imagine alternatives to desertion, to explore the adult world, and to externalize the life of the psyche—does not take shape in a vacuum. It is nourished by history. In an age such as ours, in which there exists so much inequality between opposing societies and nations (not to mention individuals), and in which, of the two poles presented—city and jungle—one possesses the technological might and cultural prestige to absorb and subordinate the other, the return of Babar must not be understood as a mere staging of the mental and emotional forces which battle for a stake in the life of the child. As Bruno Bettelheim has suggested, the child's fear of being abandoned, his need to anticipate his future role and compensate for his immediate vulnerability, are certainly authentic and inevitable concerns. But de Brunhoff's stories show that these dilemmas that every child must face are not just worked out according to abstract, ever repeating, metaphysical images that dwell in the psyche, but are grounded in concrete historical circumstances. That is where de Brunhoff got his characters, ideas, and actors. In addition to a pedagogical theory of how youngsters (elephants) are integrated into a benevolent adult world (the land of men), de Brunhoff also presented his children with a theory of history, an unconscious method for interpreting the contemporary economic and political world.

As he grows older, the admirer of Babar will not only find palpable evidence that there are "developed" countries and others which do not exhibit the characteristics of progress or modernity, and are therefore perceived as "backward," but also that there is a set of "solutions" to such an "abnormal" predicament. Even before he can read, however, the child has come into contact with an implicit history that justifies and rationalizes the motives behind an international situation in which some countries have everything and other countries almost nothing. The child may also be overcoming his infantile traumas. Or again, he may not. Such a process is difficult to verify. But what is definitely happening is that the reader is being handed an easy-to-grasp, easy-to-swallow historical version of the incorporation of Africa (and, by analogy, that of other out-of-the-mainstream continents, namely Latin America and Asia) into the contemporary world.

For this reason, geographical disguise is essential. Instead of Europe, there is a town; instead of Africa, a jungle. Although we can guess that the town is Paris, we haven't a clue to where the jungle might be located. The land of the elephants stands for Africa without overtly representing it, without actually using the name, which might precipitate an overly painful identification. Jean de Brunhoff had the good sense not to mockingly deform the countries where these adventures take place. Or maybe it was something deeper: the self-assurance that goes with being a member of a colonizing nation with several centuries of experience in the field. De Brunhoff had in mind a *mission civilisatrice*, a civilizing mission. He probably felt that his stories had to pulse with a historic dimension, implicitly had to clear the past if they were to be successful lessons in how to grow, under the gaze and approving smile of a benevolent parent or mother country, into polite maturity.

It is plausible that this very constraint limits de Brunhoff's adaptability, his capacity for reaching out to a more massive audience or attaining the popularity of other exponents of children's literature. In fact, if we contrast him with Walt Disney, the real king of twentieth-century infantile fiction, we are struck almost immediately by the absolute freedom, the total lack of responsibility, with which Disney sallies forth into the world, ready to expropriate it cheerfully with his own trademark. He is obviously not locked into explaining a land that has already been conquered and occupied by priests and the military, but instead feels free to impose his own culture, his own innocence, his own marketplace mentality on whomever crosses his path.

While it may seem strange to bring Disney in at this point, it would have been stranger to have kept him out. His work has so dominated the way in which the media treat children and appeal to them, and his formulas have gained such a phenomenal commercial success, so overshadowing his nearest competitors, that a comparison with him will always be indispensable. Donald Duck and Mickey Mouse do things that Babar, even if he is of royal blood, simply cannot do. They show the limitations under which de Brunhoff is working. But the reverse is also true. An elephant who is trying to build a utopia with the willing aid of his native brothers affords us a good vantage point from which to later understand the strategies used by the U.S. media to export its mass culture beyond its frontiers.

Disney's cartoons fairly writhe with ducks and mice that trot the globe, descending upon the very lands where Babar and his real Third World cousins were born and brought up. Through his art, Disney visits these distant regions in the same way his characters do with their bodies: that is, lacking any notion of former reprehensible historical relations, almost as if they were only recent arrivals to the distribution of land and wealth. Without such a context to weigh him down, he can exercise his commercial and linguistic domination in less colonial and more indirect ways than de Brunhoff could. In search of adventure and treasure, his animals drop in on these sites only to find them frozen at some stage in their evolution. There they are free to do what they like, which may be why Disney cartoons need fictional countries where adventures won't constantly be checked and corrected by everyday life, places where everything can, and should, happen.

Just as Disney plunders all folklore, fairy tales, and nineteenth- and twentieth-century children's literature, reshaping it in his average North American image, so he proceeds with world geography.[6] He feels no obligation to avoid the caricature, and rebaptizes each country as if it were a can on a shelf, an object of infinite fun, always good for a laugh. Disney starts with a clearly identifiable nucleus (a part of the original name or something that sounds like it, a supposedly typical characteristic) and then adds certain North American traces or endings: Azteclano, Chiliburgeria, Brutopia, Volcanovia, Inca Blinca, Hondorica, and San Bananador in Latin America; Kachoonga, the Oasis of Nolssa, Kooko Coco, and Foola Zoola in Africa; the provinces of Jumbostan, Backdore, Footsore, and Howdoyustan in India; and Siambodia, Unsteadystan, and South Miseryland in Southeast Asia—a disheartening panorama of the majority of mankind as viewed by a minority that happens to have a monopoly on the concoction of postcards and package tours.[7]

Most of these examples were created by the illustrator-writer Carl Barks in the postwar decades between 1945 and 1967, a period which corresponds exactly to that of decolonization.[8] To someone from a country like the United States, which is renewing and reformulating its own past all the time, and which considers itself as recent an arrival on the scene as many newly independent countries, the Third World is fair game. In the free flow of merchandise and ideas there is nothing wrong with cultural assimilation. To modify a name is as easy as to modify a landscape.

De Brunhoff would no doubt have rejected the vulgarity of such disfigurations. But more than that, in his books the magical disappearance of the semantic link (that tiresome word, Africa) can be attributed to a sense of history absent in Disney, a feeling that he was compelled to communicate in a world where he could not ignore his nation's responsibility for whatever had happened, for whatever would come to pass. He must have sensed the need to substitute for real history, full of accusations and contradictions, the colonial history which in 1931 was still going on right before his eyes, a parallel, ideal history,[9] a version of the westernization of those barbaric territories as he hoped his children would one day see it. His books contained a prophecy of what the author was certain would be Africa decolonized.

That history then, Babar's history, is none other than the fulfillment of the dominant countries' colonial dream. It is not something new. From the sixteenth century onward, expanding capitalism would justify its intervention in other zones through visions and literature, with the utopian hope of being able to construct a perfect mythic space where conflicts such as those afflicting Europe (at that time undergoing the tumultuous transition from feudalism) would have no place. The myth of the noble savage, together with the desire for a beneficial and providential natural environment, and the need for a Golden Age in which the crisis would resolve itself rationally and harmoniously, all provided a way to secularize the medieval religious myths of Eden and Heaven, the two paradisiacal dimensions between which the finite history of men had to unfold. There you have the educational ideal intended for the autochthonous native populations. In them would be joined the light of their natural reason (logos) and the law of civilized progress (mankind reborn after a supposedly dark millennium). A nation would be created where nature and civilization could live side by side, where technical advances would not corrupt but bring contentment, where feudal and bourgeois qualities would be synthesized without antagonisms.

The result, as we all know, was disastrous. Nevertheless, four centuries later Babar succeeded where the conquistadors had failed. Babar slips progress into the jungle without upsetting the ecological balance, because de Brunhoff omits all the plundering, racism, underdevelopment, and misery from his story of the relationship between the two worlds. This is the substitutional fantasy with which the author corrects (just as Babar neglects) the defects, pitfalls, and imperfections of actual historical developments, exposing an X-ray of European civilization's aspirations which never fades away. There's always the possibility of finding some island, some shore of the universe which is still uncontaminated, where all the positive aspects of "progress" can be reconstituted without the attendant flaws and dilemmas. Incidentally, the inspiration behind this pseudo-history that lifts us out of our daily woes and nostalgically transports us back to a more heroic and unshakable conception of the world, goes beyond just the colonization of the Americas or the later appropriation of Africa and parts of Asia. Even after World War II, when the majority of these countries gained their independence, the interventions that took place in Algeria, Vietnam, and the Dominican Republic (to name just one per continent), were carried out in the name of similar values with a rhetoric that seems to show little fatigue. We must save these countries for civilization; and besides, we can do it without interfering with their postcard existence.

So, for children then and now, the land of the elephants resolves the great contradictions in the history of capitalism. Not only is the way in which Europe handled the natives justified, but contemporary politics are cleaned up too, as we shall presently see.

But you have to be careful not to declare such fabrications lies. In the Babar books, history is neither eliminated nor ignored. It is sweetened up, its meaning changed; it is reduced and inverted, but (unlike Disney) real history is there. It can be sought after, tracked down. De Brunhoff has taken the most conspicuous aspects of African history, abstracted and removed them from their immediate framework and problematical resonances, and rearranged them to form a subconscious set of identifications. Each stage in Babar's life formally corresponds (or will eventually correspond, as the child is able to locate and recognize it) to a stage in real life, a stage in real history. Certain historical elements, picked out and isolated, are allowed to function in a different context. Having lost their real links to history, unable to accuse their perpetrators or denounce their origins, they are absorbed by the dominant interpretations, sterilized, and made neutral.

This replacement of the true by the deformed (as in a fairy tale where some usurper takes the place of the princess) succeeds because these kinds of narrations don't pretend to teach a thing, they present themselves as guileless, make-believe, nonpartisan, and far from didactic. But if the truth were not inserted into Babar the Elephant's evolution, albeit hidden and bastardized, then the child would not be able to correlate the fictional process settling in his brain with the real process pleading to be understood. In the future, subconscious comparisons will be made, and contradictions will be waved away as if by magic. But such an identification can operate only if the child is able to equate and interchange the stages he has read with those that, in effect, exist in the world as it has been built. The guises under which these stages are introduced have been changed, and their consequences have been substantially modified, but the framework and underlying order of history are there. The false system becomes the representative of reality in its entirety, which it is able to do because it includes the concealed problems of the world as it is presented to the child while he grows up. "Writing," suggests Roland Barthes, "being the spectacularly powerful form of the word, contains at one and the same time, thanks to a lovely ambiguity, the being and appearance of power, what it is and what it would like you to believe it is."[10]

In 1931, then, there were elements in the relationship between Europe and its dominions which could no longer be ignored: There was violence, there was slavery, there was plundering. Such evils have been included in *Babar*. It is, in fact, the perverse hunter who represents the abominable side of the foreign incursions that sacked Africa. Later on, when Babar and Celeste are shipwrecked (in *The*

Travels of Babar), they are picked up by a captain who gives them (note, he doesn't sell them) to an animal trainer. They are locked up in a cage and consequently lose their freedom.

European civilization evidently does contain certain negative aspects. But every time representatives of the city appear to make the elephants suffer, the Western world's good-natured, loving, positive alter ego, the Old Lady, majestically appears to blot out all negative characteristics. All roads lead to her tutelage. Whenever there is a threat of extermination and servitude from a misguided sector of the European world, there is invariably an educational, missionary, "progressive" ideal which supercedes it, gathering Babar and his herd into the bosom of the great occidental family. It's not necessary to kill the natives or chain them up; all you have to do is Europeanize them in the right way.

This can be proved by noting that every time in the Babar books Europe wanders from its own honorable ideals, the animals aren't wearing any clothes. In the first instance, it is because they reside in a primitive state prior to the discovery of clothing. The next time, it's because they're shipwrecked and appear to be uneducated beasts. "They had lost their crowns, so no one believed they were King and Queen of the elephants." Such violent moments are established as links on a chain. They form an indispensable nexus between nudity and clothing, between backwardness and development, between the forest and the Old Lady. You could almost say that it is the cruel persecution by men that urges the elephants to depend on her. Only if they progress will these devastating events not be repeated. Only if they equal Europe, and manifest all the evangelical signs of inclusion in the civilized world, will the executioner, and therefore the victim, vanish. The message is: assimilate.

The stages in the conquest and enslavement of Africa, therefore, have been incorporated in a way that changes their meaning and inverts their truth. Of course, children, we cannot tell a lie. There was some plundering, but just look how happy the elephants are now.

This procedure of admitting the negative features, and consigning them to a remote past, can also be found in a large portion of contemporary mass market children's literature, but with a different twist. In the Disney comics, Donald, Mickey, and their acolytes visit savage lands. Sometimes they reach the equivalent of the land of the pachyderms in its most Edenic state, as if they were the first visitors in history, and this enormously facilitates their penetration. They are received without suspicion and generally go back to their frenetic metropolis having procured a good dose of sun and bottled purity, as well as a hefty vitaminic jolt of raw materials and treasures which they pack into their suitcases. The innocents from the city meet those from the backlands and everything works out delight-fully. History, however, like a rotten apple, would intrude, wouldn't it. Never mind. Once in a while, the natives have already been ousted from Eden by some distant, unfortunate experience. Then Disney cannot but admit some form of consciousness that things have gone wrong, even though the ducks and rodents disclaim responsibility and decide to tidy up the depredations of the past.

Anyway, in Disney we're never dealing with some wicked hunter who killed someone else's mother. Since there aren't any mothers in Disney cartoons, it's hard to massacre them.[11] Instead, all previous incursions seem to be tainted with imperfections of a metallic nature—robbing, embezzling, swindling, unfair business deals. In short, it is property and not life which is in constant danger of being lost. The solution to such foreign predation is not to launch a civilizing crusade in the style of the Old Lady. For Disney, civilization means learning how to do business; education is the process which accompanies the interchange of goods and services. His response to the misfortunes of the past is a benign modernization of the untamed world, the application of a combination of commerce and technology that should hardly surprise us. After all, the actual evolution of Disney's craft, according to Richard Schickel,[12] progressively became a matter of engineering, the resolution of aesthetic problems by means of technical advances with the object of selling . . . happiness.[13]

Two examples serve to illustrate this point.

Feeling bored one day (a situation common to the beginning of many Disney adventures), Donald, his nephews, and his grandmother go in search of adventure in the Wild West.[14]

"The scenery is spectacular, isn't it boys?"

"Just like television, only in 3-D."

But it's not all fun and games. They are attacked by real, live Indians, who hate any duck that dares cross over into their territory. Fifty years ago an ancestral duck called (Cato Pato in Spanish) double-crossed them by stealing their land and then selling it back when it was no longer any good. Now the ducks have to convince the Indians that not all ducks (especially white ones) are bad, and that the plundering of the past can be rectified. If the mistrust produced by the former fraud can be annulled, then the races can reach an understanding and there will be a comfortable spot for the outsiders within the prevailing order.

At that very moment, two con men appear who want to buy the land for "a thousand cents." Luckily, this time the ducks are there to protect the natives. "That's highway robbery! They know how much that gas filtering out of the mine is worth!" The Indians respond by declaring eternal peace with the ducks and integrating themselves into the modern world which they no longer fear. For one thing, "a big gas company will create new jobs and pay the tribe handsomely." There will be a consortium that will resolve disputes with *justice*.

All foreigners aren't automatically bad. Their only crime consists in not paying the correct price. In other words, robbery is an extreme form of finding yourself in possession of an object without having paid fairly for it. History appears to be no more than an attempt on the part of the bad (defined as those not possessing any property) to take from those who have—the "good guys." Nobody wonders about the origin of the wealth which is the source of such strife. Just as nobody ever wonders, naturally, who will ultimately determine the fairness of the price. Of course the Indians are not selling natural resources exclusively. They are also the owners of the image they project, and tourism will permit them to put their natural essence up for sale, incidently providing the adventurers with the vacation they longed for.

In the final scene of this comic, two "wild" horses take Donald and his nephews for an exciting but safe ride, while Granny peacefully knits on the terrace of the teepee-shaped hotel, and a redskin sells native curios in the background. "Yoo-hoo," cries Donald. "If you wanna have fun like they usta, you gotta find some real Indians."

This dichotomy between the evils of past larceny and the benign, present-day intervention of businessmen and merchants is reiterated in much the same way when the ducks search for treasure in Azteclano (where else?) with the same beneficial results.[15] Centuries ago, conquistadors wanted to snatch gold from the Indians. Now the "Beagle Boys," the infantile hulking thugs who are always trying to dispossess Uncle Scrooge, are about to attempt the same thing. Fortunately, the ducks have gained the confidence of the shepherd who guards the treasure by saving one of his lambs. At first "he doesn't know how to repay such a good deed." But old Donald lets him know: "This is absurd. Conquistadors don't exist anymore." There's no reason to hoard all that wealth. The consequences of this attitude aren't long in coming. The natives discard the memory of their first bad experience: They open their doors to these new foreigners. "Visit Azteclano. Entrance: one dollar." They've been educated; they've learned how to capitalize on their resources. Once again, all the ducks' excitement is channeled into a reward of rest and relaxation: "Our adventure ends in the form of a tropical vacation."

The fact that in Disney such adventures, bridging the initial boredom and the final repose, take place in distant geographical locations, ensures that the reward, whether it be gold or tranquility, is deserved, and more importantly, obtained without working. Just as money is the abstraction of the value of the work incorporated into a particular object, so adventure is an abstraction of the effort that is needed, and endured, to produce that wealth.

Although the same types of adventures are found in Babar, with the same sense of disaffection for work, of seeing sweat as a form of suffering, they do not acquire the same monetary feeling as in Disney; rather they deal with changes in fortune—as well as rewards—which are more moral in tone. Similarly, in ancient Hellenistic adventure narratives (called Byzantine-Baroque) and their medieval and Renaissance derivations, kings (and sometimes minor heroes) are afflicted with misfortune (shipwrecks, captivity, separation, etc.) that place them on the same level as the reader, that is, below the aristocratic stratum. They then proceed, according to Wolfgang Kayser,[16] to demonstrate through their "fortitude" and "magnanimity" not only the loftiness of their birth but the justness

31

of the pile of riches providence finally heaps upon them. In de Brunhoff's second book, *The Travels of Babar,* Babar and Celeste have their own Byzantine-Baroque encounter with danger and disorder, one which threatens to cast doubt on the nobility of their characters and their progress toward modernity and humanity.

Since the land of the elephants has begun to lose its exotic qualities, and now seems exclusively like a backyard for European fun and games, Babar and Celeste have no choice but to take their honeymoon in other latitudes. In order to do this, they've obtained a hot-air balloon, as yellow as Babar's crown, in which they are elevated above all other elephants. This is a recurring theme: to rise. The first thing the young Babar does in the city is to rush headlong into an elevator, quite literally seeking upward mobility. Finally the elevator boy warns him, "This is not a toy, Mr. Elephant." It's entirely possible that behind this idea (remember Dumbo, the flying elephant) lies a basic desire to deny the body's weight, that concrete substance which keeps us forever tethered to necessity and circumstance. [17] In other books, Babar twice climbs mountains in order to ski and is invited to the land of the birds, where he receives a disguise that allows him to ignore the laws of gravity. Once he has abandoned his horizontal stance, now on two feet, his only thought is to renounce his low condition, continue rising, and make something more of himself. He climbs the stairway that civilization awards him. It seems fitting at this point to confess that one of the delights of the Babar books, as with many other successful children's books, is their graphic evanescence, the way in which the illustrator's light touch dematerializes his protagonists and sets them apart from the asphyxiating world that surrounds and threatens us.

Of course this magical sense of elevation is not an exclusively external attribute. Babar is able to rise above the others (what else would a monarch do?) because he has that extra internal spiritual dimension as well. That is the true meaning of his travels with Celeste.

A storm takes them out to sea, deflates their balloon, and leaves them abandoned on a desert island. Just like Robinson Crusoe, they will be tested, and like him they will not lose their civilized habits. [18] (They wash their clothes, prepare and cook sumptuous feasts, and so on.) Both elephants could very well have reverted to primitivism and wallowed in bestiality, like so many contemporary literary characters. But we're not dealing with the protagonists of Golding's *Lord of the Flies* or Dickey's *Deliverance*. The Europe which the elephants carry inside them is an internal, ethical, and exemplary dimension. Just as Crusoe could reduplicate the entire successful and frugal history of the birth of a managerial class,[19] so the elephants are able to overcome adversity and demonstrate their capacity to govern. So too, like latter-day Fridays, they must confront and distinguish themselves from "ferocious, savage cannibals," creatures who, unlike them, not only have never reached a state of civilization but never will. Thus are separated as in the early days of the conquest of the Americas, two types of natural beings: noble savages and anthropophagi.[20] Although these classifications are brought out of storage every time Europe invades a foreign territory (those who kneel before them in peace are divided from those who defend themselves in war), we are dealing with something more than an excuse created after the fact to justify the domestication of some and the extermination of others. European writers of the sixteenth and seventeenth centuries had long been staging the fundamental ambiguity they felt towards nature as an allegorical drama in which shepherds (who represent nature as kind and, of course, rational and courtly) confronted horrendous, savage, Machiavellian beings, men who ignored God's law and relied instead on their instincts (nature as passionate and overflowing).[21] In Babar's case, nature serves to emphasize and measure the distance between him and the primitive state he has so recently abandoned. There is no going back. It is his and his queen's education (domestic fire, rice, fish from the sea, cunning) which permits the animals (sic) to conquer the men who, in spite of the fact that they live on a small and apparently Polynesian island, are in fact clichéd Africans, just as they have been portrayed for decades in films, books, and magazines.[22] They are black, naked anthropophagi. (Or should we call them elephantophagi?)

The subjection of the barbaric Africans by the Europeanized Africans anticipates the fact that there remain sectors of the land of the elephants which might resort to force to oppose the changes that have taken place. And sure enough, in Babar's kingdom the rhinos are a long way from accepting the foreign customs of the Old Lady. While she rescues her friends from the circus to which they've been given (the first thing she does is dress her protégés, and make them rest in separate beds, watched over by her benevolent and chaste portrait) Arthur (Babar's young cousin) has played a bad joke on Rataxes, the sleeping chief of the rhinoceroses, tying a firecracker to his tail. Cornelius, ever the polite European, begs forgiveness and promises to punish the child. The rhinoceros, however, will have nothing of it and becomes threatening.

The war that follows, in which Babar consolidates his leadership, once and for all establishing the superiority of his way of life over the law of the jungle, seems to originate in an insignificant act, in the eccentric personality of one of the rhino rulers, in fact in his lack of courtesy. There is no way to explain the belligerence of these animals, except by resorting to the savagery of their basic state. They are "lunatics" who distort the facts. No other evidence is offered us, a technique not exclusive to children's literature. Just as the rhinos want to "tweak the ears of this young King Babar and punish that rascal Arthur," so thirty years later the news agencies would report that the war between El Salvador and Honduras began because of something as childish as a soccer match, conveniently omitting any reference to the multinational rivalries in the area or the migratory problems caused by an overexploitation of the land which goes hand in hand with a policy based on the production of crops mainly for export.

In such explanations, something basic to our understanding is always omitted. For instance, the war between the elephants and the rhinos (much like our familiar descriptions of the real fratricidal wars in Africa that the European way of life provoked) is not brought on by foreign powers seeking to establish the frontiers of their empires, nor by the attempt to control valuable raw materials; rather, it is the acceptance of civilized, international models which both permits the avoidance of the "barbaric" state of war and brings this particular one on. If only the rhinos too could become eminently reasonable, "Western," and mature this nasty event would never happen.

Babar's absence only serves to demonstrate how indispensable he was—a retroactive justification for his enthronement. He returns from the outside (as we shall see the superheroes do in the next essay) to establish law and order. Even though the hot air balloon fell into the sea and his crown got lost due to bad luck, Babar still has his wits about him. In the midst of catastrophic, hazardous, and unpredictable changes, Babar's capacity to generate ideas and take initiative never fails. Babar is no different here, in spite of his royal pedigree and his jungle origins, than Disney characters or superheroes or the exemplary lives in *Reader's Digest*. In all these, and so many other twentieth-century products, having a "brilliant idea" is not only what allows a contestant to win in the game of life. It is also a sign that such a victory is well deserved. The providential light bulb that flares up in so many comics or cartoons is invisibly wired to that Grand Old Thinking Cap in the sky. It is those who have been chosen beforehand (by providence and the scriptwriter) as being worthy of social mobility in an already stratified world who are accorded intelligence. Spiritual wealth in mass market literature is distributed by the same criteria that prevail in the not-so-literary world of economics. Faced with armed rhinos, Babar seizes on his ingenuity and strategic ability to outwit brute force and cruelty. With paint and wigs, he disguises the elephants' enormous rumps with eyes, noses, and multicolored hair. At a crucial moment, as the rhinos charge, those rumps rise up from behind a hill. "The rhinoceroses thought they were monsters and, terrified, they retreated in great disorder."

It is the economic backwardness of the savages which has been the decisive element. They did not know how to close the technical gap which separated them from the elephants who, with sophisticated weapons, demonstrated the importance of their link to the Western world. The adult world, too. For the rhinos are actually running from themselves: the backsides of their rivals are none other than great African masks. Those stupid animals can't even tell the difference between reality and its representation!

The small readers, therefore, can choose between two versions of childhood: They can be rhinoceroses threatened by the darkness of their own nightmares, their own faces deformed in a dream, or elephants who have advanced so rapidly they are even capable of using their own bottoms as instruments for controlling reality. Between the abyss of childhood and the heaven of adulthood, there doesn't seem to be much of a choice.

This identification of forms of evil with aspects of childhood is fundamental to the Babar stories because, as frequently happens in contemporary children's literature, it closes the juvenile imagination and its rebellious tendencies off from alternative routes. It doesn't leave much room for young minds to maneuver or go about choosing their own solutions. The roads which lead out of childhood (and poverty, as we shall see) are exclusively those which have been paved in advance by foreign bulldozers.

All insubordination must be left by the wayside. If it has its origins in a plausible misunderstanding (as in the case of the Indians in the Disney cartoon), then we are in the presence of noble savages who will have no choice but to see the light of Rousseau and climb into the sheepfold of progress. If the savages are ornery, they will have to be exterminated or caged up. This is what happens to the rhinos, in whose characterization are mixed both the primitive (the taboo of anthropophagy which they share with the cannibals on the desert island) and the simply puerile (the superstitious). What condemns them most, however, is their destruction of nature without any reason. Because of their aggressiveness, "nothing was left of the great forest. There were no flowers, no birds. Everyone was sad."

Decades later, Disney's cartoons would project these same combinations of characteristics onto the revolutions of the Third World (in Vietnam, Cuba, and elsewhere). At the end of each cartoon, as at the end of this Babar book, the natives are freed from their malignant terror and are faced with a choice—either to stick to their age-old peaceful ways or to keep up with their visitors and neighbors by leaping onto the roller coaster of pseudo-history. Of course, they imagine themselves getting onto a freeway, while they are really driving along a vicious Möbius strip in which they always pass the same point without even realizing it.

So it's no surprise when Babar appears after the battle mounted on an elephant, one of his own subjects, his hands raised in a signal of victory. The goodness of the system has now been adequately tested by its military efficiency, and the time has come to put its prestige to work in constructing a new civilized order. After the war, they inaugurate a peaceful civilization identical to that of Europe. The time has come to build the first city of the elephants. Babar's travels and his second book close with the beginnings of the next step toward colonization, not only of a continent, but of a mind.

Bruno Bettelheim has observed in his book *The Uses of Enchantment* that when fairy tales end with the protagonist as the king of a country (as ruler of his emotions and in control of his destiny), the monarch is never seen reigning. After a successful adventure, the character once again becomes an ordinary person in order to enjoy the normalcy of a satisfying life. This helps the child recognize himself.[23] Babar is not permitted such a respite. The power he has must be exercised, because he is enmeshed in both a historical reality and a dream projected onto that reality by the colonizers.

In the next book, *Babar the King*, "the dromedaries were bringing Babar the things he had bought on his honeymoon." Magically, all of civilization fits into these bundles. Babar gives a speech: "I have in these trunks gifts for all of you. I will give them out after we build our city." The elephants react favorably and get right to work. "They cut down trees, moved stones, sawed wood, and dug holes. The Old Lady played the phonograph for them, and Babar played the trumpet. The elephants opened their ears wide to hear." Babar, standing in their midst without moving a muscle, directs the harmonious division of labor, the smooth, luscious fruits of which will belong to everyone. They all will have their own bungalows, while up on a hill (higher! higher!) behind them sit a two-story house for Babar and another identical house for the Old Lady.

Sure enough, she has decided to stay in their country. During the war, she founded (together with Celeste) a hospital with a big red cross on it where she toiled "selflessly." After the battle, she returns to her initial role, that of educator ("She often told the children stories"). The charitable thrust of her activities is indisputable. When Babar decorates her ("she had been so good to them and had cared for the wounded"), she appears in a white nun's habit, which reveals that we are in the presence of the missionary spirit in Africa. But her fragile, wrinkled figure, her generosity, and her spirituality reflect something more than militant Catholicism. The Old Lady also acts as a surrogate mother figure among the family of forsaken elephants (while also performing the roles of grandmother, nun, aunt, teacher). She spreads the light of the metropolis, fount and source of all that is good, to all her "children" and "foundlings." Babar, at her side, takes the masculine role. He will be the father—if not biological, then intellectual—of his subjects, creating them from nothing, raising them up.

In Uncle Walt's cartoons, on the other hand, the paternal figure is simply left out, his mice and ducks existing within a family of uncles, cousins, nephews, and eternal sweethearts. In *How to Read Donald Duck*, we analyzed the way such an absence can be traced not only to Disney's prudishness, but also to the fact that the author perceives himself to be the work's only productive and generative force (either sexually or in terms of output). [24] Later on we will see how this structure permits the child to project his criticisms of undesirable adult behavior onto an uncle rather than subvert the authoritarian relationships in the actual home, where the father gives the orders and the child had better obey. Jean de Brunhoff doesn't need this kind of outlet. After a while, he will present Babar and Celeste with offspring, relieving them of the sort of asphyxiating and universal "sexless sexiness" found in Disney. [25] Until then, while Babar can't yet claim any progeny of his own, his entire nation acts as a putative family. He will repeat to his child-subjects what he learned in the "motherland," the secret, magical, almost Oedipal fount of his power.

"Then Babar kept his promise. He gave a gift to each elephant and also sturdy clothes for workdays and rich, beautiful clothes for holidays."

The drawing is noteworthy: Dozens of elephants entering a door, on all fours, wait in line to receive their gifts. Once they exit, the gray, amorphous mass disappears. Through the other door they emerge, dancing (like children? like blacks?) on two feet, half-dressed, presents in hand.

This is the end of an era in their utopian and idyllic history. Without a hitch, having easily beaten the rhinoceroses, they have created a city on the fringes of time, far removed from money and exploitation. They will dance until the centuries have ended.

Of course, civilization brings certain implacable laws along with it. For one thing, the elephants' day seems to have been split in half, which is further emphasized by their two kinds of outfits—one for leisure time and one for work. There will be a party on Sunday. But first they must work hard all week long to prepare for the occasion.

Clothing brings the elephants' fragmentation. The young ones go to school and "all the elephants who were too old to attend classes chose a trade." It is something which is voluntary, something which implicitly carries an immeasurable pleasure with it. The division of labor appears necessary, but it benefits everyone equally in this society based on the exchange of services. "If Capoulosse has broken shoes, he takes them to Tapitor and if Tapitor is sick, Capoulosse takes care of him. If Barbacol wants to put a statue on top of his chimney, he asks Podular for one and when Podular's jacket is worn out, Barbacol makes him a new one. Justinen paints a portrait of Pilophage who in turn protects him from his enemies. Hatchibombatar sweeps the streets, Olur fixes cars and when they're tired, Doulamor makes music." (The reader is asked to ignore the fact that Babar plays tennis with Pilophage and his wife—that is to say, with the military hierarchy.)

The arcadian myth has been made concrete. The saintly and natural life of the savages, which incorporates the conveniences of technical progress, combines both morality and civilization. This is not a welfare state in the jungle, as Bettina Hürlimann proposes.[26] This privileged space condenses Europe and its nostalgias; it eliminates the friction between developed and underdeveloped countries, between exploiter and exploited. The model that Babar proposed and put into practice has given prosperity and happiness to his people. Urban values have not ruined nature, they have perfected it. The barbarians have been integrated painlessly into the dominant economic structure, just as imperial myths have always said they would be.

European intervention has been a complete success. The shot which killed Babar's mother, the stupid war started by those savage rhinos, the cages in which they were imprisoned—they're all in the past. Ahead there is only a miraculous and excellent present of well-being and harmony for the elephants.

Thus, just below the surface of Babar, there lurks, half unconsciously, a whole theory of development. There exist backward countries which, once they imitate the more "advanced" (grown-up) countries, once they import technological know-how and begin working like they're supposed to, once they invite foreign professors and technicians to assist them, will succeed in improving their lot. You don't have to occupy these countries militarily. There's no need to exercise direct political control. It's enough to maintain economic, technological, and cultural control. It's enough if you've got internal, national collaborators. In Babar's case, the experiment is successful exactly because the elephants have accomplished it on their own.

In imagining the independence of the land of the elephants, Jean de Brunhoff anticipates, more than a decade before history forced Europe to put it into practice, the theory of neocolonialism.

This theory has been described by Basil Davidson:[27] First you must create a middle class who will facilitate the step from savagery to civilization, but whose true function is to ensure that the ex-colonies' economic system will continue to be a fragment of the worldwide capitalistic system. "The great colonial powers," writes Davidson,

almost always achieve their objectives. In one colony after another, they made sure to hand the power over to the traditional chiefs, members of a small educated elite, who were in turn allied to their own national white collar groups, all graduates of the universities who aspired to personal careers which would emulate the superiority of Oxford, Paris, or similar traditions. The colonial governors naturally weren't blind to "their Africans'" deficiencies, they simply argued, in carefully chosen words, "these were the best we could find." Having found these "best" they did everything in their power to make sure that this "government by the elite" would last. Native political institutions were twisted or turned into simulacra of parliamentary systems borrowed from British or Parisian models, and they mounted, simultaneously, full-scale propaganda campaigns aimed at convincing the

Africans that these forms of democracy were the be-all-and-end-all, and all others were inferior, impossible, or lead to "communism."[28]

Babar develops his country in accord with this dominant dream. He educates it according to modern and ultimately technocratic models, thereby demonstrating that only proximity to Europe (or the United States) guarantees success, and that when it comes to the weak and the dispossesed, you must adopt a loving, patient, and paternal attitude.

Such attitudes are possible because the poverty of some nations and the overaccumulation of wealth in others are not seen as part of the same phenomenon. It is not proclaimed that some are midgets because others are giants. Instead, the problems, hardships, and miseries of those countries that haven't yet reached a satisfactory standard of living are ethnocentrically likened to the turbulent aspects of Europe's transition from feudalism to capitalism or America's expansion *ab ovo*. Underdevelopment is no more than a "normal" stage in a "normal growth pattern" for any country that wishes to "stand on its own two feet."[29] In his classic description, W. W. Rostow outlined five successive plateaus for the countries of the Third World in his book *The Stages of Economic Growth: A Non-Communist Manifesto*: "traditional society; the preconditions for takeoff; takeoff; the drive to maturity; the age of high mass consumption."[30] All these countries need to do is "get rolling" and "take off" and their growing pains will subside.

A couple of years ago, one might have thought that Rostow was doling out a storybook version, almost a flying, child's-eye view of economics. But his Peter Pan panorama is not as outdated as it would seem. Here is President Reagan on October 15, 1981, in Philadelphia, on the real essence of development: "We Americans can speak from experience on this subject. When the original settlers arrived here, they faced a wilderness where poverty was their daily lot, danger and starvation their close companions. . . . But through all the dangers, disappointments and setbacks, they kept their faith. They never stopped believing that with the freedom to try and try again, they could make tomorrow a better day." And if anybody from the countries which are today poor, starving, and disappointed has the audacity to point out that this model cannot be imitated again because, among other reasons, the development of the United States helped to create the disdevelopment of many other parts of the world, the President can always point triumphantly to the fact that his vision is shared by many Babar rulers of the Third World.

At the end of his Philadelphia speech, he quotes none other than Anwar Sadat, on his March 1979 visit to Washington: "I am dreaming," said Sadat, explaining to the U.S. Chamber of Commerce his "mission to secure economic progress for his people" and went on: "Really I am dreaming of a drive like the drive of your grandfathers, the drive to the West. . . . Water we have, land we have, climate we have, farming we have. But we need technology, we need know-how, new ways of irrigation, new ways of agriculture. All this one can find here in America. . . . Come and be my partners, be pioneers like your grandfathers who opened the West and built in 200 years the most powerful, the richest country, the great United States of America."

Behind such speeches, exhortations, and prospects, there is an idea of development as growth, the idea that "young" economies need only mimic "older" ones. In more or less sophisticated form, it is this belief which permeates all developmental theory. In the same years that Rostow was spouting his antigravitational recommendations (1959–1960), the years the Cuban revolution burst onto the scene, another "theoretician" looked into his crystal ball and foretold reforms that would destroy the "feudal" structure that held Latin America in its grasp. "The already important nuclei of industrialization," writes Lincoln Gordon, who was the U.S. ambassador to Brazil during the coup that ousted the elected president, João Goulart, in 1964, "the gradual strengthening of the middle class and the development of a lively, if often undisciplined, group of entrepreneurs [note the paterfamilias tone] all give hope that a well-conceived, cooperative effort might, in a mere decade or so, bring the great bulk of Latin America into economic step with the modern world."[31] Unfortunately, the countries for whom Rostow made his aeronautical predictions were unwilling or unable to follow his advice. Those uncooperative good-for-nothings! And more, much more than ten years have limped by, and Gordon's modernization thesis, and other efforts on three continents and in innumerable discourses, aid programs, and bank injections do not seem to have produced a mature middle class able to bring those lands where ducks and mice sought tranquility, treasure, and lost sheep out of their "adolescence."[32]

Even though such theories might have failed in practice, folks—never fear. They can always be given a face-lift. Try and try again. Now, instead of regarding developed countries as parents to a large, squalling family of children, it is fashionable to speak of "interdependence,"[33] as if everyone belonged to one big happy grouping of brothers and sisters. Of course, some of the brothers and sisters are older and more mature, and they must treat their young wards in a characteristically paternal manner. When you come right down to it, countries are always treated as organisms with cycles that can be compared to birth, childhood, and maturity, and include all the difficulties borrowed from biology and psychology (inflation as an endemic disease, violence as a juvenile syndrome, instability of institutions as a product of an imbalance between expectations and abilities).[34]

This superimposition of the individual on the social, of the biological on the historical, is at the heart of the way that books like Babar educate children. Not only do we find out how civilization has beneficiently elevated Africa (or any other savage, strange, and alien zone), but we are simultaneously shown how playful, ignorant, adorable, and innocent beings—in short, children; in short, elephants—are ushered into and take their rightful place in the world of grownups. The psychosocial message is indistinguishable from the historical blueprint: The elephants have grown up and adapted to the world; that's what the child should do, too. While he's making this unsettling, almost unimaginable transition, he can feel reassured. It's okay to act both like a responsible adult and like a silly kid; just as in Babar's utopia you can be both African and European, man and animal, developed and underdeveloped. He can even work without being exploited and exchange goods without being contaminated by money.

The Old Lady tells her friends, "Let's work hard and cheerfully and we'll continue to be happy." If nature can enter the European world without losing its purity, then there's no reason why children should have to deny their own distinctive traits as they get older, while those already adult are allowed the distinctly nostalgic pleasure of consoling themselves on the irreparable loss of past innocence. Therefore it is innocence, the basic substratum upon which this space is constructed, that allows fantasy and reality to be reconciled without doubts or schisms. The child is not suspicious of the animal, nor is the adult. The confidence one feels about these cuddly walking-talking dolls is transferred into the account in which these animals have deposited their hopes. The little one finds himself at just the right distance—neither too near nor too far—from his models to be able to intuit that they are and are not human beings.

This first fusion of nature with society, of the animal with the historical, is the introductory step to the creation of a utopia. In this state one lives tribally, in the midst of a landscape void of artificial constructions, one that combines contemporary architecture with splendid, unpolluted lakes. Relationships between people are simple and Edenic. In this Golden Age, this uterine scenario, this maternal paradise which the myths of all human societies have retained and perpetuated, it is easy for the child to identify with both the animal and the civilized forms which he internalizes simply by being human. Elephants and children, both small savages, begin life in a supportive environment, crawl on all fours, learn how to get dressed, and finally reach a point at which they must assume greater responsibilities. In Babar's case, this learning process, which is part and parcel of all growing up, contains a pseudohistorical vision of how he got where he was, and at the same time stacks the deck in favor of a world construct which the child does not fully comprehend, but of which he does possess—like commercials for products that haven't come out on the market yet—an image.

The stages of colonial penetration, the stages in which the native assumes Western norms as his models, are felt by the reader to be the stages of his own socialization. The adult world can hang on to all its dominant formulas and pass them on to the child without creating negative antibodies as long as the formulas are permeated with simplicity. To the extent that the child prepares himself to become an adult, to become Babar, he understands that colonization (that of his parents as well as that of the more powerful nations) is highly beneficial to those who receive it, and any kind of dependence and submission is the inevitable price you pay to be admitted into grown-up ranks, to gloriously and uninterruptedly continue the labor begun by your ancestors, the Old Lady, grandmother, schoolmarm, mother church.

This confusion of individual psychological life with national historical life enhances the dominating dimensions of both. You get treated like a child for your own good, and that's how the indigenous and backward must be treated too. Those who are underdeveloped are so because of their childlike natures, not as the result of the international economic system, and all those little people need is education and technology in order to gain access to the Western, Christian, adult world.[35] By biologizing social stages and socializing bodily growth, the familial system (and colonial and neocolonial systems, too) creates a certainty that, as far as peoples-who-are-the-same-as-children are concerned, there is only one river flowing to success: namely, established values.

We've reached the end of human history. Just as elephants are men and men are countries, so are the tensions between city and country, development and underdevelopment, Europe and Africa, order and freedom, work and play, brains and brawn nonexistent, and it's possible to go on simplifying and reconciling as long as you live. Babar's utopia resolves the antagonisms that history, like a wicked stepmother, refuses to deal with. He whispers in our ear that there's no need to work them out through a daily struggle which could end up transforming our circumstances as well as our own personalities, because the contradictions (between city and country, etc.) are not irremediable.

All this is reinforced by the incredible ease of transitions in such stories. The movement from one moment to the next, one stage to the next, one historical period to the next is deceptively instantaneous—a phenomenon particularly true of Disney's cartoons. Birth and maturity, past and present, are contiguous. Erased are not only intermediate centuries connecting one moment to the next, but also the immense effort and even greater suffering which such a passage of time implies. It is a—pardon the expression—magical process. The civilized world conquers and elevates the barbarian

45

spirit with the same speed as the natural world regenerates the pure, tired souls of tourists (as we shall see in the next essay). There is no point of contact between these two dimensions of contemporary humanity, for they are conceived as juxtaposed spaces, between which it is possible to leap back and forth without any problem. Just as Main Street USA in Disneyland or Disneyworld leads to the African jungle of Adventureland and from there into the future of Tomorrowland,[36] so mass market literature represents historical change—as if historical epochs were static blocks frozen next to one another, like products on an assembly line, frames in a comic strip, cans on the shelf in the supermarket, houses in the suburbs, or cars on the highway.

Such instantaneousness has nothing to do with imagination. Whoever thinks that fantasy consists of leaps and pirouettes is a prisoner of a notion that opposes imagination to the everyday, workaday world; that supposes it to be a form of entertainment. In commercial entertainment, and certainly in commercial children's literature, everything has been predigested and defined in advance; everything has been imagined by another's mind. The spectator sits back, consumes, and is entertained, without realizing that true imagination is hard work. It is a siege to bring into being that which had previously existed only in a no-man's land. True imagination implicitly criticizes the prevailing version of reality and invites us to make our own substitutions.

It is false imagination, however, that must preside over the last stage in the history of a Celesteville, which is bound to last forever. In the city's anniversary parade, one can discern elephants dressed in the costumes of all periods and geographies: musketeers, Roman and Napoleonic soldiers, lancers, and boy scouts. Many books later the elephants will visit Bellatrompa Castle: "In the majestic vestibule, the children admired portraits of their ancestors. Oh what an elegant musketeer, says Arthur. I prefer the Roman, Zephyr says."[37]

But we know that since Babar covered the distance from primeval forest dweller to citified importer of foreign goods in his own lifetime, it's impossible for his ancestors to be either Roman, Renaissance, or Enlightenment figures. They're simply elephants. Before Babar's flight and return, they lived in the cyclical innocence of nature, breathing in a paradise outside of time and without problems, a life where one day was the same as the next. But if Africa is to be Europe's equal, it has to assimilate Europe's history as well. So a new history must be invented to supplant the elephants' disposable past. It's not enough to adopt the advanced countries' industries, languages, and machines; the natives must go further and jettison their own memories. They must even abolish the idealized version of their own conquest, eliminating all reference to the fact that one of the elephants lost his mother, escaped to the city, and returned like Prometheus, only in a modern automobile. They must forget that he was put in a cage or that there were wars with the rhinos.

Just as real subjugated peoples often had Western history imposed on them as if it were their own, so the road the elephants have taken to the present moment is astutely obliterated. It will be impossible for future generations of elephants even to catch a glimpse of the process of change which led to their country's "progress." After all, their previous books have, for all intents and purposes, been obliterated. The falsification which Babar verifies to be his own past (already a rose-colored deformation of conquest) corresponds to what Frantz Fanon has called the neocolonial mentality:

> Every colonized people—in other words, every people in whose soul an inferiority complex has been created by the death and burial of its local cultural originality—finds itself face to face with the language of the civilizing nation; that is, with the culture of the mother country. The colonized is elevated above his jungle status in proportion to his adoption of the mother country's cultural standards. He becomes whiter as he renounces his blackness, his jungle.[38]

This desecularization of his roots, in which he sees himself through another's eyes, is then used to corroborate the exact racist theory with which the colonizer originally arrived: The colored man needs the white. He has a subconscious desire to be crushed and to surrender his personality. In the same way that a woman needs a man and wants to be subjugated and possessed. In the same way the child dreams of becoming the father. In the same way the elephant dreams of becoming a child, not an animal.

Naturally, Babar's country has not been entirely Europeanized.

Although the scenery along the road towards Bellatrompa Castle is completely French, almost a carbon copy of the road Babar traveled in his youth as a guest of the Old Lady, you can still see thatched roofs and palm trees in Celesteville. Greek mythological statues, cherubs, satyrs, and sirens in the shape of pachyderms exist side by side with quick and dangerous crocodiles, untamed mountains, haunted areas, and enigmatic islands. After all, the elephants can't help but be innocent, good, and a bit out of it, because therein lies their particular charm. All that is savage has been detached from anything having to do with historical epochs or possible oppression, but just enough has been retained to facilitate the child's edification and identification.

This allows for the constant focus on modernizing moments in the land of the elephants. This is what happens in *Babar and Father Christmas*, the last Babar book, which Jean de Brunhoff had almost completed before his death.[39] The little elephants find out how children in other countries celebrate Christmas. "Don't you think that we could write Father Christmas so that he would also visit our houses in Elephant Land?" But Father Christmas doesn't respond, and Babar must intervene. "Why didn't I think of it sooner? I'll go myself and ask Father Christmas to come to the land of the elephants." He follows the Yuletide Messenger's trail until he gets to his abode. "Babar asks him to come to his kingdom and hand out toys to the little elephants, like he does with the children of men." After bringing the Old Man to the land of the elephants, where he relaxes in the sun, Babar gets his reward. He is delegated with the responsibility. "Do you know what's inside this bag? A Father Christmas suit that's just your size! A magical garment which will permit you *to fly* [my emphasis] through the air, and a sack that's always loaded with toys. You will take my place on Christmas Eve in the land of the elephants. I promise to return after my job is done and bring a beautiful Christmas tree for your children." Babar imports, then personifies, the foreign model that is naturally desired by children everywhere (elephants and humans alike) because with it come presents. The paternal aspect is accentuated, the international habit is internalized. To accept happiness and contentment is to mimic the "land of men" until you can't tell men from elephants. The

Great White Father is fused with the Great Father and King of the elephants, so that they mutually lend prestige to one another.

Babar is and is not Father Christmas. He grants gifts, but his outfit is a foreign disguise. The children sense that Babar's true power lies in maintaining proper, friendly relations with the land of men. The beings who come from outside also make themselves indispensable to the economic progress of the land of the elephants as well as to the psychological well-being of the reader who longs to see the same system authenticated and made concrete every step of the way.

Thus, Professor Grifaton, the Old Lady's brother, comes from the "outside" (the gerontocracy continues). He brings with him a series of novelties, each one admired by the elephants more than the last.[40] He goes out to hunt butterflies for his collection. He is the intellectual (or technocrat) who comes to explain to the natives what riches they possess and how they should take advantage of them. In one drawing we see his books, a microscope, a collection of scientific instruments, geometrical drawings, and a Picasso reproduction on the wall. This space *is* Europe, although certain details are always slightly off, always vaguely animal, just wrong enough to need continually more infusions of technology, science, arts, more of Europe's progress, the latest gadget. The small readers, also a bit out of touch, will identify with the elephants and specifically with their children, and will feel similar needs to constantly "modernize" and keep abreast of current trends.

A cave is discovered. It is Professor Grifaton, with his enterprising spirit, who organizes the exploration. "This cave interests me very much," the professor says. "Don't you think we should explore it, too, Babar?" So they leave on an expedition, outfitted with all the latest equipment (including pith helmets and lanterns). They find a subterranean river. "Dear commander," murmurs the professor (note the courtesy, a certain paternal condescension, a certain patient distance and warmth in his voice), "wouldn't it be stupendous if all the elephants could cruise up the subterranean river in motorboats? I've just gotten an idea to build a pleasure boat." His ideas are always met with a "Bravo," "Great," or "Here, here." The result is a boat: "an atomically propelled paddle-wheeler." Once again, sophisticated technology (nuclear) is coupled with and made more innocent by nostalgia for a bygone era, for a ludicrous, uncontaminated, and placid world of paddle-wheelers.

But what Professor Grifaton is really proposing is tourism. A distant spot in the world economic system is set aside and converted into a little corner of happiness and relaxation. Instead of industrializing the country, its "exotic" condition, its nature, and its ancient traditions are "conserved" and made into a business. It gets *developed*, but the development is photographic. The country is reduced to a postcard, a souvenir, a "memento of our trip," and the inhabitants—in order to obtain money from the tourists—must be accommodating and adjust their landscape (their natural resources) to the demands of the travel agencies. They must read up on themselves in almanacs, encyclopedias, guidebooks, and manuals.[41]

The plan is a success. "That night in the ballroom, Cornelius decorates Professor Grifaton with the order of merit, as a benefactor of Celesteville." The Old Lady's role in education and public health is now taken up by the bearer of the Scientific Word, who proposes that technology can solve any problem as long as it is applied without interference.

And what do the children have to say about all of this?

"At home, the children watch the celebration on television, in the company of the Old Lady. They are very excited and applaud wildly."

In this way, a strain of paternalism runs through all these books, though the figures be masculine, feminine, animal, or vegetable. It is true that there are occasions when grown-ups are mildly ridiculed (Professor Grifaton must endure some minor puns), but in general, the tendency to adore both progenitors and civilization is boundless. Adults and children do not ride a merry-go-round as in Disney, with one group feverishly supplanting the other. Babar's universe is stable and hierarchical. The distance and verticality of authority is, in the case of the principal protagonist, softened by various efforts to make him more innocent, beginning with his name. *Babar* suggests infantile associations (*baby, babbling*, the naive repetition of syllables: ma-ma, da-da, ba-ba), but it can also refer to *Papar*, papa, father—the future model who is to be admired.[42] At the same time, the handwriting in which the story was originally printed appeared equally infantile: rounded, a little unsteady, careful, almost arche-typal, like that of a child who's just learning to write. Perhaps the most notable of the devices intended to preserve the innocence of the paternal figure is the constant flight of birds around Babar, a subtle spiritualization of his figure, a wingèd benediction. It is something like—to make a tremendous leap—the circle of violins around the illuminated head, and voice, of Christ in Bach's *St. Matthew Passion.*

In any case, Babar's personality, once he's converted into king and authority, cannot serve as the only model for young readers. They need, and will get, animals of their own size to capture their sympathies.

At first, Zephyr, a monkey, fills this role. He becomes a compan-ion to Babar's cousin Arthur, who, in contrast to Celeste, must remain forever stuck in the red sailor suit of childhood. The monkey is a pet given as a present to the Old Lady at the end of *The Travels of Babar.* Initially, she keeps him on her lap as if she's nursing him. He's a small, mischievous being with whom children can identify, while the elephant kingdom grows and progresses away from child-hood. Zephyr also has a pictorial advantage and function. Already, at the coronation of Babar in the first book, there were a group of monkeys playing musical instruments with Arthur, prefiguring someone like Zephyr, someone who among the younger animals could be the graceful, sleek equivalent to the Old Lady among the grown-ups, providing the illustrator with a figure graphically opposed to the round, awkward bodies of the protagonists and setting them off.[43]

Be that as it may, de Brunhoff spontaneously created the "nephew" he lacked, in a tactic similar to that used by Disney, and also in Porky Pig, Woody Woodpecker, Tom and Jerry cartoons, and so many others. During this period the author had evidently not yet decided to give Babar and Celeste the progeny with which he later graced them. It is true that in the last scene of *King Babar,* during a jubilant parade, there appear as if by magic, encapsulating the future and skipping insemination, two small elephants with crowns and a third in a baby carriage. This seems to have been a reproduc-tion of the author's own family situation.[44] In the next book, however, this miraculous expansion of the family has been left out, and we instead follow the adventures of Zephyr in his own land of the monkeys, as civilized as that of the elephants.

It's possible that at that point, after Celesteville had been domesticated, Jean de Brunhoff intended to create another alternate space to go alongside it, a place as mysterious and far away as Africa had been before, filled with monsters and legends and danger. Or perhaps a surrogate Africa, populated by little brown beings performing the roles of "darkies." Maybe de Brunhoff did not realize that sometimes one must pay a price for an excess of civilization. It becomes necessary to invent yet another space where everything fantastic, perverse, and weird can be exiled, a place where we can project our dreams and nightmares. Although Zephyr's wanderings anticipate later trips made by the elephants, it seems clear that de Brunhoff was not satisfied with this solution, and it is my personal guess that its continuation would not have had much commercial success.[45]

In any case, the author (and the monkey) returned to his beloved elephants, and in the next book, *Babar and His Children*,[46] he blessed them with offspring: Flora, Alexander, and Pom. But such a procreative process—rare in children's mass literature—is made at the expense of former historical genealogy. The childhood of these little ones is radically removed from that of Babar: Their pranks, accidents, and toys (miniature lions and giraffes) are obviously those of the human species. If someone happened to read this book, without having looked at the others, he would not be able to guess the parents' past nor how they arrived at their present situation. It's almost as if we were witnessing the trials and tribulations of little ones growing up in a typical upper-middle-class French family. A series of wanderings, drawn almost in comic-strip form, exhibit the dangers which the children must overcome.[47] Certainly, de Brunhoff's "cartoons" are less competitive, less cruel, less frenetic, and less violent than their North American cartoon counterparts, but there does seem to be a tendency to build the plot around catastrophic events, which isn't surprising, since it was 1936 and undoubtedly the author could sense death welling up in his lungs. The world is now foreboding and mortal. Flora swallows her bell, and only Zephyr's tiny hand can save her from choking to death.

Alexander falls off a cliff, and only a providential tree, some friendly squirrels, and an amiable giraffe can deposit him safely back in his parents' arms. Finally, Pom goes off sailing in a hat, and a crocodile is just about to eat him up when Babar intervenes, almost like Tarzan, and puts things back in their place.

But Babar couldn't save his author, Jean de Brunhoff, who died in 1937, leaving the next book *Father Christmas* nearly finished. It's impossible to know what new adventures he would have offered us had he lived. Perhaps he would have succeeded in avoiding the temptations of industrialization and assembly lines to which his son fell prey ten years later—after the Second World War, when he resumed his father's series of books. Jean de Brunhoff wrought every volume with splendor (although he was inspired by the values we have revealed), and he also plumbed certain underwater fears and chasms which neither the child nor the adult who projected his anxieties onto that child knew how to express, and he did it with exceptional graphic talent, constructing gigantic natural panoramas and pictorial movements which, for the first time in the history of children's literature, were on the young reader's scale, achieving an almost physical involvement in their ambience of drama and joy.[48]

In any event, de Brunhoff left his son with a character at a point in his evolution where he could afford to walk away from his past and retrace it, as if it had never existed. Up to this point Babar's case has been especially interesting. He is prototypical because he has traveled a road seldom taken by other cartoon creatures. Usually they are atemporal and asexual; their countries neither advance nor regress; they were never born; they have no fathers, mothers, or permanent jobs. Yet, in the end, Jean de Brunhoff left Babar in a situation hardly different from that of other run-of-the-mill cartoon beings. By ignoring his historical origins, the stages of his genesis, he now stood poised, ready to be assimilated into the mainstream of contemporary children's mass literature. Babar, together with his family and kingdom, is ready to enter the secure territory of superficial change within an eternally stable framework, and it's hard to imagine that Jean could have taken a different path than the one adopted by Laurent.

From the moment Babar's country became equal to the metropolis, Babar acquired the same freedoms that are the privilege of any little animal born in Europe or the United States. He can now step into many roles, and he can be molded to fit all the standard versions of mass market literature.[49] Each successive incident will structurally resemble the last, and become just another in a chain of basically similar situations. This is how characters can be transformed (as has happened to Babar himself in France) into dolls, pillows, toothpaste, a monthly magazine, and a television series, although, in all fairness, not on the Madison Avenue scale we have come to expect in mass media products. From now on, his family will be standardized, practically homogenized, resembling any other family in the media, dividing their time between adventures in other spaces and incidental, everyday domestic calamities. This "Americanization" even encroaches on the original scriptlike writing, which is converted into regular print. The child can now come directly into contact with the written word, without the parental figure as a reading intermediary. But some of the magic has also gone.

Of course, the Babar books always retain a certain charm, and often a pictorial interest, which is superior to what one usually finds in similar works of the same time period. Although there are no lack of episodes in which, for example, the elephants solve a "mystery" and catch some larcenous crocodiles,[50] or occasions in which the rhinoceroses go back to their disreputable ways,[51] the general absence of monetary obsessions or of the need for frenzied interchanges in the Babar books comes as a welcome relief. Compared to the assaults made by Disney's characters with their maps and jaunts to the countries of the Third World, Babar's adventures are relatively inoffensive: He loses his crown in Paris, voyages to the land of the birds, or to another wonderful planet.[52] There is also a trace of playfulness and amiability which can be refreshing, like when his brood learns to cook or when they encounter a friendly ghost,[53] a tone which guarantees that their petty domestic squabbles will give way to the miraculous workings of chance. We are mercifully far away from the rivalries, envy, and tension that dominate family relations in Disney, and even farther away from his concept of existence as a marketplace in which each individual, while pursuing his own interests, contributes to the law of equitable distribution of punishment and reward.

54

Consequently, Babar can never be turned into adult entertainment. His adventures are always kept within the limits of paternal authority, in which universal bliss is assured by grown-up figures who never make mistakes, and are unsusceptible to criticism. The little elephants' games and secret passageways, their hunt for pet parrots and their experimentations with recipes and sauces are carried out under the benevolent and rational gaze of responsible beings. Every threat or disagreement has been played down. The young, unable to discover enough friction even to begin to dream of rebellion, end up integrated into a world of adult values which are not to be questioned.

This vision of youth is typically French, and contrasts with American culture. In 1947, the anthropologist Martha Wolfenstein, after watching French parents and children in the park, noted that

> in America we regard childhood as a very nearly ideal time, a time for enjoyment, an end in itself. . . . We do not picture children as longing for adult prerogatives from which they are excluded. Adults tend to feel nostalgic for the carefree times of childhood, or at any rate adolescence. . . . In the continual planning ahead which absorbs adults, the capacity for immediate sensuous enjoyment is often lacking. With the French . . . it seems to be the other way around. Childhood is a period of probation, when everything is a means to an end; it is unenviable from the vantage point of adulthood. The image of the child is replete with frustration and longing for pleasures of the adults which are not for him.[34]

The fact, therefore, that the French see the child as a potential adult, on his way to becoming one, and childhood as a state which no one wishes to return to, explains Babar's universe; while the child in every adult, which Americans seem to hunger for, the constant innocentization of all aspects of life, has found, among other places, a perfect embodiment in Disney. The difference between de Brunhoff and Disney, therefore, goes beyond two temperaments, talents, genres, or audiences. It really derives from underlying assumptions about what growing up means in two cultures. Later on, after we have examined other American mass media products which repeat the same sort of procedures, we will have occasion to suggest some reasons why this infantilization of the adult, this child who is supposedly inside us all, has come to dominate the culture which the United States exports to each and every corner of the globe that its contemporary technology can reach. Suffice it to say for now that Disney's world is directed, for reasons of conviction and business alike, at "children of all ages"—in other words, anyone who has cash in his pocket. Such fiction can reach farther and colonize more minds than Babar can, because it has a more ambitious and universal thrust to it, a concept of the child as a common denominator between varying civilizations that appeals to more deep-rooted dissatisfactions in today's society. It is a world more subtly peruasive than Babar's, more anguished and complex, because it tackles all of reality, intending to encompass the entire gamut of contemporary problems afflicting its readers and spectators. This is not accomplished by expelling these problems from the family or the country, as in Babar's case, where a gentle father figure must guard the gates of the realm. In *Babar the King* two catastrophes descend upon Celesteville right at its happiest moment: The Old Lady is bitten by a snake while protecting Zephyr, who thinks it is a stick; and Cornelius nearly dies in a fire. One suspects that the original traumatic nightmare of the death of the older generation, the death of the mother which caused the little elephants' escape, will be reincarnated in the new city. But that night Babar dreams that a group of monsters, Misfortune and her friends (Fear, Indolence, Laziness, Ignorance, Sickness, Anger, Stupidity, Cowardice, Despair, and Discouragement) have come to occupy Celesteville.

These monsters are, however, quickly driven off by angels in the form of elephants: Goodness, Intelligence, Love, Happiness, Joy, Health, Work, Learning, Perseverance, Patience, and Courage. The next morning Cornelius and the Old Lady recover.

Although such an allegorical, practically medieval vision can be especially comforting to little tykes who don't even know how to read, guaranteeing that the author will avoid tumbling headlong once again into the chasms of violence and loss which characterize the first two volumes, it doesn't succeed in convincing anyone who has had any experience of the real adult world—including the majority of children, who know more than we suppose, although they may be afraid or incapable of expressing it. Contemporary, commercial subliterature, for whatever age group, supplies many of its characters with a lot of the plagues that Babar banished from his kingdom and thus can attempt a full, if distorted, treatment of contemporary contradictions.

Donald Duck is a typical case. If we follow one of his adventures, we'll be able to see how he differs from Babar. In the first few frames of the episode "Safe Kids,"[55] we are presented with a meeting of the Founding Fathers of Duckland Club. "It is the duty of all fathers to watch over their children," says an antiquated female mastodon from the podium. One of the audience members is Donald Duck, who admits that if his nephews were in trouble, "I would resort to my extraordinary strength and skill to save them." He soon gets the chance to put his knowledge and foresight into practice. They are about to travel to South America ("full of danger"). Apparently we are in the presence of a protective, paternalistic attitude similar to Babar's; except, the adult world—Donald in particular—is satirized from the the first scene on. The grown-ups are ridiculous, squinting, archaic, grotesque, and mock-solemn; they smile idiotically, adopt rigid postures, and are gathered for an absurd purpose. They are caricatures of parents. In the multitude we see dogs, hogs, and human beings all mixed together. And Donald is the worst of all. His showing off, trite observations, and know-it-all answers are made even more ironic by his pathetic, scrawny figure (his feet don't even touch the floor), his imbecilic expression, and his one-track mind.

Sure enough, the following frames bear out this critical intent. On board a boat, his nephews calmly contemplate the dock as it moves away from them. Donald (boasting that he'll save the kids if they get into trouble) promptly loses his balance and falls overboard, and it is the youngsters who must save him. This situation is repeated to excess. Donald is awkward, unsteady, cowardly; he constantly makes mistakes, doesn't plan ahead, is egotistical and disorderly. His nephews must constantly rescue him from the most unlikely predicaments. His is a topsy-turvy world, a fact that is emphasized by four or five frames in which Donald is drawn with his feet up in the air (falling down, floating upside down, etc.). The adult is worthless, in spite of his grandiloquence and external gestures.

Although we should bear in mind that this is a comic genre, and that one of the functions of laughter is to shift the weight of society onto those beings who don't know how to fulfill properly their obligations,[56] there is unquestionably more to it than that. In Disney's world, children represent goodness and intelligence, and they are joined by quite a number of other small beings who are more mature than their elders and who emerge triumphant from various adventures: the chipmunks Chip 'n' Dale, the Little Bad Wolf, Dumbo, the fairy Tinkerbell, the mice Gus and Jacques, Jiminy Cricket, the Three Little Pigs, Thumper the rabbit, and Scamp the dog. In other words, he allows his readers to immerse themselves in the dream of all who are on the outside looking in—namely, to criticize those in power and expose them as eccentric, outlandish, dim-witted failures.

However, it is necessary to ask from what vantage point is the critique of Donald Duck and his foolish escapades directed, according to what standards and which norms. First of all, there are, of course, Donald's own indisputable and unfulfilled intentions: to establish an order that protects the defenseless from harm. But, more to the point, Donald is judged by the responsible actions of his nephews. They embody all the things that he should be: They are rational, provident, generous, wise, prudent, courageous—in a word, paternal.

What has happened is that Donald Duck, in his adult form, is really a child; and the little ducks, in their children's form, are really adults. The child (or the adult) reading this narrative takes to task a Donald Duck who embodies all the characteristics that are supposed to be infantile; and he aligns himself with the nephews, who symbolize the sacred virtues of maturity. To give but one example: Huey, Dewey, and Louie base their knowledge of reality on their "Junior Woodchucks Manual," where their entire universe (including, naturally, South America) is found to be defined and prescribed. There is nothing new under the sun. Everything has already been written down; everything is already known. Whereas Cornelius talks like a book, Disney goes one step further, talking like a manual.

All you have to do to make threats and dilemmas go away is to consult a dictionary of the established and the proven. Even chance, the great protagonist-adventurer of these cartoons, is subordinate to order and reason. If Donald would only subscribe to these categories, he would no longer be laughable, and there wouldn't be any discord in the world.

Once the child identifies with other children who are really adults, he participates in his own self-domination, thereby circumscribing his freedom not only to become another person, but also to invent another kind of world. In this way his natural rebellious energies—which should normally be used to question the established order and risk imagining one that is different—are neutralized. It is as if all the characters (and the reader) were trapped in a "nineteenth century orphanage"[57] where no one ever engendered them. Without an escape via biological growth, without the capacity to exercise moral repudiation, without an artistic language to shatter their drab existence, they will live forever on the tyrannical merry-go-round of dominant-versus-dominated, competing to join the club of the fortunate, the rich, and the adult. The instability of this world, where anyone can be displaced at any moment and once again have to begin his mad dash against the others, is not, however, total. For while this delirious pace is maintained, great care is taken not to raise doubts about the foundations of society or its basic tenets—there will always be one voice or one position that offers a wise word to point us in the right direction; for if there weren't, we would be in the anguished terrain of art.

People can be questioned; values are eternal.

In order to prove that this is the message, it will be useful to analyze another Donald Duck episode.[58] Donald and his nephews are sweating it out on rich Uncle Scrooge McDuck's farm. As usual, Donald complains. If he had a million dollars he wouldn't have to feed the pigs, milk the cows, or plow the soil. But Huey, Dewey, and Louie understand that that kind of whining is for little kids. "Unca Donald is hollering his head off about work, as usual," one of them announces. "I know! He's too young to understand things—that boy!" They, on the other hand, are different. They appreciate the meaning and value of work (as Uncle Scrooge himself later recognizes when he plans to raise their salary ten cents a week). "If you're gonna wear a light wool jacket, you've gotta *work* to get the wool," says one of the nephews. Another, gleefully running among the hens, adds, "If you like poached eggs on toast, you've got to *work* to get the eggs."

Donald, however, does not want to recognize that behind money there is effort. It would be easier, he says, as he stomps on a plant, to go to the store and buy "one of these doggoned cucumbers, or whatever they are." But you would need "a million bucks" for that. As he explains to his lucky cousin Gladstone Gander a little while later, after abandoning his chores, it's a question of luck. He tries to convince the lucky goose that he desires such a sum for the two of them. Gladstone does not act immediately, because in recent days his good luck has led him to a diamond ring and gold nugget. But he finally gives in, and naturally a couple of million promptly drops into those two lazy barnyard birds' hats.

As a result of this miraculous catch, the readers will have the opportunity to judge who is right—Donald or his nephews. They will also receive a lesson on the origin of Wealth (of Nations) on the side, because all those bills actually belong to Uncle Scrooge. A tornado emptied the enormous silo where the tightwad hoarded his septillions in order to confuse thieves, and they have been scattered "all over the place." The old curmudgeon doesn't bat an eyelash. He must certainly have read Adam Smith, and Voltaire's *Candide*, for that matter. "Who cares?" he says. "As long as I stay here and worry about my string beans and pumpkins, I'll get it all back." In other words, "*Il faut cultiver son jardin.*" The children also stay put when Donald suggests a round-the-world trip. Frugal, honest, loyal— their concern for the weak serves to exalt them in our eyes. "The pigs and chickens need us." Perhaps they are murmuring, "*Il faut cultiver le jardin des autres*" (You must cultivate the gardens of others, too).

Donald, in turn, is tired of being exploited, so he and Gladstone leave on a tour of the world. Disney tends never to introduce unpleasant things such as hunger, lack of shelter, cold, or disease into his world. (Just try to get these things past the turnstiles at Disneyland sometime!) So there's always been something fishy about Donald's habitual compulsions. His search for money owes more to hysteria and overindulgence than to basic brute necessity. His needs are as false as his eternal unemployment.

In this particular cartoon, tourism and leisure seem to be the prevalent preoccupations. Not just the duck and the goose, but all those who held out their hands have received their million and gone on vacation, fleeing their immediate circumstances.

Which means that there's no one left to pump gas, no one to cook at the diner, no one to drive the bus to some other place. Donald and Gladstone can't even buy a pair of boots to go for a walk! This should not come as a surprise, since workers have never appeared in the Disney universe.

However, in this case it is fundamental to the moral of the story for the workers' very absence—not generally a matter of concern in the mass media—to be brought to our attention. And Donald must be afflicted with something more than bogus necessities. For once, he must be reduced to a true state of misery and destitution. Because his discovery of his own hunger and the value of work will bring him back, as Uncle Scrooge predicted, to the farm. It seems that McDuck has the only food in a world suddenly become rich, where the pressures to produce something no longer exist. The ex-millionaire is able to recuperate his fortune by charging billions for eggs, ham, wool, and cabbage. "Everything went back to normal," the narrator informs us.

Readers and nephews (with their adult voice) have good-naturedly learned how to criticize anyone who absurdly suggests that you can live without working, as the irresponsible Mr. Duck dreamed he could do. They have also learned something else. Donald can start with a million and end up with zero, while McDuck can start with zero and regain all his vast wealth. The old geezer has rewritten the Horatio Alger story in just one episode. The fact that he loses and recovers his fortune in the face of adversaries or thieves, as usually happens in other adventures where he is reduced to penury, once again legitimizes its origins. Behind all that money there is clearly sweat, cunning, calculation, and perseverance. Now. And in the past, too. Such resplendent success sanitizes the past and places years of suffering and setbacks in a self-justifying perspective. Thus, our world, redeemed and sanctified, has been left exactly as it was when we were born. According to this theory, the amount of money each person possesses is equal to the amount of work and cunning he has put into it. There's no reason to think that it took years of appropriating other people's labor to build up that wealth, because it has just been reconstituted in its entirety right before our astonished eyes.

So we are faced with a conflict in which at the very start both competitors have been deceptively and crookedly defined. McDuck is a false capitalist, because he possesses only the abstract, external signs of wealth and not the concrete means to produce it—the means of production. Of course, on top of that, his loss appears unjust because it has been transferred into the hands of someone who hasn't got the slightest intention of working for it. McDuck would, however, be singing (or quacking) a different tune if instead of going after his dollars, they were going after his factories, banks, and land; and even more so if such demands came from the mouths of the laborers, workers, peasants, technicians, and employees who, unlike Donald, have wasted their bodies and minds so such wealth could exist. But, of course, such people are inaudible in the world of Disney.

Donald is their false representative. Donald doesn't claim McDuck's money because its accumulation was made possible solely through the efforts of him and his fellow creatures, nor does he argue that he was forced to sell himself in the marketplace because he was born into a world in which the unjust division of capital had already taken place. He aspires to a million dollars because he's a compulsive freeloader. His industrious and impartial nephews, on the other hand, keep quiet and go along with everything. They never even ask for a percentage of the profits. They keep on working for Uncle Scrooge, participating in the immaculate reincarnation of his estate, without requesting any compensation other than the inherent virtue work confers on them. This deceptive division within the world of McDuck's subordinates (those who don't work are disqualified at the outset because of their own laziness and gluttony, and those who do work have declared themselves happy with their lot) guarantees that an authentic critique on the origin of McDuck's wealth will never be forthcoming.

Furthermore, such a vindication of that cool million's return can be pulled off because the reader's natural resentment toward its initial inequitable distribution is simultaneously deflected into other channels. McDuck poses no threat to anybody, because his money has made him vulnerable and pathetic, without granting him, as we've pointed out, either the power or the means for productive investment. The relationship between the miser and his mountains of gold is completely puerile. At the same time that he jumps into his piles of coins with such playful sensuality, he's also getting a bath of innocence, since it's perfectly clear to the reader that this old man remains paralyzed in a preadult stage.

The result? The socioeconomic status quo has been reinforced, without making McDuck, from the point of view of his behavior and personality, a model for young people, just as Donald could never be such a model. The (class?) struggle between the two, each stuck in his own belligerent, deformed extreme, each recognizable but impossible to identify with, seems like a ridiculous and infantile quarrel from the three nephews' point of view.

They will grow up, industrious, obedient readers of encyclopedic manuals, equidistant from the excesses of their elders, taking care not to repeat the mistakes of the "grown-ups." Just as Babar created a kingdom where nature and development were allied, in which civilization and barbarism could be reconciled, so the little ducks present to their readers—children of all ages—the possibility of realizing the most dogged, undying dream of the twentieth century, the dream which led to the founding of the USA, the dream of working and being your own boss at the same time.

Once again they bear witness, in their individual bodies and in the body of the comic strip, episode after episode, to the same mythic, instantaneous evolution that Babar's country suffered. Such a movement, from inferior to superior, from primitive to urban, from poverty to progress, coincides with the aesthetic experience of reading that the reader has of that world, the way that he vicariously consumes the life of its characters. The reader begins these cartoons as if he were in an underdeveloped territory, with no control over events, and ends up having acquiesced to illumination, revelation, and success—thereby resolving his tensions and ignorance.

The worlds of these "animals" are sheltered from all criticism. It's not just that it's impossible to infiltrate the Old Lady's social class and raise a hand to display a photograph of a hungry child, an illiterate person, a military coup taking place, or a violation of human rights. It's not just that the ducks won't answer any questions about why the power and wealth they so shrewdly defend already has an owner. It's that the reader himself has already accepted a formulation about children's literature—it's all harmless fun—which leaves no room for any alternatives. Facing an already predefined genre, everything in the reader's daily experiences—certainly the way work and play, competition and relaxation, the interrelation of the individual and the group are structured—reinforces the notion that when it comes to children's books and comics everything should be "just entertainment." Politics, being part of a serious and solemn, not to say boring or even painful, other universe, can't conceivably be part of this. Taste, tradition, habit disallow it. Even those hallowed American values—plurality, debate, and the freedom to criticize— are forbidden in that universe.

And so, in the end, the reader himself stands at the door to his kingdom like a guardian demon, forbidding entrance to anyone who wants to ask impertinent questions; and by using that defense mechanism known as "Oh, that's weird," he is ready to repel any intruder who instigates a rebellion.

When the door shuts behind him, leaving him supposedly secure in that magical, saintly space called children's literature, he won't see the blind alley into which he's stumbled, the blind alley which is his past without history and his future without history. He doesn't see it because someone—the Old Lady; Babar; Huey, Dewey, and Louie; or the reader himself when he becomes an adult and must raise his own children—is painting the four infinite walls, the floor and ceiling, someone is painting on a very hard and very real wall a horizon that does not exist.

THREE

THE LONE TRANGER'S LAST RIDE

1 IN WHICH OUR HERO IS INTRODUCED

AS ALWAYS, the Lone Ranger rides again.

As always, he finds an obstacle in his way.

This time, it's a barbed-wire fence. The horseman and his Indian friend, Tonto, are worried because they find it near Wild Horse Valley, the last refuge for these wild horses in that part of the West. A cowboy, alarmed by the Ranger's mask, attacks them, but he is disarmed by a well-fired shot. During the conversation that follows, the man tells them that Milo Bruno, the owner of all these lands, has put up the fence in order to trap the wild horses and become even richer. "Nothing will stop him from increasing his profits with more horses."

And who should arrive at this very moment but Bruno himself, a man not afraid to use his gun, but not so violent that he doesn't care about his employees: Before shooting it out with the Ranger, whom he confuses with a horse thief, he asks his man to move out of the way.

There will be no fight. The Lone Ranger explains that all he's worried about is the valley. "It's practically the last refuge for those animals around here and it should be preserved, not destroyed." Because of Bruno's persistent threats, our hero must clarify: "That valley is a kind of national heritage. Nothing has changed it since the first settlers came to this part of the country."

Bruno doesn't seem convinced. That's not his concern.

The Ranger concedes that legally nobody can stop Bruno from entering the valley. There is, however, a moral reason. And at that moment we observe a child nearby. Bruno's action, says the Ranger, "would ruin a good natural setting and all the wild things living there, which is something that your children will one day inherit."

Once again, Bruno doesn't give in. His son, Jimmy, will inherit the money that is to be made selling horses. Nor does he agree when the Ranger points out that there are herds aplenty on the plains; those are harder to round up.

And off he goes to Wild Horse Valley.

The Lone Ranger and Tonto watch him disappear in a cloud of dust, pondering the situation. They know that the law cannot intervene and that the horses will soon have lost their happy dwelling place.

Night falls. The pair of lawmen are awoken by Bruno's men, who accuse them of kidnapping Jimmy. The Ranger protests his innocence and offers to let his assistant (who, like a good Indian, knows the fine art of tracking) help find the lost heir. Bruno apologizes and accepts. At daybreak, Tonto fulfills the Ranger's prediction: He finds the boy's footprints leading into the valley. As soon as they hear this, Bruno and his cowpokes get ready to ride, but at that very instant, as if by magic, a herd of wild horses rushes at them, and, in the midst of shouts and dust, Bruno loses his balance and must be rescued by the Ranger.

The stampede has shown them all how difficult it will be to save Jimmy. One of the cowboys suggests that they will have to shoot some of the horses if they want to get Bruno's son back.

"Kill valuable horses? Are you crazy?"

Luckily, there is no need to decide between a few more bucks in the bank or the child. The Ranger has the perfect ally to save both the son and the horses. He unsaddles Silver, who was once—and still is—the king of the herd, so he can confront the rest of the horses. A black stallion challenges Silver's right to dominion, but he is beaten back. The path is open. Now the Ranger and Tonto can penetrate Wild Horse Valley: It is full of trees, waterfalls, animal life, and birds. It is this "natural enchantment" that will be ruined if Bruno carries out his plans. "A link to our past," says the Ranger "will vanish, and soon . . ."

He doesn't finish the sentence. For above Bruno's son, whom they've just spotted in the distance, a less amicable natural threat eyes him intently: A cougar is about to pounce on the innocent boy. Since it's impossible to shoot without the risk of hitting Jimmy, the Lone Ranger single-handedly battles and defeats the cougar. He sends the rescued child, and Tonto, back to Bruno. His own problems, nevertheless, aren't over yet. When he calls Silver, he realizes that his horse doesn't pay any attention; he doesn't want to come back, intending to stay in his old natural setting. The only thing the Ranger can think of doing is to remind Silver of the first time that they met. On that occasion, Silver was being mauled by a buffalo and the Ranger's shot saved him. It is possible that by firing his gun again, Silver will recall where his true loyalties lie.

That is just what happens. Like a mouth that salivates to a conditioned reflex, Silver hears the shot and returns to his master.

The main dilemma, let us not forget, must still be resolved. Bruno puts our worries to rest. As long as he's in charge, Wild Horse Valley will be safe. He has been converted to this position by his son, who had gone into the valley in order to see it, "before I spoiled it," and is now amazed and in love with that natural spot.

The Lone Ranger thanks Jimmy for having persuaded his father to care for the wild horses and their refuge.

"Oh, the Lone Ranger thanked me" is Jimmy's last phrase, identifying the protagonist as he gallops off into another adventure, another magazine, another serial, another movie, another radio show, another book, another T-shirt, another lunch box, towards . . .

Towards anywhere, as long as it's far away from our analysis, because we're not going to follow him this time. We're going to skip the music from *William Tell* and ride in the opposite direction, reentering this latest episode of his with the same intensity that he entered Wild Horse Valley. In an attempt to find the Lone Ranger's place in the family of superheroes to which he belongs, we'll uncover the mystery surrounding his origins and the roots of his popularity.

The reader, always on the lookout for new sensations and ready to right a host of wrongs, will have to forgive us if our methods are less violent than the Ranger's, and certainly less lonely. Perhaps we can coax the audience with the promise that dismounting the Lone Ranger is not an activity exempt from danger.

Unfortunately, today it's impossible for me to provide the attentive reader with data on the exact issue of the magazine in which the episode we have just detailed with feigned ingenuousness and minute precision appeared. The first edition of this essay, which included such information, was being bound on September 15,

1973 (four days after Chile's coup d'état) when, at about 10:30 in the morning, uniformed personnel from the Chilean Air Force surrounded the printing office. With submachine guns in hand they insisted the workers surrender. Which was something they couldn't do, since no one was there except a janitor. No matter. The lieutenant in charge of the operation ordered the janitor to be taken in. And just so no one could accuse them of discrimination against human beings, they also took the books being bound, mine among them. "We're reading them," they announced every time an attempt was made to recover the sequestered originals.*

So it becomes rather dramatic to think that the first reader of my analysis of the Lone Ranger turned out to be not a man of letters but, of all things, a man of arms, what you might call a real macho. Then it becomes grotesque, almost painful to imagine that soldier laboriously reading some of the arguments on the pages that follow. Could he have grasped the paradox that he was perhaps scrutinizing his own inner face without even knowing it? That I was explaining to him the ideological causes that had motivated his insurrection to bring "order" to the republic?

Like him, there are many who dream they are Superman, the Lone Ranger, or any of the free, Christian, occidental world's countless other saviors, those who dream they are the guardians of family, property, and public decency, those who dream—without a chink in their armor—that they are the nation's protectors. Like the Lone Ranger, they use persuasion while they believe that this gets results, but they know that, if necessary, they can always reluctantly resort to a weapon that packs more ammunition.

Taking care, then, that our enemies are not planning an ambush, we'll try to convince the reader that behind the Lone Ranger's mask there lurks something more than a face.

Only the brave may follow.

---

*I cannot give the exact date of the comic we are analyzing, but we can assume it comes from the sixties or early seventies, when ecology became an issue. The dialogues, obviously, have been translated back into English and are not the original words a reader might find in the American version of the comic.

2 IN WHICH OUR HERO DEMONSTRATES THAT OF WHICH HE IS CAPABLE

A FIRST, SUPERFICIAL reading allows one to observe that the Lone Ranger confronts and resolves a central problem—the defense of Wild Horse Valley—and also several offshoots of this situation (for example, Silver's attempted escape). His physical force, his skills and abilities, his persuasive talents, and his irreproachable ethics indicate that we are dealing with a man excellently equipped to overcome any obstacle, large or small, that may get in his way. When he leaves, there remain no dilemmas or difficulties. All is quiet, and a Happy New Year to one and all.

The main interest, as in any work of fiction dominated by action, is to destroy an adversary who threatens to disturb the tranquility of the cosmos. The Lone Ranger's exploits are essential to the smooth functioning of that world, for he zaps the cancerous tumor of disharmony out of existence.

But why is Bruno's attitude dangerous? Why does the reader immediately sense that he embodies a pernicious but corrigible force? Why do his decisions unleash such indignation in the hearts of the Lone Ranger and his fans, who cry out for a rectification that will restore the equilibrium of a world gone awry?

Apparently it's because Bruno tosses his boundless greed for profit, his unbridled capitalism, right in our face. He is a man blinded by his love of money. (He mentions several times that it's of the utmost importance.) He subordinates everything (his son's future, and the future of his lands) to the search for wealth. He is a man who "has lost his mind."

So, on an elementary level, a conflict is set up between Money and Virtue. Let us note, however, that the Ranger is not against Bruno's getting rich. On the contrary, he suggests a legitimate way of doing so: Hunt horses on the plains. To attack Bruno by way of his wealth would be to go against one of the basic rules laid down by the creators and owners of the Masked Man: "Property is the fruit of labor. That some should be rich shows that others may become rich and hence is encouragement to industry and enterprise."[1]

It isn't so strange, then, that those on Bruno's payroll are considered not as a source of wealth, but only as permanent, passive, and loyal supporters of Bruno. Conflict, if it occurs, can only be between the rancher and the products of the land, the natural resources that he wants to use up, never between him and his well-treated workers. He denies the Lone Ranger's request because he would spend too much effort, time, and, therefore, money trying to round up ponies on the broad flatlands. What initially appears to be a struggle between money and virtue is in fact an antagonism between virtue and all money gotten in excess of certain limits. The rivulets of Bruno's morality have run dry, because he desires to augment his fortune by breaking minimal rules of convenience and respect. All he has to do is renounce the pursuit of those wild horses in order to once again be an exemplary figure, an understudy for the Ranger himself as the valley's defender. He'll doubtless continue reaping profits, but now he'll do it in the proper place, having earned it with his sweat: He'll go to the plains.

As we discovered in the previous essay, the same process is used to obscure—in an unconscious, automatic way—the creation of wealth in Disney's comics. The assurance that Bruno makes his fortune directly from nature eliminates a valid critique of capitalism, substituting for it another type of critique: Money's bad qualities do not stem from the social relations of production, where some own the means of production and others own only their bodies, but from the abuses owners commit against nature, their attempts to extract goods beyond certain decent boundaries. In other words, there is only one true snag which the system must untangle in order to feel clean. At the end of the story, Bruno proves not only that he's obtained his fortune by valid means, but that he's also capable of mending his ways when he makes a mistake.

Bruno therefore receives preferential treatment. Nobody doubts the legality of his claim. But as the propaganda brochure we've just quoted reads, the Lone Ranger "registers disapproval of . . . men who, even though within their legal rights, step beyond the bounds of fair play."[2] The Lone Ranger can't simply stop such plunder by citing constitutional clauses or putting his rival in jail. What he does do has been described by Don Beattie, a scriptwriter for the Lone Ranger radio program, in explaining the difference between his character and Robin Hood: "The difference is that Robin Hood stole from the rich and was a rogue. The Ranger doesn't have anything against rich people—if they've made their money honestly. But sometimes if there are some very rich or powerful ranchers who are trampling on the rights of the little people, the Ranger will have to 'convert' them so that they can see the error of their ways."[3] That is, his strategy is based on moral regeneration. He relies on the eternal ethical reserves which the landowner possesses in his heart.

One must compare this attitude with the drastic sanctions imposed on those, such as robbers, who instead of being the possessors of private property, attack it. Bruno is a *free* man, fit for the privilege of choosing, just like all characters belonging to the world of the dominant. When written laws are incapable of setting a limit on their excesses, it's enough to appeal (with the aid of a child, as we shall see) to the transgressor's hidden goodness.

Of course, Bruno's infringement and repentance can't be understood as an abstract movement of the soul, operating in a vacuum. It evokes some very precise social tensions. When he wishes to make himself richer by surpassing the rightful limits, by assaulting nature, the heritage of all mankind, he becomes, for contemporary readers, an accomplice of pollution—that demon and villain of recent decades. The public will connect Wild Horse Valley's overexploitation with contamination of the atmosphere and the water, ecological and climatological perturbations, the poisoning of the flora and fauna, the systematic disappearance of age-old resources. What the public and the magazine will *not* do is admit that such phenomena accompany capitalism (or is it just industrial society?) like endemic diseases: the need to maximize profits, lack of planning, unbridled competition, and a general lack of restrictions, controls, or specific responsibilities. The possibility that an affluent society may inevitably become effluent, that Bruno must destroy the valley in order to stay in business, passes them by.

Such a separation of the system's excesses (Bruno's mistakes) from the system itself (the legitimacy of his fortune) has historical antecedents. James Ridgeway has observed in *The Politics of Ecology* that the first conservationists at the beginning of the twentieth century were not so much opposed to the idea of "business" as to that of "bad business," since they were under the impression that only the largest corporations could collaborate in the preservation of natural resources. "In a manner similar to Thorstein Veblen, they distinguished between the efficient production engineers and the adventurous profiteers."[5]

But even though this attitude toward Bruno is grounded in historical models (which also function, as we have seen, for the ducks on their visit to the Wild West), the possibility for excesses such as his to assume a leading role in the fiction industry would have to wait until the public could feel that his problem was its own, until its outrage became widespread and everyday. Between 1950 and 1970 the number of visitors to state parks quintupled (from a hundred million to half a billion). In the late 1960s, public concern with and public campaigns to clean up the environment gained momentum, giving rise to everything from Earth Day to the health food movement and the *Whole Earth Catalogue*.

When the Ranger severely chastises Bruno, we are not only a long way from the Lone Ranger radio program of the 1930s, but almost inconceivably far from the first reactions to the devastation of European industrialization. Initially, from the fifteenth century to the seventeenth, Nature was deified and converted into a site of nostalgia—nostalgia for an autonomous agrarian structure, far removed from the city, a place where people led a supposedly idyllic way of life. This was one of the ways that a waning aristocratic and courtly ideology had of defending itself against the grinding encroachments of adverse history. After the eighteenth century there began to flourish another type of critique on the horrors of a landscape and society in transition (perhaps Blake was its first involuntary prophet). However, this attack on the ravages of "progress" actually occupied only a handful of people, principally writers and artists in the century and a half that followed. During the same years that Dostoevsky meditated on the ills of modernity, smoke was proclaimed to be highly desirable in Middleborough, England—an unmistakable sign of the "advances" made by mankind.[6] During the period when Mary Shelley projected onto Frankenstein the fears and insecurities of a divided elite coming to terms with technology, the Benthamites began to plan the first urban sanitation systems, not to oppose industrial growth, but to aid it.[7] It isn't strange, then, that the first "conservationist" initiatives slowly gestating in the United States, did not involve wholesale reforms of the system, but the creation of isolated islands in legislation and in nature which would guarantee that some land and resources be preserved while the rest was incorporated into the industrial development of the country.

In order to accept the magical metamorphosis of Bruno, moments ago a destroyer of the landscape, now the victorious custodian of its delights, the reader must begin by accepting that the world is justly divided in two: the plain, where a man can pounce upon and seize nature, and the valley, which he can enter only with a reverential attitude. Because Bruno's activity is restricted to the plain, which is never seen, the reader forgets what Bruno does on that plain. As long as he preserves the valley, of his own volition and without legal pressure, all his other decisions are sanctified and used as proof that when it comes to nature, lust for profit does reach a point of self-constraint.

Bruno's renunciation of more money demonstrates the ethics inherent in his way of garnering economic benefits. Similarly, corporations, the actual managers of the economy, must only meditate on their own little boys and girls and let themselves be morally directed by irreproachable advisers like the Lone Ranger for the world's balance to be restored. Bruno saves the ponies; oil companies save animal species, advertising that millions of dollars are being set aside to investigate methods of combating pollution (without informing the public that the millions were earned in the first place by selling all those new products that cause pollution). The valley's presence becomes a sort of collateral, a blank check for Bruno, just as chemical and oil companies present themselves in their advertising as enthusiastic beautifiers of nature, not as its violators.

But Wild Horse Valley also has other, less tangible uses. In terms of physical space, it is described (and drawn) as an oasis of perfection, of idealized nature. From the point of view of time, surprising phenomena take place there. People who enter the valley lose their temporal sense. As Bruno's son can testify, they become dissociated from that slavery we call the clock and routine. We've already seen in the previous essay how the myth of primitivism was created: out of a need for underdeveloped countries to serve as temples of a happy, primeval nature, where the daily, limiting world—with all its contradictions and improvements, its complexities and advances—ought not penetrate. Such a desire for idyllic spaces crops up obsessively every time urban life burgeons, in whatever epoch (ancient Rome or Alexandria, for instance). However, it is when mercantile capitalism expands, and especially later, when the process of industrialization accelerates, that such illusions of a place unblemished and intact become widespread, practically universal, in their attraction.

Zones such as Wild Horse Valley fulfill the same function in the media as tourist resorts in society. Within that deified Nature, harried city dwellers are able to reconcile the conflicting tensions that menace their mental life every day. Wild Horse Valley wipes out contemporary history. In it everyone is compelled, like it or not, to pass through a museum of pure and free forms, where everything is permanent and secure. While Bruno watches over the valley, any pedestrian can take an ahistorical stroll, transcending the limitations of his era to communicate with all the men of the past and those who are to come.

Thus Bruno threatens to violate his own past when he intends to rustle horses. The valley is how nature was before man arrived, and Bruno's final decision insures that it will stay that way forever, out of the reach of progress (with its positive and negative effects). Yesterday, today, tomorrow, millions of years before or after, the precise date means nothing, for we're dealing with a diorama of the West just as it was before the settlers defaced it, a place where the concrete history of the United States never happened. The valley, then, revitalizes one of North America's foundation myths, that of the frontier—the push ever westward—which has been explored, populated, and redefined now for over three hundred years. The

New Frontier (of technology) about which John F. Kennedy spoke, could supposedly be expanded infinitely, as long as it simultaneously preserved its ties with the past as a source of inspiration and security, and as long as no one questioned the spirit behind the economic and geographic expansion of the Old Frontier.

Nourishing this myth is the job of places like Wild Horse Valley: recreating the conditions of the nation's beginnings so that every Bruno's little boy can visit the past and regain the clean perspective with which the first settlers viewed that immaculate land. Represented in that valley is the inexhaustible spirit of the West in its entirety, the eternally renewable innocence of a country wishing to be, as D. H. Lawrence put it, forever young.

But what is it assumed that the settlers saw? And what, therefore, will North American children (and all the children of the world who buy North American magazines) learn about?

Pure Nature.

Indigenous North American tribes, the true first settlers, have been excluded from that retrospective, from that primeval glance. Those who were born there have disappeared.

"If Bruno and his men invade the valley," says the Ranger to, yes, none other than Tonto, "a link with our past will vanish."

In the cartoon, the Indian, like the white man, contemplates the valley from afar, from the standpoint of an advertisement for exotic vacations. His past, according to this type of fiction, is the same as the white man's, the same "humanity" embraced by the elephants when they stopped being primitive.

It seems that in this version of history the Indians are not the former possessors of the soil. They are not natural. They constitute an exception, something that is contingent. Since "aboriginal" human life is not included within the animal and vegetable landscape, history is learned apart from the actual violent conquest of the West. The true poles of history are untouched nature on one hand and white civilization on the other. It is the Anglo-Saxons and their descendents who have taken legitimate possession of that nature, transforming one part of it (building cities, industries, highways, grocery stores, and shopping malls) and "conserving" another.

Once again, reduced options.

One of the possibilities open to the Indians is to admire the valley from outside, accepting that that expanse pertains to them only so long as they pay homage to the viewpoint of the great white man at their side, in short, proclaiming this history is what appears in the textbooks, museums, and tourist hotels of current North American culture—the history in which Pontiac is an automobile and not a chief of the first Americans. The other possibility is to blend them into the landscape as one more animal alongside the cougar and the buffalo, to admire their natural, merely passive and anecdotal existence, and then put them back on their reservations. To be a shadow among other shadows, a coincidence that glides almost unnoticed along the surface of the land.

In either case, the valley's authentic owner is Bruno, who keeps it for the entire nation, including the Indians, who did not learn how to separate themselves from nature, who did not earn the rights to either the valley or the plains because they did not invent progress, money, competition, foreign incursions, supermarkets, machine guns, the light bulb, or the automobile. That is the punishment imposed upon them for not having invented Yankee civilization. If they've lost their lands, it's because they could not come up with the proper ancestors, or technical and moral writings. In the palatial mansions of the South, some of which have become relics you can visit for a dollar, the guide blushes when asked where the slaves slept.

"They slept out back," says the guide after a slight hesitation.

And there's nothing there behind the house. Those habitations, where the hands that built the house rested, have been torn down.

Each of the Lone Ranger's episodes (and every adventure in every subliterary publication) is an act of omission, a silence, a history book with blank pages. Time and time again, from the earliest age, a vision of the temple of the past is projected that purges the violence, erases the conquests, and causes all the strife to settle like the dust on the plains. The tourist visits the valley just as the reader visits the Lone Ranger's comic book: Neither of them sees the origin of Bruno's property.

Thus Wild Horse Valley obliquely, without calling attention to itself, attests to the fact that the West was subjugated by its true heirs apparent, those chosen by God, luck, or innate virtue, those deserving—even before they've set out on their journey—of that promised land. They knew what to do with it. They changed it to create progress, and when the moment came for that progress to threaten nature (lots of promise and little land remained), Bruno returned to demonstrate—along with the Lone Ranger, Jimmy, Tonto, the cowboys, and the reader—that he knew all along how to take care of that treasure. The rights to that land are established first by historically destroying its initial possessors and later supressing that act of destruction.

Starting from this premise—that the Indians are not essential to the history of the West, but an unfortunate accident—one can understand that any charitable allocation of certain territories to them is more than enough compensation. This is why, in other episodes of the Lone Ranger, when the redskins appear as aggressive or malicious beings, it is because they deny the justice of this distribution. They doubt the whites' rights to *all* the land. They are, of course, defeated.

On the other hand, there are times when the aborigines who happen to be around wish not to take possession of what belongs to the whites, but to defend the portion (minimal, to be sure) allotted them after the plunder. For example, in the adventure, "The Buffalo Herd," several white crooks have started a fire so the buffalo that the Indians live on will cross to the other side of the train tracks, a line that demarcates the territory where they're not allowed to hunt. Even though the Lone Ranger discovers the bandits just as the Sioux are about to violate the limit, the Indians are detained by soldiers anyway. "Halt. You know that, according to the treaty, no group of armed Indians may cross the tracks. . . . Go back." For a few moments, it is possible that a tempestuous conflict might erupt, since various irrational Sioux insist on opening fire on the soldiers. However, the chief trusts the Ranger, who wishes to "avoid a struggle between the two factions." When the masked rider promises to "reclaim the herd for you, but don't start any fights," the chief swears that "no Sioux will be the first to shoot, friend." But the buffalo must be recovered. They are the natives' only sustenance. Naturally, the Lone Ranger devises a trick: The Indians (unarmed) go along the line, and by using their drums (feigning a "great Indian dance") stir up such a racket that the buffalo cross back over into their original territory. Now, when the outlaws want to break the treaty by pursuing the buffalo, it is the soldiers who save the day. "Get out of here. I won't permit any armed group, be they white or Indian, to cross the track." The chief must acknowledge this sort of fairness. "Thank you. You have been just."

What the Sioux chief defends, in reality, is the justice of the white man's distribution of the lands, which once belonged entirely to the Indians. Being just with the savages guarantees that the treaty which the white man made them sign (under military duress), and which he violated and remade and violated whenever he liked, will not be altered. The one who's been plundered becomes a retroactive guardian of the laws that gave rise to the plunder. Whoever attempts to go against those laws, whether they're Indian or white, will receive their exemplary sanction.

Neither in reality nor in the script will the Indians ever again recover Wild Horse Valley. By definition, a priori, it was never theirs to begin with.

Thus, the valley is revealed to us as a center of holiness. All quarrels and contradictions have been eliminated. Ponies, and children, dwell there in "happiness." It's an "enchanted" place, even though it still has cougars lurking nearby.

Nature is not only given the task of enriching Bruno, once he consents to put a stop to his excesses; but in addition, as long as he won't fill that virgin atmosphere with smog or nuclear reactors, it will act as a moral regenerator, a fount of virtue for him. It will be the errant landowner's son, his biological heir, who will unleash an ethical revolution. This alliance, nature and child, is possible because within the story both symbolize innocence, "natural" goodness, that which has not been chewed up and aged by civilization. In human society, children embody the same values as Wild Horse Valley does in history. They are something like its ambassadors. Bruno might be wrong, but he has a family and in that family a small human being who will in no way participate in his father's aberrations. This is the salvation of the Brunos of this world: Their sons are capable of absorbing that valley's miraculous lesson. They then can change their fathers.

The actual fact that humanity is reborn with every baby, and that each new arrival potentially has the right—and I think the duty— to remake the history he or she inherits, is transformed into a purification of that history and that inheritance. To begin at zero, without personal memory, is seized as an occasion for the erasure of collective memory and history; is used to whitewash and forget the past, to which the newest arrival, whether he likes it or not, is linked.

So Jimmy's function in this series is neither fortuitous nor exceptional. David Wilson Parker, in his study of 120 Lone Ranger radio programs produced between 1951 and 1955, found innumerable children, all good, all possessing some kind of problem generally stemming from an adult's unsympathetic or egotistical attitude. The Lone Ranger's intervention invariably puts things in their place. Which isn't hard. After all, the scriptwriters forgot to include even one case of juvenile delinquency in their model, not one case in which a youngster was the hero's enemy, not his ally. Not only have the wicked had their past taken away from them; they aren't even permitted a future. And they were never children, either. Nor will they ever be. Unless they repent.

In order to show how general this tactic is, all we have to do is pay another visit to our elephant friends. In one of their last volumes, *Babar and the Wully-Wully*,[8] the children of the King of the Pachyderms stumble upon a small natural being, the Wully-Wully, who is something like their own alterego, adorable and utterly innocent. The rhinoceros Rataxes (remember him—that malignant being who provoked war because he didn't want to accept naughty Arthur's apologies?) steals the animal and locks him up, forlorn, in a cage. Arthur and Zephyr embark upon a rescue mission and succeed in regaining their little treasure. But the rhinos counterattack (like an earthquake, a hurricane, observes the narrator, placing them in the realm of natural disasters), making off with the Wully-Wully once again. It seems war is again the only alternative. However, this time that won't be necessary. Flora, the smallest of Babar's brood, decides to speak directly with Rataxes in his city. Their dialogue follows:

"Why," Flora asked, "do you keep Wully-Wully in a cage? And why did you steal him? He is not yours."

"He's not your either," grumbled Rataxes.

"You are right," said Flora, "but I am the one who found him and I never tied him up. I didn't put him in a cage either, yet he stayed with me."

Perplexed, Rataxes scratched his ear. "If I let him out he will run away."

"Perhaps," said Flora, "But he will come back when he wants to."

The last scene shows Wully-Wully absolutely free, playing with the elephants and Rataxes too. "It's really amazing," comments Babar. "Our little Flora has completely tamed the great, rough Rataxes."

I would not want to attack the implied moral: There are things that children (big ones like Rataxes and little ones like Flora) should learn to share. But while we're at it, it might be worth calling attention to procedures similar to those used in the Lone Ranger series in a book well removed from his geography and public. The fact that violence has not had to be used to convince Rataxes is a sign that he possesses sufficient moral depth to be able to enjoy that little animal (who is something like a miniature Wild Horse Valley). Rataxes, like Bruno, is a convert, not on the road to Damascus, but on the road to Elephantland. From now on he can be handled comfortably by the readers, since he respects their rights, and shares with them and the children certain natural reserves that succeed, moreover, in rejuvenating him.

If such methods had not worked, a figure such as the Lone Ranger would have had to intervene. As a matter of fact, as we'll see later on, the superheroes combine excessive strength with an irrefutable capacity to represent the natural order, to the point of fusing and confusing themselves with it. In the Wild Horse Valley episode, the Ranger is none other than the efficient executor of the actions that nature and childhood require in the adult world, in the corrupt world of history, in order to triumph. The superhero is a Jimmy or Flora with an adult body and extraordinary powers to manifest the goodness about which children supposedly dream.

However, there is no lack of danger or potential ideological friction inherent in such an exaltation of nature. For if the land is so wonderful and enchanting, if children (and heroes) feel themselves to be so thoroughly interpreted by it, what is there to prevent them (and their repentant, born-again parents) from leaving their daily lives, abandoning profit once and for all, and forever renouncing all dealings with the contemporary world? Why not live, as the super-hero does, outside of society and its limitations and create a community of loners and outsiders like those that shaped the West, or at least its myth?[9] From this perspective and beneath this cloak of fascination, Wild Horse Valley threatens to swallow all surrounding reality. The magical world of nature, which is somewhat peripheral and transient in the adventure, could be transformed into the preeminent center of aspirations. If humans find their true being there, what's to stop them from seeking their essence there too? In short, as those who retire from the world to their utopias of free communities without worldly possessions might put it: Why not be a perpetual child?

It's not a new solution. It has followed capitalism as a phantom, an escape route, and a challenge throughout its entire development, but it had never experienced such a large-scale, tenacious, and—why not admit it—dangerous incarnation as in the North American counterculture of the sixties. Outside of established power, but right in the thick of the spectacular grandeur of an opulent, imperial society needing more than what it produced within its bountiful borders in order to live,[10] the counterculture was proposing another type of society, an alternative humanity. In every sphere, their predominant ideals and their critique of what already exists demanded a return to nature, and certainly a nostalgia for a lost innocence—the possibility of continuing to be young and pure in an increasingly corrupt and aging world; to be Jimmy and convert Brunos poisoned by power and consumption.

Just take a look at some of the titles of the movement's bibles: *Small Is Beautiful,* with its worship of the minimal, of a technology (which has in effect been infantilized) enabling us to survive on a human scale; *The Greening of America,* in which a country's revolution is visualized as a peaceful gardening process, a return to the Eden we all have inside; *De-Schooling Society,* where it is suggested that unlearning, starting over is, to a large extent, the way to reduce social conflicts. You must diminish and withdraw from the services offered by civilization and become a community of adults who are ready to be children again. Such utopian attitudes, embraced by millions of people, are bound to create uneasiness and anxiety among the dominant groups. There's no problem with worshiping nature (even Bruno does it). But it's another thing to stop consuming. You can be Jimmy as long as there's a guarantee that Jimmy will one day become Bruno.

This digression gives us the emotional context in which we can ask why Bruno does not take the lesson learned by his son to its logical conclusion: to renounce the world of the plains once and for all, turn the entire West into a worthy and marvelous setting, and live like the pioneers (but without their kind of hardships).

It is the question Babar's children will never ask: Why did you leave the jungle, Daddy?

The dream of nature as regeneration has been used to save Bruno and wipe away the exploitation of past and present, but the remedies for Bruno's sickness—the valley and the child—threaten the cured patient's future. Will they turn into a nightmare that could end up destroying the very man it meant to rescue? How do you get the child out of the valley? How do you make sure that once he's grown up, the child will want to get richer on the wearying plains?

It doesn't actually matter whether the child decides to come out of the valley or not, whether Bruno continues hunting horses on the plains and selling them in the cities, or whether the valley remains obediently frozen in its assigned space. The doubts are there in the reader's mind anyway, and the magazine must address them. A fictitious structure has been erected, one that plays on the reader's emotions and leads him in certain directions. The introduction of disturbing critical elements in each adventure, in each work of pulp fiction, is what usually gives them their tension and interest, what profoundly engages the public. But in the same adventure there must appear forces that respond to those anxieties and alleviate the questioning. There can be no loose ends to tie. The final message cannot be the opposition of natural goodness to contemporary evil. Just imagine the Lone Ranger galloping in favor of valleys and children (not to mention those eternal innocents—Indians, blacks, and other "primitives"). Just imagine him proclaiming that the entire

West should be returned to the state of Wild Horse Valley. Just imagine him struggling to establish a utopia not in people's hearts but in their streets.

However, this is not what happens, because the Ranger, like Bruno, knows his limits and limits his desires. Just as Babar is innocence that has agreed to become civilized and grow up, the Ranger is Jimmy with responsibility and power; his conduct alone restores the reader's peace of mind and provides an outlet for his or her possible fears and frustrations. New contradictions have been generated by the very solution to the initial conflict. The defense of the valley and the regeneration of the landowner have opened up the eventuality that the reader or Jimmy, or both, will deviate, may demand that the prerogatives of childhood or of uncorrupted nature take precedence over society's interests and organization. If left unanswered, these loose ends will unsettle the central message, make the audience uncomfortable, punch us full of question marks.

To use the analogy of medicine once again, the Lone Ranger must demonstrate that too much medicine can cause greater damage than the original illness. This is not something that the writer or illustrator of the story is intentionally or deliberately setting out to do. He is probably not even conscious of what he's doing. He will simply try to complete his tale, to make it pat, round, comforting, unified. He will unleash, within the world of fiction itself, inside the story, a series of actions that should anticipate or forestall any doubts that may have grown in the audience from the plot's movements and tensions. Every window that industrial works of fiction opens looks out not onto another reality, but into a mirror that always reflects the same thing—the reader's own familiar surroundings.

This is what happens in the adventure we've analyzed. It is insinuated, for example, that nature contains destructive aspects; that the sun can be unmerciful; that besides toasting your skin at the beach, it can also burn it, so you've got to use a suntan lotion or some other luxurious, highly publicized mixture—that is, a product of civilization. Similarly, the cougar lies in wait for the child and someone ought to kill him. Or the horses stampede and Bruno must be saved. The fact is, nature frequently gets out of hand, and when it does, certain reservations and misgivings arise; not many, but enough for the reader to comprehend subliminally that the same nature that cleanses can, when it lacks human and social protection, when the Lone Ranger is not present, also cause great damage. For instance, Wild Horse Valley's dangerous side is not ignored: "For though . . . Wild Horse Valley was the paradise it seemed, he [Silver] had reason to know of certain sneaking coyotes and lone gray timber wolves, not to forget that tawny murderer, the lean cougar of the hills—all of whom preferred baby horse-flesh to any other delicacy."[11] Two precivilized forms come face to face: The wilderness in its cannibal aspect once again intimidates defenseless childhood.

However, it is Silver who is the adventure's only truly natural being, and also a character who genuinely corrects our notions about nature and the child. So crucial is his exemplary nature that it becomes a countermelody, an auxiliary motif which takes up more than one fourth of the episode's entire space.

To begin with, the same social relations of domination found in the world of men are reproduced in the world of nature: Silver is king there. A black creature (naturally!) tries to snatch his scepter. The white horse vanquishes the darkness (naturally!). Thus, the initial erroneous assumption we might fall into, that everything in the world of animals is free and communal, is quickly rectified. Hierarchies are tolerated there as well—stepping-stones of merit and strength, leadership and servitude. Anyone who thinks he's going to find a different, democratic conception of the relationship between human beings is gravely mistaken. Silver's world imitates that of Bruno and his men, of the Lone Ranger and Tonto. Nature is irremissibly socialized, at least in this respect.

Silver decides, once he's back at the head of his clan, to get away from the Lone Ranger and civilization. Actually, what the horse does is follow the course that the Lone Ranger and Jimmy indicate as the positive route to take. Silver is a natural being. Why shouldn't he go back to his valley, if it's so marvelous, enchanting, and unde-filed? If the Ranger doesn't want Bruno to hunt colts in the valley, why doesn't he let his own horse return freely to the land he was taken from? Poor Ranger: Not only has the landowner given him trouble, but his own horse has gone off into the protective valley. It's just as if a child molester suddenly discovers that the unknown girl in bed with him is his own daughter.

But we shouldn't be so quick to pity the Lone Ranger. He still has a few tricks up his sleeve. He's a friend of the storywriter (and the magazine's owner). He's going to get his horse back without resorting to the violence suggested by Bruno. He'll simply remind Silver of the origins of their collaboration. What happened, as you can read in *The Lone Ranger: The Story of a Backwoods Texan*, a book that recounts the origins of the mounted lawman and his companions, is that the Ranger saved Silver from a wild buffalo and nursed him back to health. Then, with an element of detachment which, as we'll see, is an indispensable feature of his personality, the Ranger let the horse go. Tonto was astonished, but the Ranger renounced any further interest in the matter. However, as the animal trotted off, the Texan called out nostalgically, "Farewell, Silver." The animal suddenly reared up on his hind legs, spun around, froze for an instant, and came back over to them. " 'Silver, my friend,' exclaimed the Ranger, stroking his neck with infinite gratitude, for the animal had offered his freedom."[12]

Silver's recognition of these particular ethical structures evidently predates his acquaintance with the Lone Ranger, for according to a different book, his wounds were caused not by one buffalo but by a whole stampede in which Silver sacrificed himself to save his herd of defenseless mares and colts. "The stallion was doomed——barring a miracle."[13] The miracle's name? The Lone Ranger, who intervenes, like a saint or a god, to protect a fellow creature, a member of the same altruistic order.

So Wild Horse Valley is surrounded. Not only by physical boundaries but also by boundaries that can only be called ideologies. The king of the untamed creatures who are free to roam the valley furiously has accepted submission as a way of life, without any kind of pressure (as long as we forget emotional blackmail, that vice of guilty relations between men which we are to suppose has an effect even on those of the equine persuasion as well). As a result, the Lone Ranger's most cherished private property, extracted (like all his goods) directly from nature is the fruit of his goodness and his offer of free assistance. Silver cannot be emancipated because, way down deep, he really doesn't want to be. In this way, any possible antisocial stirrings which the reader or Jimmy might sense are nipped in the bud. Just take a lesson from Silver, who has repeatedly had the opportunity to leave the plains and go back to the valley, but has chosen instead to reside in Bruno's world, imperfect though it may be.

By defending his own private property, his own personal stronghold, the Ranger also demonstrates the legitimacy of Bruno's activities on the plain. As long as no legal and moral rules are broken, it's perfectly acceptable and desirable for men to continue enjoying the benefits of the land and the goods to which they are entitled. The only things the Ranger owns are his abilities and his ethics, and with them he succeeds in obtaining his horse. Bruno is legally entitled to round up horses, and he also has the means (though nobody knows how he acquired them) to do just that. By limiting his search to those places which have been morally sanctioned, he too succeeds in obtaining his horses. We'll see later on that the difference between Bruno's interests and the Ranger's disinterests forms the basis for the latter's position as upholder of the law. But for now, the only thing to bear in mind, with eyes made misty with emotion, is this message and lesson for young readers: May the reasonableness and loyalty of a horse not fail the generations to come!

The adventure "Fire in Wild Horse Valley"* confirms this. Once again the magical valley is threatened. The landowner Frias wants to start a fire to trap a thieving horse which he insists lives there. The Lone Ranger (after once again being mistaken for a bandit) says that's impossible. "I'm sure the rustling horse didn't come out of here. Horses never leave the valley." Frias doesn't want to hear explanations: "Well, your horse left the valley," he says, referring to Silver. A major mistake, Mr. Frias. You obviously haven't read the Ranger's other books and magazines. You really ought to buy them. Then you would realize that the Lone Ranger's steed emerged from nature in order to advance the cause of justice and never to destroy

*Published in Chile in the early 1970s (vol. XIX, no. 231). "Frías" is probably a Spanish translation for an English surname.

private property. It's unthinkable to compare him to a misguided equine-type who has resorted to *robbery*.

Frias must defend his material wealth by destroying natural and spiritual resources, just like any other Rataxes. "The valley means nothing to him. It doesn't hold for him the memories that it holds for us, and he doesn't care about the wild life reigning there, either." Overcoming a series of obstacles which are of no interest to us here, the Lone Ranger succeeds in putting out the fire. But it's Silver's role that really concerns us, for he must defend his unblemished record. When the thieving, rebellious horse attacks Dan (another child, this time the Ranger's own nephew—in other words, the quintessential model of unspoiled youth) it is Silver who intercedes, overthrowing the assailant and saving the generation of tomorrow. Meanwhile, in the picture you can make out the imposter (a white horse, of all things!) groveling in the dirt at the king's feet. Frias shows he's learned his lesson: "Your horse defeated that crazy colt! At last the other horses will stop disappearing."

Silver is in charge of restoring order to the animal world when it gets out of hand. He saves Frias's financial life and the life of a child. The usurper is termed "crazy," a way in which the powerful have always classified and filed away contradictory phenomena. To consider such an unsettling element merely abnormal is to deny its significance—that is, conveniently to ignore the causes that produced it.

The valley was simply not meant for that rebellious creature. On the contrary, when sectors of nature fail to recognize the moral rules that permit a collaboration between nature and society, when the wilderness goes against the human order (which also means the way in which the production and distribution of wealth are organized), it becomes necessary to reestablish certain basic hierarchies and frontiers. It's very clear that Silver constantly symbolizes the limit that those North American idols—nature and freedom—encounter on the road to expansion. The limit is economic—private property—though that limit is itself limited by certain moral boundaries. As Frias puts it, "And to think that for practically no reason at all I would have set fire to that beautiful valley full of horses. Thanks to the Lone Ranger, I didn't do it." Mutual respect for the dividing line, not crossing the train tracks, worshiping the peace treaty, learning what your own place and prerogatives are, and teaching the other side its, all fuse together to ratify peace and harmony. Wild horses should not steal landowners' horses, and landowners shouldn't set fire to the horses' native valley. Everyone's happy.

But there is a difference. The robber must be reduced by force, while it is conscience that converts the owner of a means of production.

In both cases, however—the use of violence, the use of persuasion—it is the Lone Ranger who turns out to be the decisive factor. It seems the time has come to ask ourselves some questions concerning the nature of the hero.

3 IN WHICH OUR HERO ENCOUNTERS CERTAIN DIFFICULTIES IN ACHIEVING HIS GOALS

THE HERO EXISTS because a crisis exists, a situation in which someone or something throws into question certain basic laws that have to do with the way the world functions.

If that crisis is averted—and this is common in all mass-cultural works—it is because from the very start it has been set up as a contradiction to which a way out can be found. Thus, for example, if Bruno were absolutely unscrupulous—as quite often happens in reality—then the Lone Ranger would have to decide whether to use force (and trample on either the law, or what amounts to the same thing, Bruno's private property and the right to its enjoyment) or to respect the law (which would destroy the valley, and symbolically the North American dream of a community and a land open to everyone). But there's no reason for either the Lone Ranger or the reader ever to face such a conflict. For in that world of comics, the owners of the land are sentimental, have pure sons, and are capable of diminishing their gains for the good of the public.

Subliterature, in order to perform its role as comforter, in order to enable the hero to fulfill his entrusted mission, must ensure that the reader will recognize in the crisis something that concerns him in the real world, something more concrete, closer to his immediate interests than a vague archetypal struggle between good and evil. However, that recognition must take place within a carefully circumscribed social reality whose main cause and effect, links with the real world, have been efficiently broken. In the case of the overexploitation of natural resources in Wild Horse Valley, the scriptwriter has raised the epiphenomenon, the threat, but without laying bare its true origins. No responsibility is assessed, nor are processes described. All that he leaves us with is what we might term, for the sake of methodology, the appearance of a crisis, which stands for reality and represents the reader's experience. It's like handing a customer an orange that doesn't have any fruit inside—just more skin, and an artificial flavor.

In another Lone Ranger episode there is a railroad employee who, having retired and lost the will to live, wants to commit suicide. With the Ranger's infallible help he succeeds in proving his usefulness to society, saving the train from some outlaws. (It's convenient for reader, employee, and Ranger alike that there's always some villain nearby who provides an opportunity to test their merits.) That employee represents for the reader the situation of most elderly people in our world. Retired elderly workers in our everyday reality should remind us of a cruel family structure, of the predicament of early unemployment, of the wasteland into which those who no longer have the strength to work are cast. Of all this, the storywriter uses only the superficial appearance of age, its external presence, its typical phrases, its anecdotal, even picturesque, situation. Everything else has been relegated to oblivion. The reader is never allowed to confront the causes of misery and loss of will in old age and so can no more deal with them in a realistic way than can the Lone Ranger. The same thing happens in every episode of every magazine in mass-produced culture.

"I've been looking for you, Cobos. You fired me for no reason," says a corpulent, sinister character in "Thwarted Conspiracy," another adventure of the Lone Ranger.

"Gart," answers Cobos, the boss, "you know why I fired you. I warned you about your attitude, and you devoted yourself to drinking with men like Kat and Burt." Then, to drive home his point, he adds, "Even though you were in jail, I wanted to give you a chance, but you let me down, Gart."

Here's a typical situation, a real dilemma, which the reader should be able to recognize. A man is fired. Reasons: laziness, drunkenness, bad company, an unlawful past. People have been fired, it is true, for that sort of conduct. But this is only part of the truth. There is nothing here to remind the reader that people are fired primarily due to other pressures: mechanization, competition for lowering costs, etc. So the crisis that the reader witnesses (and often suffers) in the real world is only apparently, externally, similar to the one that fiction presents. It is, however, similar enough to allow the reader to automatically correlate and substitute one for the other, so that the solution given in the comic can be translated by the reader into the kind of solution that will work for his own genuine, ongoing troubles. Relief must follow. To break this illusion, one might merely imagine the Ranger confronting the problem of unemployment itself instead of a man who's been fired for misconduct; or attempting to solve the terrible trap of old age in our society instead of lending a hand to a retired employee. But such "political" imaginings are normally banned in the mass-market media.

The superhero does not have to worry about entering that world and finding himself suddenly in a basement apartment piled high with all society's filthy, undesirable, insoluble quandaries. He will always find that the receptionist or the doorman has defined the difficulties in such a way that he will be able gloriously to unravel and dismiss them, thus reaping the proper applause. An army of autonomous and undercover collaborators has already made sure that things are safe. He will not be ambushed by any scandalous challenges to his authority. Call them chance, coincidence, the morals and psychology of certain characters, the absence of certain pitfalls that would entangle him in everyday life—call them destiny and fate if you will; but make no mistake, the hero has more allies than Tonto and Silver. He only rushes to the rescue in a universe that promises to regulate itself with his aid, which shows a resolute capacity for internal health and soundness, which does not ask sticky or thorny questions. He is the last of many mechanisms, the most visible and awesome one, to act on a typical, identifiable crisis which invariably touches the reader's—and society's—nerves. That crisis not only turns out to be decidedly transitory but lacks real people, people who work and produce and struggle, people who could face those issues in a positive way. The superhero's triumph is based on the omission of the working class, the elimination of a community or collective which could transform the crisis and give it a meaning or new direction. [14]

The superhero can supplant that positive factor, those actors of real history, because the producers of wealth, as we have already seen, have either been expelled from or misrepresented in the paradise of the media over and over again. They cannot compete with the Lone Ranger and his buddies because they are not part of what is habitually considered fiction or adventures.

The only really dangerous, active element the superhero has to defeat is of another sort: the villain. Villains are easy to spot. They start off by kicking a dog, battering an old person, or insulting a child. Then they compete for the privilege of wallowing in cruelty, cunning, and destruction, seeing who can chalk up more outrages against nature, family, and property. There are times when they can be rehabilitated, when a ray of "weakness" appears, illuminating them like a light from God. This not only adds to the suspense but also confirms the claustrophobic verticality of the comic book universe: If they have enough kernels of freedom inside them, miniature Jimmies on their consciences, they may want to end up like Bruno. Once they belong to "humanity," they acquire the right to be reformed and therefore absolved. We can observe that this is not much of a choice. They can be reprimanded, vanquished, and physically disappear; or they can accept the norms of their enemies as valid and stop being unruly and refractory elements.

The gut-level disgust we feel towards such scoundrels (I'd never want to meet one in an alley without someone like the Lone Ranger to help me) should not exempt us from noting, however, that they are the only characters who are outside society and who, unlike the Ranger, question it. It is a limited, false kind of questioning which doesn't get at the roots of the system, since these characters are meant to stand for all those obscure, fluctuating, miserable forces which can really undermine the world as it is. In a word, in works like Disney's or adventures like the Lone Ranger's, it is impossible—by definition—to be rebellious *and* good. Revolution—forgive that word, I promise not to use it again—is forbidden.

So nobody can dispute the Ranger's preeminence, his right to be the only positive and active factor. The solution that he will discover for the problems that snare and upset the reader drives home the idea—which seems evident, almost trivial, to anyone who must endure history impotently day by day—that the crisis will resolve itself. The system, with a little help from its friends, will always get up on its feet again, because there exist automatic normalizing mechanisms.

This is the famous optimism of the mass media, which found its triumphant incarnation in the Hollywood of yesteryear and endless television series of today. Everything gets pleasantly resolved, with what we've come to call the happy ending. It is not, however, simply a sugar-coated, honey-tongued escape. It responds to a yearning felt by the inhabitants of the capitalistic plains, where people hunt and are hunted. The literature of the elite from Romanticism onwards attacks precisely this notion and, in contrast, wraps itself in the sensibility of man-as-victim, barely more alive than a ghost, with only his pain and his feeling of alienation to separate him from oblivion; but this is done for a select circle, using approaches and methods often incomprehensible to the great masses of people. While twentieth-century art (theater, painting, poetry, music, novels, etc.) submerges itself in the floating fragments of a marooned, shipwrecked, overproductive humanity trying to control the slightest flicker of its destiny, the art of the masses reaffirms that all contradictions can be overcome; and in the case of action comics and cartoons, it exalts conscious intervention, the fortuitous arrival of a subject who is not just active, but hyperactive—an individual who can change history and successfully manage the crisis. This is the hero.

This doesn't mean that pulp literature's function is to respond to the problems literature has proposed. The majority of those who read (and many of those who write) industrial products of fiction don't even suspect that the antihero is busy analyzing himself into paralysis in the recesses of some novel of the enlightened minority. But they are addressing the same phenomenon from another angle, inverting the writers' and artists' often pessimistic message, and denying, in any case, the revitalizing language of art.

For this reason, the comic-book hero must come to grips with the system's rupture points, the places where neuralgia is occurring, where the basic insurmountable contradictions become evident and cry out to be harmonized. In the long run, it is the problems that the reader is worried about that finally allow the social body to cure and heal itself, to show its inner flexibility and strength. From a mature perspective, it's good that Bruno has sinned, for now he can make up for it and present himself as the valley's guardian. Most likely, he would not have noticed a thing before. He's been converted from an agnostic into an evangelist. Once the Ranger has such a spiritual heir and vicar, he can go on with his journey. He has advanced.

Since the hero is the decisive element in this turnabout, he does not oppose the world, he does not rebel against its laws (be they written or secret). On the contrary, he appears as the natural and moral emanation of these tendencies. With his strength and abilities, he allows these rules to act on their own behalf, so that the system can uninterruptedly continue to reveal its incessant mechanical self-regulation.

What a seeming difference from the world of Disney, where an all-out competition exists between equals (in rights, but not in talent, luck, ideas, effort, personality, or brilliance) who vie for the prize, whether money, prestige, or love. The presence of a superhero, as external to society as a bandit—but part of it inasmuch as he shares its virtuous precepts—renders that competitive chaos and disorder an impossibility. Thus action comics turn out to be more predictable, repetitive, and boring than the works of Disney. The Lone Ranger and his superhero buddies act as boundaries fencing in all disagreements. They're ethical maps with unalterable borders or codes that have been invisibly transcribed—if you'll pardon the metaphor (I hope my prose hasn't become too contaminated by overexposure to so much pulp literature)—in every heart. The Lone Ranger puts the disjointedness and conflicts of the dominant and the good in order horizontally, harmonizing and arbitrating interests. At the same time, he puts those who vertically undermine the foundations of the existing order in their place, usually the penitentiary. (In fact, destiny, or fate, works in Disney's creations as well as in "family" shows and sitcoms on television almost as if it were a ubiquitous, mischievous, disembodied superhero, dispensing chance, assistance, coincidence, and compensation; although it is fused with the world instead of being an external lay divinity.)

If the Ranger is revealed as the subject of the action and not its object, it is because he personifies the consciousness of this process, the awareness that the system, in its search for a natural balance, will give itself the last little shove. Everything in this world is spontaneously put on the right track, destined for the correct solution. The Ranger's presence will confirm this tendency, make it possible, execute the actions indispensable for a return to normalcy. He is the last drop which, instead of making the cup overflow, calms the waters.

So the superhero's arrival is always providential. It can only take place when the first sign of imbalance has been established: The barbed-wire fence cuts off the open road; the buffalo herd crosses the train tracks; the stagecoach has been held up. The internal forces tending toward stability and goodness have momentarily withdrawn. On their own they would lose the battle. The one ingredient missing from this intricate, difficult reality is the Lone Ranger. He must turn that world into a home on the *range,* make it equal to his perfect and incorruptible person. All he has to do is punish violators or even point out their slip-ups and the West will be transformed into the Ranger himself. Then the hero will head for other horizons and other magazines, certain that he has moralized this zone in its entirety. Its ethical underdevelopment has been fixed with an injection of the Ranger's own ethical superdevelopment.

The Lone Ranger himself contains not a single internal contradiction. He can change reality, but it can't change him. He travels, smashes, shoots, leaps, gallops, shouts. The excess of movement hides the fact that he never learns how the process works. All the hero's agitation ultimately aspires to the world's repose, to its stabilization. The return of the reader's security coincides with the final frame, in which the chorus identifies the character, echoing their famous last words. Another identical episode is waiting: the fracture of order, the hero's timely arrival, fluctuating fortunes, solutions, return to repose, a new quest. Goodness, success, and fame are accumulated in every adventure, but they never add up to anything, because a person who's never been sick can never get better. The Lone Ranger rides so fast that it's hard to accept the fact that he's always in the same place, marking time. For this reason, you can read any set of episodes in any order you like. What the hero in fact desires is for the place where he's intervened to become like him: immutable and consummate.

As Senator Homer Ferguson of Michigan explained in the

Congressional Record on the occasion of the Lone Ranger's twentieth anniversary, one of the program's novelties was the fact that every episode could be heard to its always successful concluding moral or message. Those were the days when "to be continued" dominated the radio (Dick Tracy, the Shadow, Charlie Chan) as well as newspaper comic strips. The Lone Ranger's creators, however, invented a product that left no loose ends, but also, like all objects dreamed up in the consumer universe, was open for future use. It embodies a circular repetition, a superficial stylistic renovation to which the contemporary products of the culture industry tend. Umberto Eco has termed this structure, which appears as much in the melodramas of the nineteenth century as in the industrial fictions of the twentieth, "comforting," because it can modify "one part so everything will remain as it was before."[15]

As a result, changing the world does not appear to the reader as something denied by the cartoon. On the contrary, all our rebelliousness and energy, all our aggression, all those needs and instincts for transformation have been channeled into the appropriate groove, bearing witness to and participating in a just battle to overcome problems which the reader identifies with intolerable situations in his everyday life. But such movement is only apparent. Neither reality nor the Ranger have been altered. Under the guise of variation, the world is preserved in exactly the state in which it existed before the Ranger was forced to purify it of its corrupt atmosphere, return it to a sinless Eden, rid nature of human error, and clean up the natural flood in which mankind drowns. The Lone Ranger's creator, George W. Trendle, had good reason to announce that the Lone Ranger was like "the embodiment of a granted prayer."[16]

This nearly divine function has been observed by John T. Gallaway, Jr., a minister who, in *The Gospel According to Superman*, points out that the superhero changes the characters' lives without asking them to profoundly reorganize or evaluate their beliefs and values, without achieving an intimacy with them which might expose them to the anguish of a transformation. "Superman offers an irresponsible deliverance from distress because he sets out only to change the environment. His work is to reinstate the familiar, same, comfortable conditions." Among his other observations, the theologian mentions that it is difficult for a hero projected by the average person to have the effect of "altering the underlying personality of the one whose imagination has projected him."[17]

If we accept these comments as valid, we must ask ourselves if the way the superhero confronts and defeats the imbalances that he encounters corresponds to some force (or forces) that the reader identifies as operating in his life on a daily basis, some force that demonstrates a similar energy and direction. Take the individuality of the (aptly named) *Lone* Ranger, for example. Anyone born in a market society is expected to get ahead all by himself, in solitude. In addition, we are taught that many times we fail because we're not able to get the better of everyone else. The dominant ideas and the productive system itself have prepared each consumer to feel that the way in which the Lone Ranger faces painful situations, in his capacity as the great unyielding macho, is absolutely natural and commendable. Such an emphasis on personal, competitive strength coexists with an opposite and complementary tendency toward paternalism, which the Ranger also satisfies as he emerges from outside the world to exercise compassion for inferior beings. The system preaches that we must fend for ourselves in order to triumph, but that once we are invested with superiority, once we have accepted a position of authority in the hierarchy, it behooves us to lend a paternal hand to those weaker than ourselves. In superhero comics, this ferocity of competition and gentleness of compassion are amalgamated into one being.

Thus the Lone Ranger represents forces whose action the reader has become accustomed to witnessing every day. He is chance, goodness, nature. He is immeasurable, miraculous, and unattainable power. He is a reality that corrects itself, that won't allow pain or disharmony to triumph. The Lone Ranger is the son of all that is natural and legendary.

But these same basic traits appear in every mass-cultural production, and listing them would be nothing new. In *Mythologies*, Barthes already defined the majority of them, calling them the rhetoric of the bourgeoisie, "a group of fixed, regulated, insistent figures in which the various forms of mythic meaning come to be arranged."[18] One must ask oneself: What makes the Lone Ranger special, which means understanding either the deeper reasons for his popularity or, which amounts to the same thing, the need on the part of a vast segment of the public for a character that obeys precisely those particular features. Since the Ranger does not appear alone, but is accompanied in his illumination by a veritable throng of superheroes, perhaps we can discover the secret to every last one of them. Now that would be an epic accomplishment!

The Lone Ranger is defined as a person who seeks and imposes justice, who will not rest until every human expanse has submitted to order, to his order, his prophylaxis. To do this he has donned a mask and uses silver bullets ("as a shining symbol of my implacable justice"). He is also physically and intellectually overendowed, although he does not exhibit the supernatural characteristics of Superman. He prefers persuasion to force, but he tends to be compelled to use violence in order to redeem most situations. There are limits, however, which he seems to have imposed upon himself. He never kills anyone (and he rarely injures or draws blood),[19] and he never violates the law. Although he always wins, he receives no reward. He gains no benefits from his abilities; rather he offers his services to the entire community. He doesn't have a salary, either, since he isn't a member of any police force. He satisfies his needs, which are minimal and basically bellicose, by means of a silver mine of which he is the lucky owner. Nature, therefore, supplies him directly. An old-timer works the mine. ("Listen, my friend. Half this mine belongs to my brother's wife and son, since he was killed by bandits. I only want enough for my needs and my bullets. The rest is yours.")[20] He is accompanied by a loyal Indian and a white horse, Silver. Years later, a nephew Dan is sometimes included.

Among all these characteristics, which are duplicated in one form or another by other protagonists of action comics, there seems to be one that stands out: the mask he never takes off. Batman, Zorro, the Phantom, in addition to their cowls all have another personality. Superman, although he doesn't wear a mask, is at least disguised, so that nobody knows his assumed identity (Clark Kent). It's evident that once these heroes put on their masks, they perform in a manner similar to that of the Lone Ranger, but the fact that the object of our attention does not have at his disposal a daytime side into which to retreat places him in a situation which, begging the pardon of Sartre, Camus, and Kierkegaard, we shall call a "boundary situation." The perpetual presence of this mask is an extreme in the annals of superheroes, and one which, by definition, cannot be surpassed.

The reason given by the Ranger himself for his situation is that he's been officially pronounced dead. (Tonto faked his grave so that the outlaws who tried to kill him when he was a Texas Ranger would not look for him.) "And since I'm officially dead . . . I will stay dead to the world so I can accomplish my task without obstacles. I will cover my face with a mask and I won't rest until I hand those criminals over to Justice."[21] The 1981 film *The Legend of the Lone Ranger* repeats these arguments in a more or less similar manner.[22] It can therefore be supposed that an attempt is being made to represent the anonymous nature of justice, the dedication to a cause that reaches the point of abnegation and the renunciation of everyday aspirations. The man from the backwoods of Texas is dead, and he only exists insofar as he's undergone a metamorphosis.

But this explanation for the mask's origin did not come into being at the same time as did our hero. It is a legend which was added on almost two decades later in order to satisfy the listeners' curiosity and to give their idol verisimilitude. At first, in 1932, when George W. Trendle and his associates were inventing the character, there were neither concrete motives behind this attitude nor a personal history that could explain it. "The hero," we are informed by a company pamphlet that relates how he was dreamed up, "should be a man of mystery—someone who, *for some reason* [italics mine] decided to hide his true identity. He should be motivated by a burning desire to help the forgers of the West and do it, not for his own personal gain or credit, but out of pure love for the country."[23] It was the same when the *Detroit Evening Times,* giving information about the character's appearance, restricted during the first few months to regional radio stations, told its readers, "None knew from where he came and none knew where he went."[24] And in 1936, in Fran Striker's first Lone Ranger book, "No one knew from whence he appeared and whither he afterwards disappeared."[25] As late as 1950, the reasons given weren't anecdotal but almost metaphysical:

"He wore the mask at all times, even when he was alone. . . . He wanted it to be a part of him, rather than an awkward hindrance."[26]

But that's just what it was, though—an awkward hindrance.

As far as the rest of the superheroes are concerned, it is their other identity that brings on their headaches. Someone is always just about to discover their secret. But maybe what they're really afraid of is becoming like the Ranger. If it's ever revealed that Clark Kent is Superman, that Bruce Wayne is Batman, etc., the only alternative for these protagonists would be to abandon their sunny, laughable, mundane side and—having killed that private, often cowardly identity—fall into the Ranger's situation of exile and wandering. This is a frightening possibility, since their secret personalities are not as great an obstacle to the interests of justice as the mask is for the Ranger. For example, Don Diego is occasionally threatened—maybe fifty percent of the time—with the possibility that someone might discover that he is really Zorro. This is not an option for the Ranger. There is not one adventure in which he doesn't run this immediate risk, almost always within the first eight frames, because of the specific way in which his total devotion to his cause is symbolized. The Ranger has to triumph *in spite of his mask*, he must prove his honesty and dedication because he wears the mask.

The initial reaction to his mere presence is almost invariably an attempt to attack him. "That mask is as good a reason as any." Instead of being recognized as a representative of goodness and impartiality, he is stigmatized as wickedness itself. No one around him ever puts their mistrust aside, and they end up accepting his aid with reservations. How many times has he been accused of being responsible for the very acts he seeks to eliminate! Barely is there an infraction of the law and they want to toss him in jail. If he's a witness, they don't believe him. He must earn the opportunity to save everyone else, struggling as much against the mask he himself has chosen to wear as against the disturbers of the peace.

The only case, in the corpus of adventures we've read, in which he takes off the mask illustrates this situation.* Someone is extorting

---

*"An Effective Disguise," published in the early 1970s in Chile, vol. XX, no. 266.

part of the railroad workers' salary as "protection." Since they don't want to tell Tonto about it (he's attacked by the foremen), the only way out is for the Ranger to disguise himself as a worker, as a result of which he realizes that it isn't the foreman who's been robbing the workers, but a group of outlaw-gangsters.

It never occurs to the workers to ask whether someone other than an extortionist could possibly be appropriating their efforts in real life, because they're only interested in defending their rightful salaries. In addition, they're incapable of organizing a resistance on their own or even asking for help from the law, so the Lone Ranger must disguise himself. At the moment he arrests the delinquents, however, he puts the mask back on. Naturally the criminals make fun of him: "You can't prove a thing, and no worker would risk accusing us." During the trial, they tell the judge, "The masked man should be put in jail. We're the respectable ones." This forces the Ranger once again to assume the role of a worker who accuses the robbers and obtains their conviction.

This entanglement demonstrates the difficulties inherent in the permanent part he has chosen to play. He could not have chosen a less appropriate road toward assisting justice. Disguising yourself as a bandit in order to infiltrate a gang of outlaws can be considered a neat trick (as borne out by the comic *Plastic Man*, untold TV series, thrillers, and spy movies); but presenting yourself to the agents of the law, or to those left destitute by the same bandits, in an outlaw getup is one of the all-time examples of insensitivity. If you want to win the race, you don't tie your feet.

Does he tie his feet?

That depends. Perhaps therein lies the originality and profound attraction of the character—the demonstration that with bound feet he runs faster than those whose feet are free, that the Lone Ranger, mask and all, can succeed where others have failed. In actuality, the Lone Ranger reproduces the myth of bourgeois social mobility which, in the previous essay, McDuck brought to life. It all begins, remember, with the theoretical equality of conditions. Then some people, through their merits, reach prosperity; and through this competition in which the best win out, all of society is protected and plays a part.

In the Lone Ranger's case, the hero starts from below zero. He starts with an apparently insurmountable hurdle, which would discourage anyone else. Let this be an invigorating example for each and every reader. Your handicap doesn't matter. It doesn't matter if you're an outsider, if they treat you like a criminal, a dangerous element, or if they don't have any faith in your abilities and intentions. Your qualities will all be proved in time. Meanwhile, just like the Ranger, you must earn the right to success. You can overcome natural or artificial limitations as long as you're bold and good and are sure of the fairness of your actions. That's how all currently rich and powerful men created themselves: by working hard, against adversity, and against apparently insurmountable odds. If you start out being inferior to everyone else (and we should assume that this includes many of the people who regularly buy this type of magazine), you could learn a thing or two from the rhythm and direction of the Ranger's own rise to power. Which just goes to show that if you don't succeed in living up to this model of mobility, then you simply don't deserve it. If after a great deal of effort they still don't trust you, if you're still an outsider and they still don't believe you, you can be sure that you're dealing with an individual problem of your own making; it could never be the way the world is organized.

That's how the mask ends up being a point of contact between reader and protagonist, the emotive mechanism that allows a projection to take place. It has often been claimed (perhaps too often) that comics are fantasy, dreams of violence, an escape from everyday life, the sublimation of repressions which haven't been truthfully dealt with, the "seduction of the innocent" (to use the title of Wertham's book). What we've shown, however, is that this type of fiction flees *toward* reality, that comics represent it as they both falsify and reflect it. What interests us, though, is that such a process is only possible if the reader can identify with the protagonist.

The Lone Ranger combines two tendencies in the mythic tradition of the legendary cowboy:[27] the community builder and the solitary rebel. He retains the advantages of both types and resolves their ambiguities in the same historical period in which so many other superheroes were doing exactly the same thing. At the very same moment that he distances himself from society and becomes independent of its fetters, he also guarantees its values and the status quo. He is simultaneously a rebel and a conformist, or, repeating the words of the previous essay, savage and civilized. Using Will Wright's categories of analysis from his excellent *Six-Guns and Society*,[28] we might note that we're dealing with a hero who reconciles individualism in the marketplace with the established values of the community. But the reader's identification with this is not simply a projection of deficiencies in his social status. The Lone Ranger also reproduces and reinforces the reader's aesthetic experience. This sort of hero begins each episode as an object, a passive extreme of action, since he never generates the problems he has to face but finishes the adventure as its authoritative, domineering subject. While he acts, he finds himself at a crossroads similar to that of the reader, extremely asphyxiated by his mask.

In this way the Ranger's transformation from object to subject reproduces the reader's experience of reading the same adventure. The protagonist's action and the reader's catharsis (which, if Aristotle will forgive us, is what we'll call it) simultaneously unfold and mutually fortify one another. The reader goes from ignorance to knowledge, from passivity to the comforting realm of what's-going-to-happen-next; the tensions and lines of movement that are generated are pleasantly resolved as the reading continues, until it finally concludes in the repose of the final frame—so much action resulting in so much tranquility. All these aesthetic characteristics imitate, anticipate, and sustain the Ranger's own actions, which begin with uncertainty, conflict, the possible loss of life and ideals, and end with a final victory, after which the world goes back to sleep and snores peacefully. Such fiction provides a way for the reader to have the experience of overcoming his condition of being an object, his alienation. Once the Ranger gallops out of the reader's situation, the reader can avoid confronting some actual crisis which truly worries him. He's freed from having to transform himself into the subject of his own story.

It appears that at long last we've discovered the Lone Ranger's secret. All heroes seem to share, in one way or another, this mechanism of identification. The hero is an inferior being who becomes superior, in some way representing all those left behind and below, enthusiastically worshiping him. Otto Rank has studied the phenomenon,[29] delving into its psychoanalytic and symbolic roots, which he believes to be based on the (collective) imagination resulting from the rebellion and appeasement of the child within the family. This myth allows the hero (Christ, Romulus, Moses, Amadis—and Superman, too) to be born under unfortunate conditions, raised by adopted parents of humble extraction (or sometimes animals), and chased by those who ought to love him—all acts that nevertheless do not stand in the way of his triumph, the recognition of his superiority and kingly countenance, and generally his representation of divinity. This myth, systematically present in the legends of all peoples, has heretofore been explained by giving psychological or archetypal reasons.

Without denying the possible validity of such exegeses, I would like to suggest that aspirations such as these seem to be the rule in all societies that are divided into social classes. From time immemorial, oppressed groups have projected onto their heroes the idea of a being who fractures the status quo and comes up from down under. Perhaps this is the basic, structure-building dream of all human beings who must experience in disguise the struggle between those who monopolize power and those who have nothing, other than their own unavoidable bodies and often avoidable dreams of a better, different world.

The impulse behind these myths is unquestionably rebellious and democratic. In order to domesticate this mythology's least tolerable aspects, the dominant sectors have always taken advantage of their monopoly on language and their control over what does or does not happen to written memory. They assign a stabilizing, conciliatory function to the hero, either uniting everyone—oppressors and oppressed alike—around him as the founder of a nation or a religious figure, or dispersing the repressed community into floating bits of individuality while giving them the illusion of personal social ascent (like Cinderella). But the explosive potential is always there. Even after the content has been made official and twisted, each generation goes back and reinvents or rediscovers in the ancient myth the need for change; and in each generation the myth (and the oral tradition out of which it is constructed) is once again reinterpreted, subdued, domesticated, in an attempt to remove its critical direction. But never before has there been a situation like that foisted upon universal consciousness by the mass media of the twentieth century. We're no longer dealing with a collective, whispered creation; we're no longer dealing with historical characters that have been adopted and recreated by the great majorities wishing to defend their right—at the very least—to dream. Industrial fictions *invent* commercial characters who drain that history of all its defiance and discontent. The popular masses that consume the myth in its newest form have not participated in its origins, in its development, in the battles for its modification. The superhero descends upon their brains just as magically and ubiquitously as the mass media penetrate their homes.

Have we reached the end of our road? Is this the myth we've been looking for? Or will the face hiding behind this mask turn out to be yet another disguise? Could the Lone Ranger have another secret identity which he refuses to divulge?

If you want to learn the answer to these and other questions, tune in to our next episode. . . .

4 IN WHICH WE FIND OUT WHO OUR HERO WAS AND WHAT HIS TRUE INTENTIONS WERE

UP TO NOW, THE Lone Ranger has appeared to be the representative and executor of ideological tendencies and mechanisms spontaneously prevalent in the reader's world. However, the Ranger also has a specific mission—justice—and he achieves it because the local authorities cannot solve their problems on their own. Apparently, the protagonist combines his interest in a good fight with a desire to impose order, harmonize points of view, eliminate whatever is disturbing or out of place, always on behalf of traditional criteria and values. The Ranger acts in the name of an ideal, perfect "justice," perpetually ready to be that impartial arbiter who takes no part in the dispute.

Hence, disinterest is essential to his effectiveness. His salary is justice and virtue his reward. He is understandably nature's favorite. He asks only for that which he absolutely needs to continue to function and carry out his mission. Whatever nature has bestowed upon him is invested in the public's well-being and never used for personal gain. In this way his imposition never appears as an arbitrary or oppressive act, but more as the consistent manifestation of an order which, by being far removed from secular points of view, can achieve a complete accord. Since he doesn't participate in the system's benefits, he is able to construct an authority respected by the reader, and ultimately esteemed by all the other characters, too.

Once his function in the literary work has been examined, it becomes clear that, as far as the reader is concerned, there is only one force in the historical world whose existence and actions are presented in the same way: the State.

Despite the fact that the Ranger is carrying out all the functions of the State, utilizing the same methods (persuasion and physical force, which are in turn endorsed by a capacity for violence), regulating the world, putting a limit on the excesses of private property while defending it, objectively arranging discordant points of view, the reader nevertheless feels that the protagonist is not an organ of repression. He's not even experienced as a social force, since he extracts his dynamic qualities from nature, from the diffuse and ubiquitous valley which he concretely defends in the episode we've primarily focused on.

This is how the Lone Ranger, as well as the other superheroes, represent the ahistorical laws and eternal values begotten of the immutability of Man. He is, on one hand, the ambassador of the Divine, without ceasing to be, on the other hand, individuality, immediacy, *persona*. In George W. Trendle's words to Mary E. Bickle, the woman charged with the task of writing his biography, "It's our job to keep the *perfection* and keep him believable."[30] Or in our own words: The common man becomes the State. Via the mask, the reader can delegate to that "I" all his energies as a subject, because the superhero's enormous capacities and virtues are relativized by certain faults or weaknesses that allow the reader to get close to him and to feel he knows him. For Arthur Asa Berger, one of the functions of Superman's schizoid other personality is that every once in a while his powers must be democratized; for if they were given free rein, they could lead the superhero in the direction of aristocracy based on his evident superiority.[31] That is what separates the nineteenth-century superman of Carlyle and Nietzsche, a member of an elite scornful of the masses, from a native of the planet Krypton or Wild Horse Valley, who is consumed not by philosophies, generals, and kings, but by the little guy, with his penny-ante problems and heartbreaks.

Our protagonists' weakness is not a tragic one. The anonymity and obscurity of which the Lone Ranger or the dark and nocturnal character of Batman or the Spirit are a part constitute a bridge stretching toward the reader, fashioning the superhero's opposition to, and his point of departure from, the official and public apparatus which also plays a part in these comic books. Although Superman's origins or Plastic Man's accident are exceptions, in the majority of cases superheroes are voluntary strangers, outsiders on the verge of being outcasts. The Ranger's mask is the guarantee of his marginality, of his private life, of his rejection of the public state's impersonality. Even the Superman of the first few episodes had a similar beginning. "He was wanted by the police for taking the law into his own hands."[32] And Plastic Man's other identity is that of a gangster.

The superhero and his particular configuration tend to reproduce the ambiguity which the defenseless person suffers in relation to justice and the regulation of his life in a stratified society. The Lone Ranger and his friends replace, complement, and reflect the reader's attitude toward the State, that mixture of distrust and awe. As in everyday life, the consumer witnesses the self-regulation of a political and economic system that follows its own supposedly inexorable and routine laws, and in which he normally participates at a distance and very infrequently. Through these action comics, though, the reader is allowed to participate in the actual administration of the laws that hold sway in his own world. Once the reader has personalized and projected those laws onto the protagonist, whom he feels to be one of his own kind, he eliminates the contradictions and problems that afflict him. The State, which is daily more divorced from those it claims to represent, passes, by way of the heroic (active) subject, over to the consuming (passive) subject.

It's no accident that, alongside the formal system of representative democracy and universal suffrage, the star system has come into being. It was the next logical step in the configuration of the public personality—the character who through his anecdotal individuality crystallizes the aspirations deposited and accumulated in him and appears on the scene, making history (or at least making the headlines). At the same time it is the average citizen who is presented as his helper, lending a bit of a hand, like Tonto, a little help, like Robin, on the long and difficult road. Like the mute that accompanies Zorro, he participates in the making of decisions to the extent that he fully identifies with that character. This is how each individual overcomes the remoteness of the State. In each episode the reader works out his life and problems, and then does it all over again, exercising his democratic rights through someone else's action, and orchestrating his own sense of crisis through a mythic figure. The reader becomes the state and assumes its functions; he fictitiously appropriates the history of which he is the victim and object.

110

Shaping the world and history in action comics is not, therefore, an act of rebellion. The basic activity which all men can accomplish is to let the law and its trustworthy representatives decide for themselves how they're going to settle problems. It's enough consciously to give your approval to the Lone Ranger's solutions. That's all that's necessary. It adds one more grain of morality to the great reserve from which the Lone Ranger extracts the energies he needs every day to ride off on Silver toward the plain of good deeds.

The Lone Ranger's mask permits the law to be presented free of all its defects. Day after day, the reader must put up with the State's remoteness, its bureaucracy, its limiting (and frightening) force, the incommunicability and hermeticism of political phenomena, the making of decisions that override his desires as well as his interests. The superhero is able to carry out all these functions of law and order, but without throwing up the barriers and distances that antagonize and separate the State from the people it claims to represent. In this regard, the State generates in every potential spectator of an action comic or an action TV series a resentment and at the same time an aggressiveness which the superheroes come to stifle and absorb.

The mechanism which seals and directs the reader's identification with the protagonist is, paradoxically, the incessant appearance of the public forces of law and order themselves within the comic. In the back alleys of the reader's mind, the State is seen as exercising its functions by means of an apparatus (police, army, prisons, etc.) that ultimately controls all attempts to deviate from or question the normal outcome of the social order. This public force appears in every episode of adventure comics. However, the force that exercises the actual military functions of the State in comics, the force that has the physical capacity to intervene fairly, to reduce the enemy to impotence, to annihilate its problematical nature, is the superhero, that being who takes great care never to kill (and frequently never to wound even lightly) his adversary.

The function of the public authorities in the comic book is precisely to be incapable of doing anything except make fun of the hero and occasionally pursue him, nearly bungling his sacred mission. They are shown to be utterly inefficient. The cavalry always arrives too late; the sheriff gets drunk; sometimes the figures of "order" are

111

corrupt; the police chief wants to jail the wrong man, etc. Naturally this minimization of the deputies of authority never goes past a certain point. In the end, the guilty will be handed over to ordinary justice, and the protagonist will never break the law. This process of hostility toward and collaboration with the law was present in the first detective stories and novels, where the romantic ideal was made flesh in the person of the private eye. It is interesting to note that from that same era the first modern hero with a double identity arises, the Scarlet Pimpernel.

Thus the public power appears inert and inefficient, dependent upon the individual will of a certain anonymous citizen for its ability to ensure control of reality. Without that cooperation on the part of the superheroes and, further, without the incessant moral and dramatic subordination of official authority to that lofty and perfect citizen, order, justice, and social peace are impossible. To complete the inversion, the individual, the persona, the loner—that part of the reader which in actual life is almost certainly passive, limited, and eternally frustrated—appears in the story as active, dominant, hegemonious, and a source of real power, necessary to really govern.

The mythical American West is a perfect setting for such a psychodrama. After all, the public forces of law and order are necessarily scattered and insufficient. A way must be found to impose the law more spontaneously—by means of a universal (let us not say vigilante) goodness concentrated in a few fortunate hands. The frontier puts the moral reserves of the American nation to the test. This is the theme of innumerable westerns. Where there is no detachment of armed forces, men can nevertheless impose an order on their own, or to use Cawelti's words, turn the Desert into a Garden.[33]

As you can see, the thesis that's being whispered and upheld is always the same. The State does not oppose its own constituents. It exercises its mandate for the benefit of society as a whole. Justice is not only not arbitrary but is actually protected by private individuals, figures with whom the reader can live and whom he can get to know, who will correct and reinforce the defenders of those public powers each time they cease to administrate well or fail in the performance of their duties.

The public forces which exercise their primordial functions in the capitalist state, but which only during times of acute disobedience or insubordination appear with all their repressive characteristics unveiled, have been redefined here as auxiliary institutions, mere helpers. They exist merely to consolidate the positions which private beings (superheroes, other characters, and readers) have already won. The customer is king. The military apparatus is no more than a domestic employee that belatedly upholds the justice which the system itself invariably continues to secrete, the balance and consensus achieved through history.

The superhero is fashioned in a manner that allows the common man to gain access to the workings of the State, exercising upon himself the internal military repression which quiets doubts, and all this without renouncing his resentment towards the public authorities. The protagonist's marginality expresses and concentrates a distance and distrust of the State while his superpowers and invincibility express and concentrate the awe and fear of state power used to carry out these tasks. No one is trying to destroy the State, just to do what it is supposed to do—only better, more efficiently, and first.

These comic books channel the reader's critical potential in two divergent directions which end up confronting one another on the field of action: The reader can either rebel tangentially, as in a competition or a race, accepting the prevailing norms and demonstrating that one can realize them better than the apparatus that is feared and venerated; or he can rebel head on, and end up being defined by that wickedness known as criminal behavior or madness, which will be justly repressed by the superhero and his enthusiastic ally—yes, the reader himself. The pent-up aggressiveness of the consumer-citizen is split into two irreconcilable bands—one which is fostered, permitted, rewarded; another which is "rebellious," destructive, and generates more disorder. Good and evil, a bifurcation which at this stage could make us yawn. Alas, we've seen it all before.

The reader represses himself, taking a stand against the common enemy, which is his own potential lack of submission, his own "evil," his own search for true justice in a world where there is none. He's split in two, and one side annihilates the other.

113

The proof that this opposition between the two functions or dimensions of the State is a mechanism of political domination can be found in the fact that the superhero, in times of war or national emergency in the real world (when citizens feel loyally represented by the State, bound together by a catastrophe or an emergency), puts himself at the direct disposal of the country's armed forces. He loses his "independence."[34] Superman, in the forties, fights the Nazis. And the Lone Ranger, more or less at the same time, catches a "German" spy. (How's that for time traveling?)

At any rate, the Ranger conceives himself as the answer to a permanent emergency. He is an institution, like the State, at the service of all. That's why he can trust his disciple, Bruno, hand him the keys to the kingdom. The landowner can round up horses (and probably underpay his hired hands) on the plains precisely because he's become the guardian of the entire country's common heritage. The Ranger is not at Bruno's exclusive service, but he is the precondition for Bruno's just preservation of nature. In other episodes he defends similar men from other enemies: rustlers, thieves, violators, con men, and even foreign spies. The reader can live everyday life through the Ranger, as long as there is ample room for the State to intervene and pass on certain benefits to underprivileged groups.

For this reason, too, the Lone Ranger, and any other protagonist, incites the reader's sympathy. Because in fact he imposes, naturally and without exerting himself artificially, certain sanctions against the economic interests of those in the comic book who represent the dominant class.

But are we ourselves not falling prey, with all this analysis, to the same errors of abstraction and evasion of which we are accusing the industrial fiction media? Are we not, in treating the superhero as a model that proves a hypothesis applicable to general situations, leaving out that dimension which we have proclaimed to be essential, the dimension which the protagonists of mass market fiction usually steal from their readers?

Isn't it about time to wonder how the Lone Ranger, as a specific series, is the product of an era, of a society in particular?

Isn't it time to open the door to that dragon we call history?

5 IN WHICH OUR HERO EXPLAINS WHO HIS PARENTS WERE AND TO WHICH FAMILY HE ACTUALLY BELONGS

THE FIGURE OF THE Lone Ranger appeared between 1932 and 1933, in the midst of the greatest crisis that capitalism had ever endured.* In spite of his name, he did not appear alone. Buck Rogers preceded him by a few years, and as the decade wore on, he was joined by Superman, Batman, Green Arrow, Sergeant Preston of the Yukon, the Green Hornet, Flash Gordon, and many others.[36]

It can't be a coincidence that such protagonists were brought to light at a traumatic historical moment when an entire system seemed to fall under "a sickening paralysis,"[37] and certain limitations on the current monopolistic economic system became visibly necessary. The only instrument available to regulate the health of the economy, while integrating into society previously ignored segments of the population via social benefits, was the State. Its actions, however, could not be confused with communism, that great North American nemesis, where the individual loses his "freedom" and is completely subordinated to the public apparatus. So the same era that excreted Nazism created, in the United States, a different application and variant of power. The acute and catastrophic crisis could be straightened out through enhanced State intercession, and controlled by its citizens, without loss of their democratic freedoms or their individual rights. Presenting . . . Superstate.

Or did I say Superhero?

The seeds of the superhero existed before the crash on Wall Street, and can be exhumed from the melodramas of the nineteenth century,[38] but not until the 1930s could there emerge superbeings

*The Lone Ranger began as a radio program in Detroit in January 1933 and quickly was broadcast across the nation. By the end of the decade he was syndicated in comic strips and books had been published about his deeds. Comic books followed shortly thereafter.

who were representatives of the average citizen, of the man lost in the crowd, of the isolated consumer, who is the victim of laws which terrify him more for being incomprehensible than for being implacable. We're not just dealing with another collaborator within the self-regulatory mercantile system.[39] When faced with the collapse of the market economy, drastic solutions are necessary.[40] The newly created superhero naturalizes the social forces to which monopolistic capitalism readjusts, pointing and dreaming a way out of the crisis: the cautious but decisive intervention of the State; military and moral expansion of the system; total participation in social benefits; fiscal assistance for technical progress and projects for the public welfare. The Lone Ranger's two weapons are concession and repression, persuasion and force. He makes use of them in precisely the period, as Paul Sweezy explains, when

> The State must expand its power and functions. Although these two methods can appear contradictory, they are in fact complementary, finding themselves mixed in varying degrees during different periods. . . . Thus do we observe the simultaneous growth of the instruments of force designed to guarantee internal law and order and the extension of social legislation in the form of workmen's compensation, unemployment insurance, old age pensions, and other things along the same lines.[41]

The last day of the year that saw the Lone Ranger burst across the radio waves at a gallop, December 31, 1933, John Maynard Keynes directed the following words to Roosevelt in an open letter in the *New York Times:* "You have made yourself the trustee for those in every country who seek to mend the evils of our condition by reasoned experiment within the framework of the existing social system. If you fail, rational change will be gravely prejudiced throughout the world, leaving orthodoxy and revolution to fight it out."[42]

The market's automatic mechanisms did not serve to avoid disaster. The State appears as the only one that can, and should, intervene.

It was necessary for the average citizen, both the one inventing the fictions and the one devouring them, to find in works of entertainment a brand-new, mythical, up-to-date person who would act out the solutions to the dilemmas, who would be the representative of "a conscious intervention ever more extensive, ever more regular, ever more systematic, in order to save this regime."[43]

For this purpose there were two North American heroes available who, though they had remained separate for the previous fifty years, would now be combined into one super body. Each one of them possessed an enormous attraction for those who wanted to survive, and succeed, in the U.S. economic system. The first was the man in the mask or with a secret identity—whom we've already beaten into the ground. He was the hero who had been removed from what is normal, set apart from the community, with obscure, dangerous, solitary associations. In this way he represented the tradition of the rebel as a romantic outlaw (who, from Jesse James to Clyde Barrow, captured North America's sympathy and imagination) in the same period that both gangster and monster movies embodied the citizen's feeling that the system was remote and inaccessible.[44]

The fact that the superheroes are conceived as morally untouchable saints is what permits them, in spite of finding themselves cut off from society, to embody both the ambiguous stigma of the outlaw and the other central, North American myth, more basic to the building of the nation—the optimistic odyssey of Horatio Alger: *from rags to riches*.[45] It was as if Roy Rogers or Gene Autry had put on a mask.

This type of protagonist could certainly not have been imagined except at that moment when the mass media, through its commercial and technical development[46] had begun to resemble a sort of superhero of the emotions, a cognitive correlative to the common man's participation in the regulation of economic laws. During the same years that politicians were establishing a bridge to the entire country through the mass media (to such an extent that Wendell Willkie was chosen as the Republican presidential candidate for his talent in opposing the style of Roosevelt's "fireside chats"[47]), the need for fantasy among those aching and abandoned millions, adrift in the economic swamp, was being answered by the industrialization of fictional worlds. Just as channels were created for public opinion to feel like an agent of intellectual vigilance controlling the crisis, and consequently escaping what Frederick Allen called "the confusion and dismay of readjustment," so too was the marketplace giving readers and listeners a form of vicarious participation. Just as the superstate, just as the superhero, the superconsumers saw the crisis extinguished in an atmosphere of leisure and entertainment, defeated by means of their new power and worship by proxy of stars.

If this specific form of heroism had such precise historical causes, does this mean that, once the series' fundamental structure had been fixed, it could not be changed in the face of new, pressing needs and in accord with changing times? Has the Lone Ranger series cyclically reiterated the same assumptions and mechanisms, or does it, too, experience a historical development, adapting itself to different circumstances?

I have the impression that it is very hard to alter the way in which the hero defeats the contradictions, the means by which he restores the destroyed equilibrium, or the dynamics he puts into practice as much in order to achieve identification as to overcome the dilemma provoked. That tends to be relatively invariable. What does get modified is the problem itself, the way it is aired, the point of rupture which becomes visible as it cleaves a concrete historical moment, and the definition of the adversary we must conquer. The superhero, jelled into certain familiar forms, seems in more or less the same, imperturbable way to confront the different anxieties that have given way to one another over the years.

One example is the Wild Horse Valley incident. Such a place does not get preferential treatment in the first few Lone Ranger programs. Nor did the initial books that duplicated the Mounted Lawman's origins place special emphasis on the fact that Silver had once belonged to an enchanted valley. This feature began to be accentuated as the overexploitation of nature began to preoccupy readers, authors, and public opinion. Another example: Essential to the series is the contrast between the Ranger and those who resemble him, false representatives of the outsider, but whom he must suppress. In "The Capture of Silver," the assailants arrive on a white horse and a pinto, and "the villain on the white horse wears a mask." The Lone Ranger succeeds in proving his identity when the impostor is not able to mount Silver. Once again nature recognizes and comes to the rescue of one of her own ambassadors.[48] The same thing occurs in dozens of episodes, greatly facilitated by the risky way the Ranger distinguishes himself from everyone else. However, we're interested in showing how that typical procedure doesn't change, given that it makes up the basic narrative structure, while the definition of the antagonist does change, or can, if the need arises. In "Villain with Long Hair," a bandit named Peter Kiel, accompanied by Indians, makes his assault mounted on a white horse, wearing a mask. "I mistook you," says the child survivor of the massacre to the Ranger, who is greeted with gunfire, "for the villain, since you're wearing a mask and riding a white horse. But I remembered that that guy had long hair."

This key feature is crucial to the outcome, but it is crucial as well to our discussion. This adventure's original publication date was 1955, a year in which long hair was synonymous with the outrage of rock 'n' roll and juvenile delinquency. Long hair is as essential to Peter Kiel as the mask is to the Lone Ranger. "I swore I'd cut it off if I ever got captured." But those scraggly locks will be the fundamental factor in his downfall. "The Lone Ranger," says the narrator, "dodges his aggressor and covers the man's eyes with his shaggy hair." He then takes away his knife. The child—in the magazine and in reality—must choose between two models: the anonymous, unclean longhair or the Lone Ranger with short, neat hair. As the reader readjusts his consciousness, the Ranger goes on defeating the varying historical forms of competition, always for the clean cause of Americanism as a way of life and as an example to the world.[49]

Maybe the Ranger would have been surprised that his friend Superman's first rival, in his 1938 premiere episode, was a capitalist arms manufacturer who manipulated "wars just so he could promote the sale of munitions." Although Superman still didn't know how to fly (he could only jump an eighth of a mile), nor did he have X-ray vision, he easily defeated his enemy. However, Norwell, the arms maker, is allowed, as we might have suspected from our experience with the Brunos and the rhinos, to repent. "Let me return to the U.S.A. I've grown to hate war." Superman responds, "Okay. But you've got to quit manufacturing weapons." He gets satisfaction from observing how morality triumphs. "From now on the most dangerous thing I'll manufacture will be a firecracker," announces the reformed industrialist.[50] Although Superman's intervention against the war industries is more violent—and more direct—than the Ranger's against the destroyers of nature several decades later, both episodes confirm our notion that they arbitrate, like the State, in disputes which otherwise would have no solution. In spite of this, in the succeeding episodes, as the character gained popularity and his authors began to accommodate commercial tastes, Superman would begin to do battle against evildoers who did not exhibit such well-defined class origins: gangsters, mad scientists, Martians, midgets from the fifth dimension, whoever might possess the technological and magical resources to make the man of steel vulnerable and create the illusion of suspense. This evolution of his imitates that of many other characters in comic strips, including the very first, *The Yellow Kid*, in the previous century. "To flow freely into the main-stream of culture," Les Daniels explains, "the savage intensity would have to be diluted."[51]

Of course, changes in the choice of adversary can also be the fruit of a more progressive vision of society. In the United States today there is a tendency to reject the insulting racial stereotypes so common in the thirties and forties. Just take a look at *The Travels of Babar*. Remember the cannibals who wanted to devour our King and Queen of the Elephants on a tropical island without realizing that they were dealing with already civilized flesh? Years later, for Babar's fiftieth-anniversary celebration, when this adventure was reproduced with several others in a single volume, the caricature of the blacks was suppressed, just like that.[52] In any case, Babar is not alone in this business. A black faun who polished boots (!) as part of Beethoven's *Pastorale*, in *Fantasia*, the Disney film, was carefully edited out of contemporary rereleases.

Beginning in the sixties, the same thing happened to the Indians. In the 1981 Lone Ranger film, the producers and screenwriters had to take into account public awareness of the native American's plight, a dimension that did not even exist in the character's original version. The fact that whatever problem the hero has to face—in this case the rights of certain minorities—varies depending upon the situation, doesn't mean that the solution has changed. The same purification of the present and placing of the burden of guilt on the past which we observed in Donald's family's visit to the West in the previous essay, by means of promises absurdly put into the mouth of Ulysses S. Grant, are symptomatic of the fact that it is easier to modernize and update a series of difficulties with which the public identifies than to modify the supreme formula by which these conflicts are resolved.

The same thing is true of the superhero's characteristics themselves. Once they've been fixed, any substantial transformation brought about in response to the way consumers feel their idols should act appears impracticable.

It should come as no surprise, then, that the film we've mentioned, in which a hero of the thirties repeats with a straight face the same mechanisms fifty years later (instead of playing them for camp as *Superman* I and II did), was a huge flop.

But how is that possible? Could it be that our hero was not immortal and invincible? Could he be humiliated by something as transitory and frivolous as the times, the tastes, and the whims of a fickle public?

Before accepting such blasphemy, let us propose instead that he was defeated by other heroes. Or, if such a solution is still too degrading, let us say that there is a conspiracy (doubtless communist and international) to change the way in which spectators have gotten used to having their heroes portrayed.

A brief summary of this new type of protagonist—however fragmented his (and her) image or transient our conclusions—suggests that, compared to the current crop of stars, our Masked Rider didn't stand a chance.

First of all, the hero has begun to be satirized. In part, such a phenomenon must be understood as an internal, stylistic movement, an ironic nostalgia with elements of pop and camp, in which the media become more and more self-referential, possessed of a private history to which they can refer before resorting to reality itself. No matter whether it's *Saturday Night Live* or *Raiders of the Lost Ark*, this tendency converts the titan into a parody, and compels the author, and often the superhero, to exhibit his self-consciousness by way of jokes and comments, winks and tricks which he shares with the public. This type of humor was latent in the actions of many heroes, including Superman's one-liners, the contortions of Plastic Man, the type of situations confronted by the Spirit; but this wry vision of their own invulnerability has been emphasized to the point of becoming the main event.[53]

The satirization of the superior man on the current TV series *The Greatest American Hero* had antecedents in Batman's new look during the sixties and the evolution of Superman on TV in the fifties. "While *Adventures of Superman* was originally played straight, the later episodes were mostly tongue-in-cheek or outright comedies."[54]

It is a road which the Lone Ranger's antibodies reject. In contrast to Hopalong Cassidy, who laughed and clowned around, or his homonym Butch Cassidy, not to mention the Sundance Kid, our hero was somber and serious right from the very start. A joke will never pass his lips.

But if such sarcasm is becoming more acceptable, it is also due to the fact that the hero has reverted to being more mundane, immersing himself, whether in his public personality, or secret life, or both at the same time, in the dilemmas of the common man. We're not just talking about Superman getting married in *Superman II*. The fault or weakness in the hero, which was the mechanism of identification, is made more profound. Instead of schizophrenically being projected onto the other half of his being, it becomes a part of the hero himself.

In addition, at the end of the sixties and the beginning of the seventies, physically handicapped heroes appear, like Ironside, who's a paralytic, or Longstreet, who's blind. But that's an extreme, just as is the Hulk, whose physically superior side is a monster and ape who emerges against the protagonist's will. That vulnerability of the hero is consolidated, more than anything else, in an insurmountable, undisguised drift away from society. The protagonist is cynical and distrustful when faced with established power, which is shown over and over to be corrupt and irresponsible. The first frames of the Ranger, when someone makes a mistake and assumes he's a criminal, invade the totality of the work. Entire series are built around the persecution and pursuit of the innocent (super) person. So, not only is it becoming more infrequent for the police, the government, or the sheriff (if he even exists or matters) to appear at the end to accept the order which the hero has succeeded in imposing on his own account, but increasingly in the films of Clint Eastwood or Burt Reynolds (or in less sinister, more lighthearted form in *The Dukes of Hazzard*) the threat comes from inside the public forces of law and order themselves. The heroes have not only lost their omniscience, but also the vocation and hope of that omniscience. They are manipulated and tricked to the point of not being able to tell their friends from their enemies. Robert Ludlum's heroes, for example, tend to be ordinary citizens who discover inside themselves, after terrible trials and perhaps irreparable losses, an almost supernatural force to keep on going.

In a world like that, it's possible, though not inevitable, for the hero to exude violence in an almost technical manner, without feeling responsible for it, thus tending to be morally neutral, almost narcissistic, as Lasch might call him. This instrumental, nearly professional vision of the capacity to kill, in which the pleasure was in the execution, in the well-oiled gears of perfection, also made the hero disposable. He either reaches the limit of self-destruction, or—which was inconceivable a few decades ago—he is led directly to death. Perhaps in 1959, when, as a result of the suicide of actor George Reeves, the man who played Superman, the newspaper headlines jokingly announced that Superman was dead, they were unwittingly anticipating all the new heroes who at the end of the film expire almost apocalyptically. I suspect, moreover, that were it not for commercial necessity (having to repeat the series or resurrect the hero and actor), more protagonists would be finished off at the end, instead of merely being tortured to the brink of death. It is rumored that Mr. Spock, killed in *Star Trek II*, will be brought back to life like Sherlock Holmes.

But perhaps the most essential transformation has been the supplanting of the individual hero for a plural, multifunctional hero, a group of interchangeable human beings performing as part of a greater unit. Will Wright has analyzed this phenomenon in the western (*The Wild Bunch, Butch Cassidy and the Sundance Kid, Eldorado, Big Jake, Rio Bravo, True Grit,* etc.).[55] But this collective, in which there is no central, dominant character but a group, was already anticipated by the Blackhawks in the comics and later in *Mission: Impossible* and *Star Trek* on television; and today it has its maximum expression in the multifaceted *Star Wars* team. Even a solitary hero like James Bond, who makes no secret of his independence and even rebelliousness, operates within an institutional structure without making decisions as to his objectives or goals, and completes his mission efficiently without any regard for the methods he uses.

Finally, the hero is able to survive as a commercial success to the extent that technology takes his place—not only insofar as he performs feats which are worthy of machines or to the extent that the machines themselves are the true protagonists—be they robots, cars, or motorcycles—but also to the extent that new audiovisual techniques themselves, what have come to be known as special effects, end up attracting a larger crowd than the hero. Even the western, that last stronghold of antimodern existence, has had, in the seventies, a television series, *The Wild, Wild West,* in which the heroes play around with gadgets and become technologized, inhabiting a locomotive moving through the vast prairies in search of adventure.

Poor Ranger. It isn't surprising that in a world such as this there's no room for him.

It seems ironic that the history which he has scorned so much, which he has sanitized so much, which has passed him by without influencing him, has turned out to be the factor that made him into an anachronism. It is society that has changed, focusing in particular on a tenser, more complex relationship between the citizen and the State.

Whereas in the Depression, as Godfrey Hodgson has observed, people wondered how to solve their problems, they now feel compelled to wonder whether problems can ever be solved.[56] The last fifteen years have destroyed the existing consensus on economic growth, on how to handle social problems, and on how to conduct foreign policy. It is likely that such a malaise is not something transitory but, as Alan Wolfe has argued, the consequence of an impasse that does not yet have an answer within the framework of the forged alliance and compromises promoted by the New Deal.[57]

Like a small businessman using outmoded, archaic methods, someone like the Lone Ranger is out of place in an age when power is disputed and shared by a State that is corporate and corporations that are ministates. Just imagine him having to comment on a description of his country by a President of the United States as "a pitiful, helpless giant" (Nixon, April 1972), and you'll realize that it is not the best of worlds in which to demonstrate his particular talents. The years of the Lone Ranger's extinction are the same ones in which the prestige of that greatest of institutions, the Presidency, was being eroded; in which nuclear arms, having become synonymous with the absolute power of destruction, tended "to immobilize rather than fortify their possessors";[58] in which the apocalypse gets not only closer and more intimate, but merges with daily life, while "the instruments of violence" have become "morally neutral."[59]

How could you call morality "irreproachable," once the spectators "had learned that there was moral ambiguity where they had once thought that the issues of right and wrong were clearest; that their own motives were not above suspicion; and there seemed little that political action could achieve, however idealistic its intentions, without evoking unforeseen and unwanted reaction."[60] How do you represent a domesticated and channeled rebelliousness, the secret condition to which each person aspires, when the State is actually becoming more secretive and impenetrable, adding more powers that no one controls to a world where technology and the corporations deprive each actor in the social process of his ability to think for himself and consider his responsibilities; when the country is full of genuine rebels who for the first time are questioning, in large numbers, the validity of North American dreams and institutions? How do you legitimize yourself as an aloof, powerful figure at the same time as the countercultural question-raisers are being integrated into the marketplace, incorporated as figures and ideas that can sell products?

We're much too close to these events to be able to predict whether the Lone Ranger's eclipse and the downfall or transformation of his colleagues signals the end of one era and the beginning of another or whether they have forever altered the way the North American people presents reality to itself. Anyway, the years have taught us to mistrust interpretations that are too global or all-encompassing. In the presence of such ambiguous, well-behaved, confused, introverted superheroes, mere survivors in a vaster structure which defines them and assumes responsibility for their actions, superheroes who know so little about their own goals and morality, who vacillate between violence and jokes, and sex and violence, it seems fitting that we, too, show ourselves to be cautious, professional, and able to savor the sweet exercise of uncertainty.

However, we should be granted the right to ask a question that recalls the words used to end all the kiddy matinees of Zorro, Captain Marvel, Batman, and so many others. As the locomotive or buzz-saw inexorably moves towards us, the question that opens our last episode: Will this be the end of our hero?

6 IN WHICH OUR HERO BIDS FAREWELL

FOR THERE *ARE* PLACES where the Lone Ranger, with his clear and irresistible solutions, with his unlimited expansion of power, his unruffled belief in the American heritage, is alive and very well, thank you. I'm not just referring to Ronald Reagan and his millions of followers, but to other, more distant lands—the countries of the so-called Third World. The same action comics which have a reduced public in their own country continue to reap dollars on the miserable shores at the outer limits of the global village.

The ways that the Ranger steps into an unbalanced, debased reality are interpreted by those on the receiving end in these countries as more than standards of conduct. What is being fed to this particular consumer—as in the Babar books and Disney cartoons— is a path of development, a way of closing the gap with the metropolis. The basic structure of this type of fiction (from a Third World point of view) is as follows: The providential arrival of a superior being to a confused and ontologically inferior reality permits the elimination of the problems, and as a result of his actions and his return to his mythical point of origin, the world is left elevated and identical to his own being.

It is actually a structure that preserves. But for a reader in a peripheral country, infested with what to his eyes appears to be backwardness and to other eyes chaos, that structure is one that changes the universe. And the very fact that the superhero comes from afar makes him, in such areas of the world, less a rebel or an outsider than an authoritarian father who has at his disposal the miraculous, generous possibility of reordering reality. The fact that these protagonists—whether they're from the West or from the stars—concentrate in their body the potential of science and the machine, reinforces the tenets of modernization, the far-removed and inexplicable creative force of technology, which soothes away pain and setback.[61]

For Third Worlders, the political and economic message embedded in these cartoons is to make catching up to the rich country and becoming identical with it a national goal. In such works of entertainment, whispered to both ghetto dwellers and the cocktail set, those who buy television sets instead of eating and those who buy color TVs with money taken from those who don't eat, all messages fuse into one: "Inferiority" and "backwardness" can be traced to the fact that the solutions and values embodied by the superhero have not been taken into consideration. Sickness can be eliminated with an injection of foreign culture and, of course, the importation of capital and machinery.

The fact that the protagonist is an outsider, private, anonymous, and pursued, facilitates the identification of the reader in poor countries. But more important to this process is that falsely rebellious being's companion who is himself truly an outsider in contemporary society. Ever since the first melodramas (as you can see in Eugène Sue's work), at the master's side there appears a servant figure who does not surrender to the inseparable unity with his master "with the stupid, puppy-dog submission of a slave, but in a conscientious, independent way."[62] The superheroes appear in an era when such ties no longer present themselves as natural, and their partners don't yield to simple aristocratic relationships or sign contracts with them. They are problematic and rebellious beings who come from submerged but seething zones of reality. They have agreed to subordinate their energies to the superhero in order to better serve their own pure, essential natures. The Lone Ranger has at his disposal an Indian; Batman, like Green Arrow, has an adolescent; Zorro, a mute; Mandrake, a black man; Buck Rodgers and Flash Gordon each have a woman. All who are mutilated or vexed, all who are excluded from power, either too young or too old, all who are resentful and sensitive, all the exploited, and all the potentially disobedient have their place alongside the Lone Ranger.

The assistant presents all the picturesque and folkloric characteristics of his marginal being. Tonto is, conveniently, an Indian without a past, all the better to effect the reader's placement and identification, his touristic encapsulation of the present. He speaks like an Indian, loyally follows the trails of people that must be found, has a sniffer that anyone could envy, says "ugh" whenever it's convenient, sends smoke signals, and knows all about medicinal herbs. A postcard. A caricature. He even cooks. Practically a woman.

Practically a woman.

In fact, if the superhero amalgamates in his masculine—but asexual—figure the features of mother and father, of authoritarian intervention and natural valley, it is the assistant—regardless of his physical form—who assumes the role that has traditionally been assigned to the woman in our society. This subordination is inevitable. Just as the wicked have no other alternative in becoming true human beings but to aspire to the dominant norms, so women, in order to get some access to power and initiative in that world of virile wills, must become men's assistants—or in the case of the female superhero, a man. No matter how much femininity aided superheroines like *Wonder Woman*, or later *The Bionic Woman*, or *Charlie's Angels* in exciting criminals—and viewers—while giving them a false sense of security (in other words, woman as object), the solution at which they finally arrive is the same (state) violence they would have had to use had they been members of the opposite sex. If they do not adopt that role, they will have to continue to function obediently as trusty companions and better halves.

Just as in Disney or Babar, mass market fictions that employ violence find it essential for the way in which the imagination constructs the universe that these types of works originally be intended for a younger public. The characters that are able to arouse the children's sympathy are always produced from the dominant sectors of the national reality, like a kind of infinite reserve of images of subordination. In focusing on childhood, vast underdeveloped territories—invisible within the borders of their own central country, visible in faraway dominions—are continually being reinvented.

Thus, the continued success of this type of hero in the countries of the so-called Third World was unconsciously prophesied by a reporter of the *Newark Star Ledger* on September 27, 1951, when he sampled the public's delirious reaction to the Lone Ranger's arrival at New York's Madison Square Garden: "There wasn't a youngster in the place who didn't wish he could trade places with the Lone Ranger's faithful Indian friend, Tonto."[63]

The newspaperman was only confirming what the hero's own

129

creator, George W. Trendle, had anticipated when he perceived the need of a companion for his lawman: "It had to be someone as free as the Ranger himself—someone who wouldn't detract from the glory of the Ranger, someone who would talk little, contribute much."[64]

Talk little. Contribute much.

The Lone Ranger's inventor was succinctly exposing the essence of the theory of domination, whether it be of countries, social classes, or individuals.

The Word is taken away from the subjugated, and they are required to work.

The Ranger can be successful as long as those sectors accept that definition as valid, as long as they keep quiet and make their contributions. In other words, as long as they agree to function as Tonto.

The superhero, the way he originally appeared in the thirties, is backed up by the myth of territorial expansion and unlimited morality, the right to intervene out there with as much impunity as he has used to impose law and order in here. His greatest success came during what Alonso L. Hamby called the imperial years, from 1939 onwards. His existence depends, then, on something more than maintaining a national feeling held together by the superiority of a way of life and organization, more than the justification that it's perfectly natural to implant that way of life on all the other peoples of the world. It also depends upon his *capacity* to do so. The way I see it, it is the restriction of this last factor, more than the first, which has caused the traditional mass market hero, as we've defined him, to reach a crisis point.

More or less during the same years that the capacity to inflict that kind of will began to erode, together with the ability to imagine it as being a clean and unambiguous act, a joke was making the rounds among kids in the United States.

In that joke—and jokes in general, although the somber, serious Ranger would never know it—are keys to the way people really feel, think, and search. The Lone Ranger and Tonto are fleeing from a savage tribe. Suddenly, they're surrounded and there's no escape.

The Ranger draws his gun and informs his lifelong companion, "Well, friend, it looks like we're done for."

Tonto looks him straight in the eye.

"What do you mean 'we,' Kemosabe? What do you mean by this 'we,' paleface?"

Behind that other face, their enemy's face, which is so pale, you can make out the much darker faces of many Indians.

Tonto has decided to talk.

FOUR

THE INFANTILI-ZATION OF THE ADULT READER

MAN DOES NOT LIVE by fiction alone.

Let's leave invented characters to one side for a while. Even though the Ranger gallops, Babar grows up, and Uncle Scrooge McDuck recovers his fortune—and they do it in a way that secretly allows the reader's imagination to absorb dominant ideas and suppress anything bothersome—in the end, we're dealing with mere entertainment.

Facts are another thing altogether—hard, cold facts, the rulers of reality.

A magazine like *Reader's Digest* does not roam the celluloid plains. It won't tolerate fables or illusions. Its readers received only authentic, irrefutable facts. An entire staff, large enough to produce a number of smaller periodicals on its own, is dedicated only to the task of checking and rechecking each little piece of information, circling whatever is potentially dubious, consulting both oral and written sources, tracing every detail to its hiding place, investigating to the ultimate millimeter and the penultimate quote so the magazine will never have to make a retraction, never be corrected or admit a mistake.[1]

Reader's Digest presents itself as infallible. So we're not going to exhaust our scanty, exiled resources in an attempt to contradict that centralized abundance of data. We don't deny that "in only three minutes [a Mirage] can ascend to an altitude of 11,000 meters and reach a velocity of Mach 2.2, or twice the speed of sound" (April 1971), or that the Briare aqueduct is 662 meters long and that it "carries the great Loire-Seine canal over 14 granite pilings above the Loire River" (ten years later, April 1981). And if we can't measure the speed of a Mirage or count the granite pilings in a French canal, we're hardly in a position to dispute the assertion that Anton Schwarzkopf, father of the roller coaster, was born in July 1924 in the little German town of Münsterhausen (July 1981).

To doubt these details would not only be useless, it could also be considered blasphemy. Somehow or other, more readers enter the *Reader's Digest* temple of knowledge than any other site (read: publication) in the world. They renew their faith through monthly communion with it. For someone to sift through and examine the icons on its stained-glass windows, the doors to the sanctuary, the altar, or the pulpit would constitute an act of aggression.

It would be even more sacrilegious, we suppose, for a critic to dare to analyze the building itself, its entire architecture—in other words, to note the way in which those facts and so many others are organized and foisted upon the consciousness of the congregation.

It would be like hooking God up to a lie detector.

However, in all modesty, the man writing these words has also made a pact with truth, although I do not write it with a capital T, nor do I pretend that my sense of it is infallible. With trepidation I feel it is my duty to profane that secular cathedral and wonder out loud, in the middle of the service that gathers the priests of knowledge and the faithful waiting to be enlightened, if the evangelism of the *Reader's Digest* is not, although referring to a verifiable daily reality and not a fictional adventure, similar in a very basic way to what we've already glimpsed in the previous essays.

In any case, the believing, credulous reader has no reason to feel uneasy about this assault. He's used to looking at life as an act of perpetual survival in the face of repellent attacks. Characters in the *Reader's Digest* are frequently besieged by hurricanes, packs of wild dogs, bears that have escaped from their cages, communist and Irish terrorists, collapsing buildings, Arctic and tropical climates, and they always succeed—thanks to their faith in God, thanks to their own integrity—in surviving. We're sure that *Reader's Digest* itself, assaulted in an equally intemperate way, driven to the brink by someone who is not North American, who writes in another language, and who professes "foreign ideas," will also know how to stay afloat and continue giving its readers the imperturbable quota of information they so desperately need.

Besides, our examination of the *Reader's Digest* is disqualified in advance since it bears an indelible stigma: It is an analysis which cannot be summarized or condensed. By definition, then, the magazine's readers wouldn't even understand what we were talking about.

In fact, the reader who buys the *Digest* does it, among other reasons, to escape intellectual analyses of just this sort. He wants the world comfortably transmitted without previously having had to question it. He feels the need to master—without being a specialist, without having to open other magazines or, God forbid, books, without creating big headaches or stretching his brain—certain portions of thought that seem to him indispensable. Using the *Reader's Digest* as a kind of combination bridge to and colander of knowledge, the reader receives "the best of current reading" in "an article a day of enduring significance, in condensed booklet form." In other words, the *Reader's Digest* selects (the magazine's Portuguese and Spanish name is *Selecciones*) and distinguishes among thousands and thousands of publications. These are guaranteed to go beyond the transitory, the merely trendy, in order to be able to remain in the reader's mind (and on his shelves). It makes no difference whether the majority of the articles were originally produced for *Reader's Digest* and planted in other publications so that later it would appear as if the *Digest* had adapted or summarized them. The main thing is for the reader to have the impression that the editors have searched through the entire spectrum of contemporary writing the world over, just as Disney's ducks explored the globe in search of riches, or the Lone Ranger in search of wrongs to right. Whatever is worthy of great consideration, of being a statue in each person's inner museum, is thus set apart from what you can forget today or tomorrow. *Reader's Digest* is a tourist guidebook for the geography of ignorance.

That's why it's a booklet. It's meant to be more than a magazine, because although it retains its modernizing, up-to-date outlook, it can be saved for constant reference, but less than a book, because although it can be found in any library, it does not frighten off its acquirer with a voluminous, austere, academic aspect. It has all the advantages of both: just the right happy (communications) medium necessary to carry out its function, and within reach of the pocketbook as well. This balance guarantees that the magazine constitutes a sanctuary just as far removed from sterile intellectualism as from the throwaway products of a consumer society. Its format reveals the hybrid environment in which it appears, the kingdoms it wishes to reconcile: It's either a magazine or a book, it's neither, and it's both, according to whatever is most convenient for the reader. At this exact crossroads the newspaper and academic mentalities converge, and novelty and stability, sensationalism and domesticity succeed in living together as one another's cute little concubines.

And so with every installment, this microcosm occupies all the frontiers reality opens, with an accent on the latest information to arrive from those outposts. After opening the booklet we find on its title page a jumble of themes on the most diverse topics. It replicates a fragmented reality, reproduces the world's division in separate little parcels identical to those the reader is used to finding in his daily experience. Every area is clearly delineated and set apart from the others, separated from any possible global cohesion. The apparent autonomy of the various chunks subterraneanly reinforces the image the reader has formed of his own cognitive potential in a world where everything changes at such a feverish rate, where specialization has grown to traumatic proportions, where nothing ever seems to reach a level of coherence or integration.

Of course this asphyxiating isolation is not admitted as such. On the contrary, it permits the *Reader's Digest* to transmit an illusion of pluralism (which never ceases to be a theme and never invites a dispute because different positions never truly confront one another), while offering the reader totality in entertaining, short, assimilable portions. Nothing is outside of this miniworld: geography, biography, history, medicine, politics, anecdotes, architecture, art, world problems, family relations, the latest technological advances, botany, advice, diets, quizzes, jokes, vocabulary, religion—sections which, despite their apparent diversity, are monotonously repeated from month to month, year to year, decade to . . . Will it be centuries? While it simulates a chimera crammed with information, the *Digest* can tackle each section without relating it to its lateral compartments; it can articulate the problems described as if they were absolutely isolated and the teachings extracted as if all qualitative links to whatever else has been learned in the rest of the magazine were completely severed.

In light of the fact that the previous written source of each piece is supposedly a book or specialized essay, it is the article's origin itself that ends up justifying this partiality of cognition. The reader is filled with the Spirit (of knowledge) on condition that he first accept the crushing atomization of this knowledge into spaces and boundary lines previously defined by society. In other words, *Reader's Digest* makes use of these technically inevitable divisions which capitalism has imposed on intellectual (and material) labor, which were necessary for economic development and a dominion over nature, but which also validated, a posteriori, the mental subdivision of those wishing to approach that knowledge. The truth in pills, pockets, closets, and immaculate compartments—the infernal consequence of an economic system that isolates a man from his job and alienates his humanity—is converted by *Reader's Digest* into an unquestionable precondition for authentically getting to know something. Only the chaotic enumeration of scattered elements can assure the individual his revelation. Clearly this model is possible because, underneath the monthly anecdotal variations lies a profound structural unity. Each "selected" piece cannot help but repeat the same language, procedure, technique, and ideology as all other pieces. The same flag, climate, and geology are cyclically reiterated on all the apparently independent islands.

But there are other motives. Since a fair number of the articles confront some problem that has become a crisis in contemporary society—for example, the armaments race, hunger, drugs, juvenile and urban delinquency, atmospheric contamination, the generation gap, chronic underdevelopment, or communal living—once one theme is separated from another it becomes difficult for the reader to sense how all these contradictions might derive from the same indivisible system, or how each fragment that he's being urged to tuck away in some corner is none other than a symptom of a considerably graver and more generalized crisis. Moreover, since the *Digest* is able to gain the upper hand in each distressing situation, it achieves a miraculous and prophetic transformation of the world's discordances. A problem is not presented in order to investigate its causes or unravel its origins. Quite the contrary. It is placed before our very eyes so we can see how, in some model place together with the inspiration of some exemplary citizen, that problem has found a path toward solution. There is no lasting contradiction generated by such a system. In fact, there isn't even a system. There are only cases which someone has learned how to face successfully, and which various imitators can resolve with symmetrical dedication and by identical routes. As long as they read *Selecciones*.

This method of dealing with problems was in vogue ten years ago, when I first approached this topic, and it is still in vogue today. In the May 1971 issue of the Chilean edition of the *Digest*—which I used as a prototype for an in-depth examination, putting myself in the place of an ordinary reader who opens to any page—all the dilemmas were miraculously resolved, as if a magician had pulled the same rabbit out of thirty different-colored hats. Pollution was denounced and overcome in theory in "The Oceans are Dying." "Revolution in Agriculture, Promise of Abundance" triumphantly augured the end of hunger. Congestion on the highways and crashes were explained in "When Alcohol and the Steering-Wheel Meet." Consciences were eased when it came to job-related accidents in "Riku Ruopsa's Trial by Fire."

The fracturing of events and the need for solutions demand, instead of prevent, a repetitive structure. Every section looks like every other, just as every issue looks like the one that preceded it and the one that will follow. Ten years later we can choose any 1981 *Digest* and we will find the same phenomena and the same average figures who, by means of their tenacity and drive show us how to struggle against adversity—from urban renewal ("The Most Famous Marketplace in the World," May 1981), the sexual abuse of children ("Incest, the Ultimate Taboo," February 1981), poverty ("I Was Santa Claus," December 1981) to the generational struggle ("What Every Child Should Know," October 1981) and depression (September and June and August and November, and boredom and weariness and . . .).

To spare the reader the monotony, to say nothing of the depression, of the etceteras, however, it would be better to stick with one issue, maybe even one article. It was my intention to choose one, at random, from 1981.

But here my readers must allow me to recount (especially since we're dealing with *Reader's Digest*) an anecdote, a personal glimpse, a memory which will illustrate and hopefully entertain.

I wanted this essay to be a continuation of the one I'd written on the *Reader's Digest* of 1971. I thought it would be interesting to compare the two crops, observing the changes that had taken place after a decade. Such an intention was dashed to pieces by the invariability of the magazine's model, especially inasmuch as it conceives of itself as permanent and, as we shall see, practically everlasting. To all intents and purposes it has not suffered a major alteration in the ten years in which not a few things have happened in my life and in the world.

But I had a small surprise. The package I asked for from Chile came with thirteen copies: the twelve from 1981 that I had requested plus one extra. Someone had, at random, by coincidence, or perhaps through some inscrutable design, slipped in the April 1980 issue. In honor of superstition, or maybe as a way of exorcizing it, I read that fugitive folio, the one that didn't fit into my chosen series, right away. To my astonishment, it went perfectly with my ideas about the *Digest*, confirming them one by one. The issues from 1981, which I read afterwards, also supported those hypotheses, but none of them approached to such an extent the Essence of the *Reader's Digest*; none of them encompassed such a rich, vast, and prototypical range as the April 1980 issue.

I must confess, I fell in love with that orphan issue.

After some vacillation, then, I decided to adopt that installment as my basic specimen, the Issue that condenses all issues; although, of course, I'll refer to its identical twins from 1981 whenever appropriate. If at first I hesitated to take this step, it was because such methods have more to do with sentiment than science. It was not originally part of my investigation to include in the corpus (or corpse) I had studied a copy from another year. After all, didn't I see *Reader's Digest* as a compendium of contemporary learning, a rigorous magazine, an illustrator of advances, a mini-encyclopedia sworn to the task of stamping out ignorance, and yet I was allowing myself the liberty of such a personal, spontaneous, discriminatory act.

But I thought that if the *Digest* can read all the articles in the universe (as well as all the books, speeches, and jokes) and choose only those which most served their purposes, didn't I perhaps have the right to do the exact same thing? Besides, if some critic decides to throw out my conclusions on the basis of this decision, I can always point out that, in choosing April 1980 I was yielding to a mythic, almost Christian structure, and the *Digest* itself would approve of such devotion. Somehow an archetype that was hard to ignore had fallen into my lap: one Leader and twelve disciples, one Voice and twelve echoes, one Copy and twelve followers.

That's life in these United States.

And with that, my tale ends. (Maybe we should call it "Are You Superstitious?" or "My Most Unforgettable Issue.")

Returning to our analysis, one of the features in the April 1980 issue that most excited me was something depicting that old nemesis and cause of so much grief for our Lone Ranger—pollution. "Plants On the Offensive Against Smog" focuses on the decision made by Andy Lipkis, who at fifteen knew that California's atmosphere was condemned to be dirty and unbreathable, to plant trees. No one paid any attention at first. "He visited several businessmen and solicited funds to put his plan into action, but he didn't succeed in convincing them about the seriousness of the problem." However, he must have been brought up on the Lone Ranger and must even have read the episode discussed in the previous essay, because he decided to implement his idea on his own, and with perseverance, he got other people to go along with him. Several years later, with the contributions of many citizens and an ad campaign in the *Los Angeles Times*, things changed: "The businessmen reconsidered the idea and contributed jeeps, tools, and an office." The last scene could have been written—or dictated, if the other seems too miraculous—by our friend Silver: " 'And to think,' commented one of the tree-planters, 'that in another hundred years maybe other kids will be sitting at the foot of our trees.' "

Their efforts, and Andy Lipkis's, too, are admirable. Less admirable is the *Reader's Digest*'s narrative strategy. Smog is the consequence of a situation that isn't described. Since there aren't any causes, there can never be a solution that attacks the roots of the problem, only its residue. It's as if a doctor, upon discovering that a patient has cancer, were to give him medicine that got rid of the symptoms, leaving the tumors to grow unmolested.

The *Digest* not only addresses such social problems in a disconnected and separate way in its pages; just as disjointed and facile is the way in which it recommends that the mental and emotional upheaval caused by the dead-end persistence of those problems can be overcome. Ten years ago, in May 1971, it was suggested in two articles ("Tranquility Without Tranquilizers" and "Put Your Worries to Work") that you didn't need to change the world. All you had to do was to loosen up and comfortably adapt to its imperfections. If that didn't work, you should just realize that tension is a good thing, a dynamo that can give you energy. "If we could only succeed in taking advantage of our worries instead of letting ourselves be consumed by them, in the long run we would end up having fewer anxieties, and that will help us in our work. But let's not worry about that now, there's plenty of time for that later." In April 1980 the solution was hypnosis ("Hypnotism: Potent Therapy").

So the social is reduced to the individual, and the individual to individualism.

It is a tactic that is depressingly, tiringly repeated over and over again. In "Graduation Into Society" (March 1981), we learn how to fight against juvenile delinquency. You should do what a Danish sea captain did, even though no one agreed with his ideas. He reformed a group of youth by utilizing the ancient traditions of the discipline of the sea, sweetened with a touch of love. As you might expect, after fighting wind and seasickness, he achieves his objective, and is finally helped out by companies, corporations, and government bureaucrats, who "regret" not having come to his aid before. In every issue there's another missionary, religious or secular. It might be a clergyman who turns youth away from their bad habits ("A Priest in Hell," June 1981) or a man who decides to release a trapped fish back into the sea ("Free That Fish!," September 1981). In this obsession for reducing everything to its individual dimension, you even wind up personalizing collective entities like cities ("Manhattan, Neurotic and Fascinating") or countries ("China Goes Shopping"), both from April 1980. Even a mineral gets this kind of treatment ("Gold and Its Secrets," December 1981).

But this feverish individualism does not imply variety. On the contrary, such a solution can only work because the publication has reduced each person to a recipe made up of the usual ingredients.

Before he or she can appear in the pages of *Reader's Digest*, each human being must pass through an implacable process of selection, editing, condensation, and remodeling, just as if he were on an assembly line of the intellect, until the final product conforms to the specifications of a common human denominator—the "average man" who supposedly lurks deep inside every one of us.

This ordinary hero from the *Digest*, who demands that everybody be tailored to fit his silhouette, doesn't need to be famous. However, he should have a certain potential to be exceptional, although he would never admit to it. He deserves our rapturous attention, nonetheless, because some unforgettable aspect of his personality is just waiting to bloom forth ("Thanks, Hazel," April 1980), or some strange, unrepeatable event has already happened to him ("Buried Alive," April 1980).

Any human being, any reader, then, can gain the right to be immortal. He doesn't need to perform any noteworthy or public service, or be a genius or a star. It's enough to be "my most unforgettable character," the archetypal section in which a trivialized being is perpetuated by the fact that he is remembered by some other equally trivialized being. This also explains the plethora of humor sections in the magazine, submitted directly by thousands of readers. Everyday experience, which abounds in oral and communal tradition, flowers anew in a fixed situation that everyone can share. That moment of existence which is amusing and out of the ordinary is given eternal life, as long as it doesn't transgress the reader's habits of identification. This kind of treatment can be extended to include an entire country ("Life in these United States"), a way of life ("Humor in Uniform" or "Campus Comedy") or the human body itself (which becomes an extraordinary appendix to the routine, statistically neutral personality of a man: "I Am Joe's Cell," July 1981). In *Reader's Digest* even the close at hand has the potential to turn into something momentarily exotic, different, memorable. Without losing balance and normality, we're all exposed to the singularity of the unusual, and thus the glory of a written commemoration.

For identical reasons, whatever is faraway and famous is reduced incessantly to its most comprehensible, immediate, not to say vulgar, form. The normal being is lifted up through the unexpected, and the exceptional one is lowered to accessibility. Of course those mysterious and strange features of a personality, a country, or a particular deed are never lost. The monotony of the reader's repetitive life demands the sensational and the marvelous, just as long as it's viewed from the windows of an air-conditioned tour bus. The unparalleled adventure of the illustrious human being is feasible only on condition that he simultaneously undergo a bath of simplicity and abbreviation. Sometimes, without abandoning his colloquial and affable tone, some luminary tells us of something simple and touching that happened to him, and this makes the reader feel at home with that "outstanding" personality. These anecdotes democratize the superior being just as the split personality or mask democratizes the heroes in comic books.

Whatever the reader might not be able to handle is never presented. He should invariably be able to discover himself just as the other guy, the protagonist, is discovering something else; and there's always something to be discovered—a new medicine, a dinosaur, a relic, a scientific invention, a formula for success, even a work of art. But the biographical trajectory is always more important than the actual discovery. Goethe's loves (April 1980) mean more than his works; or rather, his work is a pretext to treat a giant like him in a familiar manner, since, regardless of his lofty life, he too suffered from problems which we've all had to cope with on our voyage through life. Lerici, the explorer of the Etruscan world ("Lerici and the Etruscans," May 1971) was much more fascinating than the Etruscans' lipstick, or their museum of dust and solitude. How much did he spend, how much did he earn from the enterprise, what obstacles and misunderstandings did he have to overcome—that's what's important. In "Trip to a Lost City" we focus on the heroic individual who crossed a desert and risked his health to visit some ruins (April 1980).

Each person's work, the consequence—it is claimed—of a life dedicated to doing good deeds, and therefore crowned with success, serves more than anything else as a source for gossip, dinner-table conversation, and decoration. So there's no reason to get upset if you can't understand the work of these men and women, no matter whether it's a work of art or a technological advance. Nor should the strangeness of geography or of an epoch throw us off. In "Baja California, Magnificent Desolation" (April 1980), the author succeeds in paring a bewitching and hostile landscape down to its bare bones: "Being there is, if not childhood itself, then the ideal of how we wish it could be." Not content just to reduce a Mexican province to a state of infancy, she goes on to make things even more familiar: "Baja California is everything: uncivilized beauty, hardship and challenge, the human spirit, the capacity to live on whatever is at hand, the joy you conquer on the road." Only after having ensured, then, the anthropomorphization of the land from the point of view of the common and ordinary—a particular state of mind—is it possible to go back to whatever is exceptional about the place: "It's something more than a land of plenty. It is in another place in time." (In "Wales, a State of Mind," September 1981, we are assured that "it isn't the landscape, or even history that shaped the country's way of life, but its people.") Thus, no matter how distant the reality being presented, the human model carrying out that expedition, taking that step, performing that deed, always reassures. Even if it's impossible for everyone to make that gesture or complete that life's work, the reader can imitate the determination, the spirit of competition or compassion, and the basic morality in his own life, or he can make that distinguished existence his own by having it reduced to his own terms.

The giant has undertaken his odyssey precisely because in his everyday life he's a man just like any other man. He has complied with the ethical laws of the universe. His secrets have been revealed (with an exotic aura that maintains interest, of course) and his mysteries are shown to be mere eccentricities which prove innocuous since they haven't hindered him from winning fame and fortune. If he is knowable, condensable, abridgeable, then his distance can't be a threat or a disturbance. In this way, even that person farthest from the reader and his passive situation, someone who is as a matter of fact active and unique, is a mirror of emulatory behavior for all men, he is—if you will pardon the expression—a creature of laughter and tears. Although it may seem paradoxical, the very fact that he is basically a common man is what has permitted that "uncommon" man to rise and conquer.

We can find the epitome of this structure in the personality of the founder and proprietor of *Reader's Digest*. I will not quote the multiple testimonies sprinkled among various books. "Dewitt Wallace," asserts his obituary (July 1981), "showed himself to be a genius gifted with the rare ability to see and feel like the common man. Even so, he considered it a privilege for his magazine to be welcomed into so many homes around the world; just as he undertook the privilege of being able to contribute millions of dollars to charitable causes." This is how the Founder and his *Digest* end up founding a dynasty in a single Copy. Both extremes of humanity, geniuses and ingnoramuses, need the bridge and intermediary which is the *Reader's Digest*. "*Digest* articles," proclaims the dean of a prestigious university in the northeastern United States, "provide one of the most pleasant ways I know for the mathematician to supplement his symbols and the child to evolve upward from his comics."[2]

The readers correctly sense that the *Digest* is their home, and they send in their collaborations, jokes, experiences, and anecdotes, as we'll see shortly. Everything is thinned down to "I": I did this, I knew him, I was in such and such a place. And every ego geometrically shares the same preconceptions and possibilities, every human being becomes *common* (and *commun*icative) in hopes that his small and transitory existence can become universal in the illustrious money-making pages of the *Reader's Digest*.

Thus, the magazine imposes the belief that each person should have confidence in his own experience, in that irreducible fact of his own good sense (I'm telling you, if there's one thing I've learned, I have a lot of experience, son). No one can call that into question. Of course, they forget to mention that that nucleus of experiences to which we give so much credit, that morality which is our spokesman, is neither natural nor in the domain of universality, but rather it has a social origin.

Reader's Digest dotes on "you yourself," you know, your common sense, public opinion, the man on the street, what we all know, what no one in his right mind would disagree with. All this makes it easy to forget that such a "human" approach is a product, a convention. When faced with a problem or upheaval, one resorts to solutions that have been transmitted from the past, those stamped

147

"valid" through tradition. Note the curious correspondence with Descartes, who discovers the "I think" only because at the same time he can insert that "I" into a body of common ideas handed down from a more prestigious past. But the magazine does not elaborate its theories in the abstract. It puts them into practice every day for millions and millions of human beings. If these ideas were good enough for your grandparents, they're good enough for you—which supposes an eternal warehouse (or garbage dump) of wisdom that has ahistorically helped all men. (In its articles on archaeology, anthropology, and history, the magazine particularly lapses into this vision, accentuating the "common" identity that time has been unable to erase.) These canned "knowledge preserves" will not only always be there, but have found in the *Digest* their natural repository and legitimate heir. Every person dramatized in the *Digest*, no matter how exceptional, can be reduced to the same common and individual experience as long as he yields to goodness. In his turn, every reader, no matter how ground up in the gears of everyday life, can always read his own, almost biographical, sketch in the magazine.

Admiral Richard E. Byrd expressed this—as both the common and outstanding man that he is—in a testimony about the morally therapeutic effects of the magazine during a five-month stint in the Antarctic: "The six *Digests* I had with me seemed written exactly to fit my situation and needs, and I wager that *Digest* readers in a million situations all over the world have the same feeling of service designed with them personally in mind."[3]

Let us leave the good admiral reading and rereading his six copies, and doubtless loaning them to his faithful subordinates as they contemplate a landscape of white desolation; noting only that Admiral Byrd and the chorus of awed and self-satisfied spectators who observe him are locked into a profound collaboration, a perfect standstill, a seesaw balance of rights and interests suspended in midair.

Everywhere you look, the readers have invaded the magazine, either through their representatives, run-of-the-mill people like themselves, or through superior personalities who have been translated into averageness. This "common man" is not only a point of departure and a road for the magazine to travel, but also a goal at the end of that road, an objective to be aimed at and attained. Starting from the fact that the reader needs to be informed, that he is unaware of something which is essential to his survival in a constantly changing and alien world, the *Digest* delivers, together with its discreet parcels of information, tranquility. "To acquire knowledge is not easy. Few of us have the time. You can acquire a broad understanding of the world—a liberal education—in a pleasurable way, by reading the *Reader's Digest*."[4] This means that it is assumed that everything is decipherable for that average man through "selections," many of them re-edited by "experts" who, however, as their colloquial and happy use of language indicates, are just like you and me. Through the *Digest* the reader can be informed about everything, without having to lose his status as a "common man." He accumulates knowledge, but he does it in such a particular way that he doesn't permute his being—that irreducible thing known as his daily routine, the sacrosanct perspective (full of prejudices) which confirms his regularness.

Just as with the superheroes, knowledge does not transform the reader; on the contrary, the more he reads the *Digest*, the less he needs to change. Here is where all that fragmentation returns to play the role it was always meant to play. Prior knowledge is never assumed. From month to month, the reader must purify himself, suffer from amnesia, bottle the knowledge he's acquired and put it on some out-of-the-way shelf so it doesn't interfere with the innocent pleasure of consuming more, all over again. What he learned about the Romans doesn't apply to the Etruscans. Hawaii has nothing to do with Polynesia. Knowledge is consumed for its calming effect, for "information renewal," for the interchange of banalities. It is useful only insofar as it can be digested anecdotally, but its potential for original sin has been washed clean, along with the temptation to generate truth or movement—in other words: change.

The *Digest* is a stomach that digests without having to evacuate. Knowledge miraculously disappears when it threatens to pass into the intestines, giving any indication of decomposition or growth. You can chew whatever you like, as much as you want, as often as you like, without suffering from cramps or getting full. Why make an effort? The future and the world are yours, because the unknowns are not all that great. The common man is consolidated in his mythology and collective representation; the universe, conveniently segmented, is no longer a mystery or a threat.

These characteristics are not coincidental.

In order to function, North American society requires that each person believe that the world offers unlimited opportunities, and that everyone is equal to the task of conquering that magical horizon. Over and over again, *Reader's Digest* portrays human beings who in spite of the most unfortunate circumstances, social or physical (there are an abundance of blind people, mutes, deaf people, paralytics, people who've been in accidents or gotten lost somewhere), somehow manage to succeed. In May 1971, this is how the magazine preached the message to its Chilean readers through one of "my most unforgettable characters."

> [My father] had no way to send me to college, so that problem was taken care of for him. But in a certain sense, he "sent" me to college after all. One afternoon, when I was sixteen, we were on the front lawn. It was a beautiful day. "My son," he said, "look as far as you can see. It is a big world and it's all yours. The only thing you've got to do is launch yourself into it and make it your own."

Of course, in actual fact that dream won't come true for everyone in the current social and economic system. Rather, every person is turned into a small cog, madly competing with everyone else in order to subsist, alone, distrustful, an expert all by himself in the corner. That person is offered everything, but little is actually "delivered." He's given thousands and thousands of keys, without ever being told that they're all for the same door.

The *Digest* achieves what society cannot achieve in reality. It compensates for these men's failed dreams by recreating the Homo universalis that bourgeois culture has raised to the mythic level from the Renaissance to the present.[5] For one bubbling, fantastic instant, each person is transmuted into a know-it-all, without having to be modified by that knowledge, without conduct or practices being affected by its use. The reader can master the universe segment by segment, month by month, advancing without changing places, like a Hollywood train that instead of going forward keeps passing an imaginary cardboard landscape. In fact, the separated and fractured person continues to be a solitary creature (with his equally solitary plots of wisdom), but he is represented to himself as integrated, synchronized, a cumulative whole communing with the other readers.

On a different level, the *Digest* satisfies another need in the same specific way: that of consumption. Every industrial product in our system of renewable objects stimulates the buyer to consume something that is always the same under the appearance of being different. In terms of the *Digest*, this is true not only for the magazine as object, month to month, booklet to booklet, but also for the very knowledge it extols. Contemporary man lives stimulated by novelty, enticed by the sensation of searching for the unique, for that which breaks the standard mold, as long as he can ingest it in its most repetitious and tranquilizing form.

But there's something else that bolsters the *Digest*'s position. The inhabitants of capitalism are taught to believe that it is ideas that generate the real differences between men. It is those ideas which account for progress and explain success; therefore, it is fundamental to know more than the other guy if you want to win and get ahead. We've already seen this structure operating in Disney and the superheroes. In the first promotional material on the *Reader's Digest* this notion was expressed very openly: "When a man stops learning, he stops living. Knowledge means power; the well-informed man is the strong man."[6] More ideas must be produced and consumed. They must be digested faster, by the minute, to allow the reader to go farther on that fuel. All these appetites are unavoidable if the system is to work; but it's not possible for the dominant class to truly oblige these desires, whose realization is limited by the very economic system that stimulates them. From this clash emerges the *Digest*.

Fast ideas are like fast food. It's not the taste of the meal that matters, nor the care taken in cooking it, no matter how much the business claims to love its customers. This sort of food and these ideas exist to be digested and not eaten. The swiftness of their preparation corresponds to the swiftness of their consumption. With this brisk digestibility, the magazine is, in fact, responding to the right to know (and to eat?), which has been theoretically proclaimed as the heritage of the entire population since the inception of capitalism.

Since the corrosion of Europe's feudal system, with its unfettering of economic bonds, a certain degree of knowledge (greater and greater, as time went on) was promised to all citizens and workers, so that a hierarchical world which had been previously fixed and defined could now be explained in "freer" terms.[7] Infinite knowledge, as in the Faust legend, was dangled in front of everybody's eyes, as was the power that supposedly went with it.

Of course, this excessive faith in science was accompanied by an equally powerful mistrust in it. Hyram Hayden has noted that, next to this humanist, rational, harmonious vision of the universe, which sought both the diffusion of ideas to all and change through the application of technology, there coexisted what he calls a counter-renaissance, an antinaturalistic trend, which muttered that wisdom was demoniacal and eccentric.[8] In other words, knowledge was seen not only as a democratic force, a leveler of men and a creator of opportunities according to merit, but also as something very difficult and dangerous to obtain, something which separated a select few from the rest of mankind. Knowledge was not only progress; it could also be turned into a curse—something not only unavailable but even undesirable.

This conflict has come to a head in the twentieth century in a mass society that continues to offer eternal improvement to everyone without really satisfying anyone, and it is answered by the *Reader's Digest* in a brilliant and extreme way. In that unpretentious booklet something is accomplished which the real world cannot tolerate—the microcosmic conversion of anyone into a universal expert, Artistotle resurrected on the corner newsstand. Knowledge, for all it promises and does not deliver, for all it builds and all the progress it makes right before our astonished eyes, for all it prohibits and does not distribute, is transformed into a good fairy, a magic wand, and a comfort in time of need. Aspirin has been extracted from a headache.

Everybody has the right to understand reality. This notion is reproduced by the magazine itself through the very fact of its massive circulation. No one is barred access to *Reader's Digest*. It is sold almost everywhere, and it's inexpensive. There's no discrimination.

Whoever wishes to learn can have recourse to that unique school and that series of successive and seemingly identical texts. All secrets have been leveled so that the reader can take on the month ahead, if not with the necessary knowledge, at least with the illusion that he possesses such knowledge. The Superstomach already knows everything in advance and will grant its consumers whatever amount might be beneficial and decent.[9] The reader has handed over his representation to the editor of the *Digest*: that super-common-reader who has read everything ever published.

The inspiration behind the *Reader's Digest* is very clearly a political project, which—aside from the extreme conservatism of its public stance—can be noted in the type of communication that it suggests, in the type of relationship between reader and producer. It is democracy as it is practiced in industrial societies, but especially in the United States. To participate is, above all, to consume, to be a completely economic man. To participate in politics is to be a radio, television, or newspaper spectator; to participate is to deposit a vote every few years, certain that we are also voting when we dig into our pockets and wallets every day.

It's no mistake that, although the magazine began in 1922, its great leap in circulation did not take place until the thirties, when two of its fundamental editorial structures were erected. The first was the aforementioned endlessly fragmented reader participation by way of thousands and thousands of anecdotes, jokes, and "original and authentic stories about personal experiences."[10] Simultaneously, the tactic which would take more precedence as time went on was in the process of being formulated—namely, that of previously planting the articles they wished to publish in other magazines.[11] During a period when everyone felt "depressed" because of a crisis over which they had no control, the magazine was handed over to its readers so they themselves could be the reporters of their own invariable daily experiences.[12] In return, the reader handed over to the *Digest* his right to know for himself, to investigate; he let himself be represented by the Magazine that Selects. The Depression put into practice forms of communication that permitted citizens to overcome their vulnerability and at the same time have faith in the normality of their lives.

Thus, each partial, fractured explanation circularly reaffirms the basic paternalism begun by the act of reading, the unanimously vertical direction of knowledge, which is passivity but never activity, absorption but never praxis. The magazine knows for, lives for, decides for, and orients the reader. And since he's "in" the magazine, his personal experiences get preferential treatment, helping create a structure of mutual confidences that will never be broken. This is how it happens that even those who might disagree with the magazine's political attitudes, its crude anticommunism or opposition to liberal social reforms, can enjoy the rest of its (supposedly apolitical) sections.

The *Digest* strains out the tense and hostile world without removing it entirely. Everything that doesn't appear in its columns is already lacking in interest. And that's that. The magazine can speak for the common man because it is the common man quantitatively endowed with power. In essence, it doesn't know any more than the most ignorant of its readers. It simply has more data, more personnel, more talented common men and women working for it and centralizing information. What it hasn't lost, though, is its simplicity, its comfortable and friendly tone, it's good humor, its prudent happiness. It hasn't gotten academic or sophisticated. It hasn't made its language more intricate. It isn't incomprehensible and it doesn't use a specialized vocabulary. It applies the same sieve to each of its protagonists, selecting from them whatever is adaptable. Lewis Thomas's optimism is fine, but not the complexity of his thought ("The Doctor Who Prescribes Optimism," March 1981).

Its language is like one of its characters. Fame hasn't spoiled it. There's no reason for knowledge to get lost in terminology or make human beings appear strange, either. *Reader's Digest* itself demonstrates that in spite of its gargantuan learning (yes, it is a digestive banquet, and Rabelais celebrated the art of eating in the same years that others celebrated the art of knowing), it has not varied its everyday habits. Crises, advances, and novelties can leave us stronger but with the same personality as before—a demonstration borne out by being able endlessly to renew intimate and immediate contact, by being so nice. Superior but equal. Receiver and transmitter unalterable, with perpetual, frenetic, circular movement between both.

This democratization of the acquisition of knowledge by means of translation into the common man's tongue fulfills other functions. By serving as a bridge between the technological elite and the great majority that lives waiting for this advance, as much for a source of news as for their personal well-being, the *Digest* promulgates an implicit thesis on the division of knowledge in the real world. The *Digest* informs its readers in an egalitarian way. In just such a way must the practical effects of this knowledge be distributed in the real world, with the very same wisdom and security that the magazine utilizes. As a result, each reader can re-embark on the road to success by reacquainting himself with the democracy of learning, by having at his disposal (after submitting to a reading which levels all things) the minimal, irreducible, and necessary basis for continuing to win or lose the battle for money, fame, or affection. Everyone ends up on the same stratum; everyone knows the same thing; they've all been exposed to identical purifying opportunities by reading the magazine. What happens next is up to each person's individual talent, to the natural inequalities that can't help but justify the emergence of social inequalities. Whatever society has contributed to each of us disappears, so that we can all compete and demonstrate our individual worth, our undeniable capabilities, and then the *Digest* will level everything once again, and so on.

The *Reader's Digest* gives the buyer the eternal right to go on competing and not get left behind. It is useful for living. Through its magical medicine, its gnoseological vitamins, this magazine erases the differences in the actual, hierarchical distribution of knowledge in this society with a stroke of the pen.

In this context, it's possible for the *Digest*—not only in its own messages, in its reports on science, but also in the way it communicates them—to suggest that the distribution of technology is in and of itself neutral and objective. Each of the magazine's readers has the same access to news and advice as any other, so surely the latest medical advance will come into his life as promptly for a reader who lives in the Recoleta district of Santiago as it does for one who lives in Kansas City or New Delhi.

But this fair, impersonal, generous distribution, beyond all ideological boundaries, actually conceals what I would call a trap. It is clear to me that, according to the *Digest*, technology only favors those who have already adopted ethically correct attitudes. Of course, the characters circulating through its pages always obtain success, and this is supposed to be the result of their happy discovery and application of knowledge. But that success, it turns out, is seemingly subject to a determination of the protagonists' goodness and integrity. On one occasion after another, the magazine focuses on the moment that knowledge, and especially the latest technological fad, steps in to solve the problems that have been posed. However, on every single occasion where science intervenes, it is emphasized that the person about whom they are writing *deserves* what he's gotten (for strictly irrational reasons). This underscores the certainty that the distribution of the benefits of science (as of every other positive thing) has been carried out in accordance with each person's previous, predestined conduct. Whoever relates this to the Protestant ethic and the spirit of capitalism wins a prize.

It's obvious that those who don't subscribe to the prevailing norms in values or conduct will not be able to receive the magical results of technological advancement. The moral division of the world precedes the sharing out of the bounty of knowledge. Like a great witch doctor that sanctions, the *Digest* knows that its readers will behave themselves.

The moral subdivision we've just mentioned is reproduced in the very structure of the magazine. There are several sections dedicated to speaking directly to the reader, offering interpretations and advice, at times in question-and-answer form, that quite often are actually useful. But the context in which the *Digest* offers this information has been preset by the transmitter-receiver structure of the magazine and by the "guidance" in the rest of the articles.[13] The magazine, repository of that which is known and knowable, puts its trust in every reader's ability to absorb this information from a perspective that has already been internalized and isn't going to be questioned. He already knows how to behave if he wants that information to be worthwhile, to give results.

Indeed, once the intervention of science is personalized, or once each journey through biology or astronomy is made into an individual, touristic adventure, surrounded by anecdotes, courage, tears, smiles, and "personal snapshots," science itself ends up being converted into a thaumaturgical thing, the fruit of sorcery. Science gets close and familiar through individual experience, it becomes communicable; but this is also what makes the possibility of truly understanding it more remote. (The same thing happens to nature in Disney films once everything is anthropomorphized and turned into "storytelling."[14]) Modern man's notion of his own impotence is reinforced, even while the distance and terror that could distress him enough to question the world, and himself, are soothed.

It's evident that at bottom, behind all that progress, novelty, and illustration, the *Reader's Digest* bases its domination on a moral territory ripe for invasion. Divine justice and the eye of the *Reader's Digest* editor fuse with one another. Just as an article's central figure receives the benefits of science and success, thanks to his individualism, uprightness, and ability to excel, so the reader receives the magazine's advice and helpful hints, understanding that they won't do any good unless he demonstrates by way of his personal conduct (first demonstration of this conduct: buy *Reader's Digest*; second: sit down and read it; third: discuss it with a friend) that he is the legitimate recipient of such foreseeable goodness, and that the faith the magazine has placed in him will one day be justified. We're all part of the same community.

Hence the everyday, sentimental tone, the tearful advice, the calculated communication that poses as frank conversation with the reader in his easy chair—all these constitute the substantive, emotional grounds on which the *Digest* expects itself to be believed, like election propaganda or a lover baring his heart. If you go straight to the heart, reason will follow later. Then knowledge will cease to be incomprehensible and a threat. That's why you smear yourself with sugar and melodrama.

The famous *Reader's Digest* optimism therefore reveals something more than some automatic, typical North American attitude, that of a happy and simple people who arm themselves with cheerfulness in order to gain control over the uncertainty of the future and the challenges of unlimited space. Optimism is a communication strategy, a way to relate to the reader in nonrational terms, in terms of faith. Reader and magazine alike share the belief that there is a solution to every problem and that everything that happens has a reason and a meaning. "Our basic thrust is our belief that people want to be better each day than they were the day before," explained Mr. Hobart Lewis, chairman of the *Digest*'s board, to BBC interviewers. "It's a puritan philosophy if you like, and we believe in a work ethic, and the perfectability of man . . . and our great success comes from the fact that we do trust people's instincts to want to improve themselves. On every page of the magazine you will find something in there which will help you to be a better person."[15]

The reader must apply such a philosophy to each of his daily activities. We've already seen this kind of thinking in action on those occasions in which the most complex social and economic problems were translated into the most smiling, chewable simplicities. And we can get a glimpse of it in the advice and suggestions that invariably culminate every article, the concrete practice of optimism in formulas and recipes. The reader is expected to appeal to that attitude in the most painful, even inexplicable, circumstances of human life. As the BBC commented in the interview mentioned above, the *Digest*'s version of life is one that "sees a solution to every problem . . . heroism more than misery in every disaster."[16]

People must move after living in the same place for thirty years; they have prolonged illnesses; they grow old in solitude. In every circumstance, there's a reason to be content, or at least there are lessons to learn. The same with the most ferocious disasters: earthquakes, retarded or mongoloid children, the sudden death of a loved one. If a young person dies in an accident, what stands out is the happiness of being able to use his organs for a transplant ("Transplants: Chronicle of 35 Dramatic Hours," December 1981).

There are issues that exaggerate this tendency. The September 1981 issue seems to specialize in young people or children who die. A son who dies of cancer at the age of twenty-one is in reality "being born to eternal life" ("Simply, an Act of Kindness"). The same issue, dealing this time with a little girl who dies: "I suffered and felt a lot of pain when I lost you. But in the end that anguish didn't get the last word. It wasn't a loss, but a victory. Because love got the last word: 'The Lord is my Shepherd, I shall not want.' And we're all very well protected." To complete the trio, in "Roses for Yolanda," it's not so important that a baby girl dies of poverty and tuberculosis, but that other children now have the opportunity to show their kindness and send flowers to the funeral. Just so you won't think that this issue has a monopoly on this theme, and just so we don't forget our April 1980 issue, we should say that there too, in "Improvised Coffin," a newborn infant dies, allowing the narrator to give her a doll as a grave present.

In its search for examples of reassurance, the *Digest* even comes up with historical periods as uncongenial as that of the Black Plague which decimated Europe's population. No matter, civilization was reborn: "Mankind walked through the valley of the shadow of death and proved to be indestructible" ("The Plague that Decimated Europe," March 1981). Since in the same issue there is also an homage to the men entrusted with the task of handling the North American nuclear arsenal ("Nuclear War: Finger on the Button") perhaps it also serves as a consolation that the nuclear holocaust may not be so terrible after all.

Optimism, therefore, is not only an emotion; it is also an instrument to be used for the purposes of approaching the world, of communicating it. By putting the brakes on his own doubts and sorrows, by refuting in advance all the internal and external voices that question the workings of the universe or the social system, the reader demonstrates that everything is comprehensible and that, once he understands the laws of reality, he counts. We are constantly advised on how to banish psychic imbalances through control of our thoughts. Depression, explains the *Digest* of October 1981 ("Are You Depressed?") "derives from wrong thinking. . . . We're all capable of controlling those ideas that plunge us into unnecessary sadness. . . . You can control your state of mind by using this simple treatment based on common sense."

The best medicine, then, is *Reader's Digest* itself. Bainbridge, in his critical book on the *Digest*, relates several cases of persons who administered the magazine itself as medicine, and he mentions that Herman H. Bundeson, president of the Chicago Board of Health, prescribes "an issue of the *Digest* to a patient suffering from worry, fear, or hypochondria"[17] eight to ten times a month. The main thing, as the magazine itself points out with incredible candor, is to reach a point where "we convert our unfriendly dreams into useful friends" ("Learn How to Control Your Dreams," February 1981).

So right ideas are going to save us. The mere fact of having them, thinking them, participating in their gestation, is proof that we're not condemned to wallow in bad dreams by day or night.

The great men, the geniuses, the stars—all demonstrate the same thing. Their journey, from anonymity to success, depends on the fact that they subscribed to a system of positive ideas that already existed. Their celebrity grows as long as they, like the reader, make the trip from ignorance to knowledge.

In the life of the common man such a redemptive structure is not absent either. Obsessively, in every episode, a situation is repeated in which a victim lies in danger, in the dark, and there are those, frequently God himself, who pull them out of the abyss. The darkness could have descended upon them at birth (blindness, paralysis, deafness) or could be due to an accident that befell them at home or in some remote spot. The outcome is always the same. Utilizing their perseverance, and with others' help, they succeed in coming out ahead. Even in the most inhospitable locales there's always a dog, a child, a policeman, a monk, a bird, a patrol, a librarian, even a flash of lightning—that is, a representative of God—to hear their pleas.

If the field of ideas is divided, then, for the *Digest*, into absolute ignorance and sapience-that-explains-all, then humanity must exhibit a similar structure: Some are survivors, others saviors. Some allow themselves to be saved; others help them survive. Once the survivors have been saved, they're converted into saviors of everyone else. It could be because they've dedicated the rest of their life to such a crusade, or it could be that the *Reader's Digest* turns them into exemplary models, causing these evangelists to propagate the formulas of redemption. Just as the reader emerges from lack of culture, so do common men get out of danger. Just as the *Digest* illuminates the ignorant, so should its readers attempt to rescue those who are in danger of sharks and sickness alike. Knowledge and action are equal and confused.

It is a very grave matter when a public man transgresses that code. This is what happened to Ted Kennedy. In the same April

1980 issue in which Hazel, "my most unforgettable character" ("Thanks, Hazel") sacrificed herself for forty years in order to bring books to a little town without a library, in which a team of people fought a wild battle against time and the dark in order to rescue Al Summers from a landslide ("Buried Alive"), in which archaeologists—naturally North Americans, since the locals never realize what treasures they possess until their colleagues "enlighten" them—pull a civilization out of thin air in Thailand ("Possible Cradle of the Bronze Age"), in which the millionaire inventors of an apparatus essential for the extraction of oil from the black depths of the earth later use their money for charitable purposes ("Oil, As If by Magic"), in that same issue, Ted Kennedy is subjected to scrutiny ("Is Ted Kennedy Reliable?"). It's the typical *Digest* situation, but in reverse. A woman falls into a river; her companion doesn't save her; she doesn't survive.

It seems clear that Kennedy probably was selected, from among many famous men who don't lead particularly blameless lives, for contingent political reasons. His liberalism and possible candidacy for the Presidency must have made him a tempting target. This discrimination on the part of *Reader's Digest,* which claims to publish only articles of enduring significance, is obvious. Many other scandals or problems of prominent politicians have not been chosen by the *Digest* for scrutiny. But this is not only because they happen to be conservative. The attack on Kennedy is indeed of "enduring significance," inasmuch as it feeds into the structure of communication and behavior that the *Digest* reiterates in each of its episodes and articles. It never goes outside the habitual norms. It doesn't directly attack Kennedy for his ideas or policies. In a world where Hazels and Goethes set out to enlighten mortals, where men go in search of lost cities and workers are rescued by their own kind, the senator from Massachusetts failed in a crisis and ceased being a possible "savior" of others. What's worse, once he supposedly used his power to protect himself, he stopped being a common man. He's not democratizable. For the *Digest,* the height of his fame and fortune doesn't match his moral altitude.

As you might expect, one of the *Digest's* favorite sports is mountain climbing. Characters climb hills at night, do alpine climbing on rocky summits, save people making an excursion to the Alps, Mount Kilimanjaro, and Mount Sinai (where they happen to give aid to some poor Arabs), and in general rise in a manner even more obsessive than that of our elephant friend Babar. We're not only talking about physical ascent. Here is a vision of human history composed only of victims and those on high, the heroes.

This category is so universal that the *Digest* projects itself as a savior, in a practical way, and not exclusively on the basis of its spiritual elevation. According to Schreiner, the cases are innumerable in which it has been "credited specifically with the saving of a life,"[18] and he mentions the November 1973 issue, in which dozens of testimonies are published in order to prove how a *Reader's Digest* article helped people recognize and survive a heart attack.

It isn't strange, then, that this path from darkness to light also reaches back to the societies of the past. Ancient cities are as astray as a lost Arctic explorer or as helpless as an old man who's had an epileptic fit and can't talk on the phone to ask for help. Almost as if they were places waiting to be put on a pre-existing map of contemporary ideas, they struggle towards immortality when someone heroically "discovers" them, gives them the appropriate therapy. An entire civilization is treated like an elderly patient who, in spite of years in an asylum, can still sing, dance, and garner applause. The past survives thanks to a "savior."

And if this sort of thing occurs in the lives of individuals and celebrities, if it occurs in contemporary society and among forgotten archaeological remains, it should come as no surprise that the same acts of salvation are universalized planetarily and serve for underdeveloped societies as well. After all, that philosophy ought to be applicable in countries where the *Digest* auctions its redemption monthly in so many languages and editions.

Just as a tiger can attack a German zookeeper, just as a woman despairs when her child falls into a river, there are countries and vast sectors of humanity who live under the constant threat of danger and attack. The successful nations (the United States, Australia, Switzerland, and Israel, to pick some examples from 1981) have already demonstrated how to solve those problems.

It's not easy, the *Digest* admits, for exotic zones and poor ones to adopt such attitudes. The strangeness of their customs makes it difficult for them to earn and accumulate knowledge in the usual way. They are reluctant to accept North American tutelage. Add to this the oppressiveness of adverse climates and the more significant mugginess of their brains.

Of course the *Digest*'s optimism prevents it from suggesting the notion that these peoples are condemned to failure in perpetuity. On the contrary, in every issue there appears a case that contradicts this assumption, an individual who demonstrates, as Babar did, that it's possible to climb the ladder of fame and success. Ten years ago, for example, the May 1971 issue showed in "Elda and Its Footwear Fair" what the economic solution to the problems of "backwardness" was. Roque Calpena, a lone man, succeeded in converting an abandoned village in Spain into a prosperous commercial and industrial center. Methods: Import North American machinery; let businessmen direct the operations as they see fit; have ideas, ideas, ideas; modernize and study; acquire a morality above suspicion; and only afterwards receive help and medals from the government. "Undoubtedly Elda's case offers us an unmistakable lesson: with work, perseverance, business sense (and a man like Roque Calpena, who's already making plans to export footwear to the countries of the Eastern Bloc) you can take advantage of energies which today lie dormant in many places. There's the road opened by Elda, and the entire nation will benefit once they take advantage of it."

Years later the *Digest* has discovered some other miraculous self-made men. Let's take "The Tabajara Indians: Musical Geniuses of the Jungle," from the April 1980 issue. They were so deep in the jungle and ignorant that in 1932 when they came upon a guitar in the jungle they "didn't know what it was," and they looked inside a box (a record player) to find the singer. "Since they didn't know anything about kerosene lamps, and understandably even less about electricity, they took the lighted houses for stars." Such savage beginnings make their road to celebrity even more surprising. First they learned to play folk music ("They still can't explain how they did it today") and then they went on to classical music ("We learned how to play classical music the same way parrots learn how to talk"). Such a step from barbarism to Bach is symbolized in everything they do, including taking off their ponchos and feathers and putting on dinner jackets to play a toccata and fugue. This instantaneous transformation, taking place practically right in front of the television audience or those in the auditorium, is what the *Digest* offers, like Babar in a can, to its Third World readers. Fast food. Fast ideas. Fast development. They become "civilized," and as a reward they receive the applause (and recognition) of the public at the center of the world, and their immortality in *Reader's Digest*.

Something similar happens to Haiti ("Painting of a Valiant People," February 1981). None of this country's art was worth anything until Dewitt Peters, a North American, stepped in, encouraging local talent and unleashing "a veritable artistic explosion." Afterwards, the price of these paintings soared in the New York and Parisian markets, permitting an artistic renaissance. Just as God rescues a child from blindness, just as an archaeologist redeems a forgotten civilization, just as the *Digest* saves the reader from ignorance and pain, so opulent society comes to emancipate these people from backwardness. "Lately, Haiti has opened its doors wider to tourists and foreign businesses. There's no doubt that this will affect its painters and from now on Haiti will preserve art as a way of life and livelihood. And art that can be appreciated is good proof that neither poverty nor politics can dampen the spirit of a valiant and happy people."

Thus, neither poverty nor politics is essential to understanding what happens in Haiti or what's going to happen either. The Tabajara Indians' dinner jackets hide the Amazonian forests where they were born. Every underdeveloped people is like a child learning to grow up, like a paralyzed violinist learning to play, like a mother that lost her child but not her faith, like an old man who gives thanks to God for all the springs he's been able to see. If, in passing, unjust situations are mentioned, well, just as with Disney or the Lone Ranger, that's all in the past. If yesterday the men who carved the totem poles in British Columbia were robbed ("The Fabulous Talking Trees," September 1981) today they're appreciated, their work sold, and they receive the fervent homage of journals and universities, not to speak of that of Winston Churchill and Bing Crosby. The purification of the past goes with the abstraction of the future. Progress is conceived of as if the real world were formally identical to the *Digest* itself, all symmetrical spheres of the same Plan: You've got to accumulate isolated changes just as the reader accumulates ideas, and both are modifications that needn't change the affable face of the universe.

So besides acting as models for its less fortunate brothers, such examples confirm the universality of the *Reader's Digest* solution. I can imagine that the magazine does not want to admit that there could be alternatives to its point of view, that it is not just one opinion among many. Everything foreign can be reduced to the well known, the simple, the optimistic, and the close at hand. The most mysterious past, the labyrinths of science, the enigmas of art, those exotic, faraway places, everything has to be comprehensible to the common man. All he had to do is apply the rigid, leveling norms (supposing them to be a product of the natural and biological storehouse of all men) of the Christian, occidental vision which has given optimum results for millenia and which has reached its culmination in contemporary North America. He must imitate, in his colonization of the strange spaces of thought, the *Digest*'s attitudes not only towards foreign countries but also towards the editions published there.

Starting in the sixties, it became unavoidable, for commercial reasons, for some of the articles for those editions to be created outside the United States. But the magazine devised a system

> to make certain that whatever the subject, whoever the writer, wherever the events took place, any article in any edition of the *Digest*, would meet the same technical requirements as to length, structure, readability, and have the same philosophical point of view as those in the United States. The essence of the system is simple: *all* purchases of articles for foreign use must be approved by Pleasantville [the *Reader's Digest* headquarters], and *all* articles must go through Pleasantville editing.[19]

The readers commune, then, with the *Digest* itself and with the illustrious men of the past and present who, in spite of being established in the exceptional nature of their talents, duplicated in their own lives the ethical backbone that any consumer can reconstruct in his own life.

However, outside this illuminated circle of the chosen ones—

which potentially includes ninety-nine percent of the human race—outside of this safe circle of covered wagons, strange, dangerous, and antihuman beings are agitating. Their moral perversity is proven by their distance and incomprehensibility. They are beings possessed. They have dealings with dark powers. They indulge in eccentricities, exiled from the rational progress of the *Digest* and from everyday life. Incapable of discovering anything, incapable of being discovered or simplified, how are they going to be able to share in the benefits, presents, and advances the magazine offers? They are destroyers and parasites and terrorists, so far removed from comprehension, so incalculable in their motivations, so errant in their conduct, so outlandish in their customs, that nobody could imagine they could be right or that they have a right to represent other ways, other visions of humanity.

In a system of communication where science is subordinate to goodness, and where goodness is defined, after being made flesh in the everyday life of every individual, as a rejection of any political, social, or economic change, criticizing established values can't be understood as a form of knowledge but merely as senseless destruction. To know is to conserve. The attempt to transform the world through an outlook that questions it and denies it not only doesn't enrich science but leaves its practitioner outside human norms and normality. Criticizing is condemned in the name of optimism; in the name of a positive and vacuous image of the world; in the name of the prior hierarchical distribution of knowledge; in the name of a bureaucracy of pseudo-erudition; in the name of a totalitarian control masquerading as sentimentalism and "letters from our readers." Rationality and its dispersed fragments belong exclusively to the seraphic universe of saviors.

It's possible to suggest, then, that *Reader's Digest's* famous anticommunism goes beyond a mere political confrontation stemming from the conservative ideas of its owner and founder. The magazine helped inaugurate the Cold War in 1943 when the USSR was allied with the U.S. against Hitler,[20] and it has continued it up to the present day. Ever since that time, in every issue there's usually an article that openly attacks some aspect of a socialist country (in April 1980, in "Poisoned Umbrella and Political Crime," the Bulgarian government is accused of being responsible for the violent death of an exile in London). In various others, one can find oblique insinuations spread throughout. Some of these accusations are certainly merited by what happens in many socialist countries. There is, undoubtedly, much to criticize. Criticism, however, is not the *Digest's* final goal; rather, it is the eradication of the opponent, if not physically at least mentally. Such demonization, I would think, derives from more than the defense of North American strategic interests. Attributing all the evils imaginable to socialism, as it is now practiced in so many regions of the world, is part of the *Reader's Digest* communications strategy, since this is how all alternative interpretations of the world are eliminated via previous moral condemnation. A satanic adversary can have no worth whatsoever, and any critic of the world who offends the *Reader's Digest* and professes Marxist philosophy automatically lacks credibility. There's more. Once it supposes that an international conspiracy cooked up by Moscow or Havana or both is about to ambush some unsuspecting country or individual, creating disorder, havoc, and problems where everything used to be calm and idyllic, the *Digest* has already incorporated political systems into its theories about catastrophes and salvation. Communism is a hurricane that comes from outside, without local causes, and falls upon families and latitudes like a plague. But it is more insidious than a natural phenomenon that comes and goes. It is made up of ideas—a cardinal sin for the *Digest*—wicked, discredited, diabolical ideas.

So nothing good can come of that world. There's no possible dialogue with its members. If something positive can be found, it must be because there are those who, even in the midst of that antihuman storm, have accepted Western values. Thus, maybe China can save herself from the disaster of the Cultural Revolution because she "goes shopping" (April 1980). The same attitude was expressed in various issues that I read in Chile in 1971. In "The Great Circus of Moscow" (May 1971) all good comes from the basic Russian genius, their individualism, their caring attitude, in spite of the commissars, the whips, the gray and closed-in life. "In spite of the Russians' vaunted classless society, in the Soviet Circus the star system holds sway." A title in the April 1971 issue alone, "Siberia, the Sleeping Land Awakens," suggests darkness and dawn and men who wake up to another vision. There, Akademgorodok, a great scientific city, is displayed as a success only because it is uncontaminated, isolated from the malefic influence of the rest of society, because competition and privileges are permitted there. "The further one gets from the Kremlin, the more the majority of Soviets show themselves to be free and cordial." The solution for the USSR, then, is its North Americanization, its conversion into a space worthy of the *Reader's Digest*. Life, at least in this article, is judged on how near or far it is from the industrial model of the West: "In Yakutsk there are more private automobiles per inhabitant than in Leningrad or Kiev."

Underdeveloped countries, therefore, cannot undertake socialist experiences if they want to grow or come out of their misery. Science, knowledge, or technology can save those who lie in the shadows, just as any number of redemptive figures rescue accident victims; but first those peoples must earn that aid. They must warrant it with their own daily existence. Help—in ideas, in machinery, in capital, in angelic, outstretched hands—is only destined for those who previously have consecrated the division of the world into good and bad in the terms proposed by the *Digest*. Technology will be able to help those straggling countries as long as their inhabitants educate themselves, and have at their disposal indispensable knowledge and moral purity; in other words, if they imagine themselves as *Reader's Digest*s in miniature or as one of its protagonists lost in a storm they can't control or flung headlong into a hole that nobody dug.

And who can give them that knowledge on a massive scale, in a scientific and economical form, so they can fertilize their opaque minds?

The *Reader's Digest* of course.

The natives can keep everything that's anecdotally aboriginal, touristy, and exotic. The main thing, underneath the Tabajara Indian's poncho, or on top of it (if we put on our dinner jackets and whistle Bach) is that the universal warehouse they are now cultivating inside them should keep on growing and connect them to the superior humanity embodied by North America and, hence, for them to receive those benefits without a major upheaval. As long as they read, they'll progress. As long as they are reduced, and resign themselves to be reduced, to being "common men," leaving their everyday superficial originality intact and unpolluted, they will miraculously advance in comfort and per capita income. Since the cause of underdevelopment (personal, social, or national) is the fault of ideas that obscure and disorient the minds of the "backward," the solution can be none other than to feed them with correct ideas and never to attack the local and international socioeconomic causes of their situation. If they "digest" these notions, their meals will arrive all by themselves. If they "select" their friends carefully, abracadabra, a house to receive them in will pop out of the ground. If we "read" what we ought to, we can save ourselves.

In order for the *Digest* to evangelize all of humanity like that, in order to be able to communicate with readers in rich countries and poor countries, in order to set itself up as the interpreter for lost and found civilizations, not only does it have to consider itself an infallible missionary; it is my contention that it must also, as part of the same process, unconsciously conceive of its readers as children. Bainbridge points out that "the articles read like stories in a primer,"[21] but my own views would go further than that. The *Digest* supposes its readers (all of them, without exception) to be motivated, as children seem to be, by an essential goodness and infinite simplicity, with the certainty that, like Bruno inspired by his little boy, we are all capable of repenting and having faith in whomever is responsibly and adultly explaining why we must behave in such a manner that everything will turn out all right.

In fact, the *Digest* offers its readers all the wisdom of maturity without any of its dilemmas. Knowledge, for this magazine, is not an experience or learning process that demands true growth, that implies change. Knowledge can't be confused with responsibility. With *Digest* in hand, one can be powerful and dominant just like omniscient beings, and good and beloved like defenseless creatures. We can keep our juvenile optimism without having to give up the progress and material well-being that comes with subordinating the world to our science.

Actually, what the *Digest* hands its readers is an extraordinarily worthwhile and universally marketable product: immortality. What each of us dreamed of in childhood, in adolescence; what we gradually had to abandon as experience whispered of other horizons and filled us with limits; what we let ourselves dream still. We're told that we can know and still preserve our innocence, because we digest, although we do not eat, the fruit of the Tree of Goodness, which isn't the same as the Tree of the Knowledge of Good and Evil. Paradise has come back to Earth. The *Digest* assumes and internalizes the voice of God, as long as the public accepts the role of Adam prior to Eve. In that voice are joined authority and sentimentality, the reason of the father and the affection of the mother, creating a family atmosphere in which we are protected from tempests, extinction, and doubts. Being of an encyclopedic bent, the magazine is "warmer and kinder, and less pretentious, than many of the human beings with which [sic] the readers have to live."[22]

This is how it responds to the illusion of the child who does not want to die, who wishes he could grow up without the risk of disappearing one day. Faust has been converted into Adam, but without the conclusion drawn by Goethe's character from experience, and found in all the medieval, Renaissance, and modern versions of the legend: Knowledge is synonymous with an encounter of your own limits, and therefore, with death. The *Reader's Digest* doesn't draw this conclusion, although it aspires to all knowledge. You can believe without ceasing to be a child and you can know "all that's worth knowing in life"[23] without suffering radical alterations, without dying every day and having definitively to die at the end of all the everydays.

So it isn't strange that the infantilization of the adult reader is accompanied by the limitation of the range or effects of death. To die, for the *Reader's Digest,* is something that happens to everybody else, never to oneself. Time and time again, with catastrophes, work-related accidents, mines caving in, or mountain climbers falling off cliffs, the focus is on the survivor and not the dozens of victims who have succumbed. Or, to use the sort of language *Reader's Digest* tends to sweeten our mortal life with, funerals serve to murmur promises of a spring which gathers up the leaves of autumn that fall to the ground.

170

Life is dreamt without death; digestion is dreamt without evacuation; knowledge is dreamt as consumption and not production. Therefore eternal youth is the *Reader's Digest*'s ideological goal. Death is eliminated and the reader rejuvenated, in knowledge and life, because the common man being perpetuated is the permanent North American, deified as the eternal representative of all humanity, present and future, near and far. But we're not just dealing with an ideological and narrative strategy, a longing and an attitude. The *Reader's Digest*—always practical—also presents immortality as an obtainable goal, a utopia to be realized.

In every issue the medical sections (which occupy a disproportionate amount of space in the magazine) lavish advice, pills, and technological advances, giving the reader therapy and hope which, in addition to alleviating the pain, have the more important effect of prolonging his life. Medicine is science applied to the body in order to save it, just as technology is applied to the underdeveloped world. Already in the first article of the first issue of *Reader's Digest*, the article that led off the *princeps* edition of 1922, the objective of not aging was being proposed. "How to Keep Young Mentally," was the title of that first promise.

Death, when it is portrayed in the *Digest*, is conceived as a passing on to another world, a world with no more earthquakes or savage beasts or communist agitators, a world for which we Digesters have been preparing ever since we were born. For this reason, in a magazine devoted to optimism, the superabundance of old people in the articles, together with the way they're presented, is not at all surprising. Being in the final stage of life doesn't mean fearing death or illness. These people are serene and peaceful, satisfied with their second childhood, as Malcolm Muggeridge explains in a religious article, introducing the April 1980 edition ("Thy Will Be Done"). Senility for him is a "process of preparation for eternity, in which one gets accustomed to the circumstances one will find there." In other articles out of the same issue, the same philosophy is repeated. "When a Man Dies, Will He Come Back to Life?" Everett Dirksen at the grave of a friend answers yes. An octogenarian is shown keeping fit through diet and karate in "Watch Out for that Old Lady!"

Not content merely to colonize the past in its own image and

171

likeness, to level all individual lives to its own ethos and anecdotal style, to put all foreign countries in the same little North American pigeonhole, to shrink the bubbling variety of human oral tradition down to "quotable quotes," the *Reader's Digest* now colonizes the Beyond.

Those who dissent are left outside of its heaven and the Divine Presence. In "God or Coincidence?" from May 1971, the author relies on the North American astronauts to reaffirm his faith in the existence of a God. "Those men could have intoned a eulogy to their own selves," but like "three modern Magi," one after another they recited the first chapter of Genesis. The future and space together are not enough. You also need human nature and the traditions of the past. "When I find myself groping in the dark, when I am hounded by passing doubts, I go back to a very simple thought. Maybe some might call it idle and even childish, but it always works for me. . . . I think of the great minds who in the course of twenty centuries have believed in Jesus, the Messenger of God. I'm in good company with them. And I go through life (as I hope the reader does) following a path of hope."

The oldness of the past and the candor of the present moment, the weight of twenty centuries and the airiness of those who float through sidereal space drive home the certitude that the *Digest* holds the keys to the Kingdom.

The magazine has met its readers. It is not responsible for our generation, but it does agree to protect us from internal and external threats, now that we've put ourselves in its hands. If its readers are children, then the magazine—without having consulted Walt Disney, I assume—acts as an uncle.

Every issue is new and up-to-date, and every issue is connected to infinity (in space, time, and spirit). This idea of infinity is once again practical and can be demonstrated concretely. The *Digest* offers the reader "an article a day of enduring significance." When he finishes the copy he bought, it's already time to buy a new one.

This means that the reader has all his time and all his knowledge occupied until the end of time. An article a day, a second childhood a day, a contraceptive idea a day, until the end of life and all his days. From now on there's never any need to be without either an example from or a copy of the magazine, which will reiterate the same fictional structure from one episode to the next, from one magazine to the next, from one year to the next. It is almost as if the *Digest* were a totality, extending forward and backward as far as the eye can see. A paradise on North American earth till the end of the world, and North American earth in paradise till the end of all time.

As long as the isolated and scattered faithful renew their faith through the ritual of reading and through that other ritual which is subscription and purchase, the *Digest* is there to reassure them, superior but so close, so familiar, such a good friend, so entertaining, such a part of our lives.

In an absurd universe, *Reader's Digest* guarantees that common sense, reality as it has been taught us, truly exists. In a world where history calls for change or uncertainty, *Reader's Digest* soothes the reader with a reflection of his own unquestioned nature, his own Wild Horse Valley, his own secret stream.[24] In a violent society, *Reader's Digest* . . . On an incomprehensible and rebellious planet, *Reader's Digest* . . . In a universe where they say God is dead and it's whispered that human beings will also have to die someday, *Reader's Digest* . . . In a . . . On a . . . Our *Digest*, who art on the newsstand, between the newspapers that know less, far away from books that only simulate knowledge, thank you, thank you, our *Reader's Digest* on Earth, deliver us from evil thoughts, deliver us from death and responsibility, from the abyss and the boredom, save us from everyone else and save us from ourselves, save us . . .

Amen.

FIVE

THE INNOCENTS MARCH INTO HISTORY... AND OVERTHROW A GOVERNMENT

IN SANTIAGO DE CHILE, every Wednesday on my way home, I used to buy a children's magazine called *Mampato*, and each evening, before putting my six-year-old son Rodrigo to bed, I would read it to him. It was 1973. The Allende government was fighting for its life. We were fighting for ours. There wasn't an instant to spare. Nonetheless, I always managed to keep that Wednesday appointment.

In the repetition of this act there was undoubtedly a sense of despair. To cling to a pattern or a schedule, some landscape untouched by violence, when things are falling apart, is to make believe that a semblance of normalcy remains somewhere, awaits us someplace. It is possible, however, that I was doing more than indulging in a family ritual on the brink of disaster. There may also have been a pinch of intellectual curiosity in my reading activities.

On the surface, there was nothing special about the magazine. It contained all the usual material of a semi-educational sort: nature studies, little vignettes on Chilean history, cutouts, puzzles, mazes, jokes, some comic strips from abroad, do-it-yourself sections. But *Mampato* was not only the name of the magazine. It was also the name of a boy, a character whose feats—to be eternally continued in the next issue—occupied four central full-color pages, as he and his friend Ogú, a primitive, overgrown caveman, ventured into the far future to battle the tyrant Ferjus. It was this story, drawn exclusively in Chile itself, which began to interest or should I say to obsess me.

As we read, each Wednesday, it began to dawn on me that what I was reading in the comic mirrored what was happening in the streets of Santiago. While Mampato and his friends went about the business of overthrowing a tyrant in the year 4000, Salvador Allende, the democratically chosen president of the real Chile, was being similarly branded "tyrant" by rather less fictitious forces seeking to oust him.

177

For a person who had already written books and essays on mass subliterature for children, and on the childish aspects of the adult media, this was a unique opportunity: to watch a comic strip intervening directly, albeit covertly, in history. I had assumed, and still do, that such fictional forms influenced people, especially youngsters, through a code of half-hidden values, which helped them adapt to reality by blurring out, or perhaps by falsely acting out, its dilemmas. I had therefore focused my attention primarily on the covert structure of the work itself—how it functioned, its meaning, and how it established certain formulas for success which could be popularized and incorporated into other versions and variations. I felt it was important to denounce the dominant model behind mass culture, the techniques, precepts, implicit educational views that shaped the consumer's imagination and dissolved his critical faculties. Although such a model was useful, displaying the invisible ideas that inform our everyday mythology, it was itself no more than a construction. Once this model has been inferred from the texts and frozen into a common denominator applicable to so many other media representations, it was easy to forget how it operated in reality: reacting to threats, defending the status quo, absorbing and reinterpreting the latest problems in neutral terms, trying to offer explanations for a seething, conflicting stream of troubles. By concentrating on the finished product, and trying to discover the ideological foundations behind it, I had separated it from the historical movement and matrix where it was produced and received by living human beings.

It was clear that behind each individual work there lurked, if we are allowed such melodramatic verbs, a consciousness industry. The owners of the economy and the State were also, of course, the owners of the means of definition, transmission, and reception of culture. They were a class. But I had not asked myself specifically how emotion and intellect came together, and under what circumstances, to spawn such works; what people, under what particular strains, with what degree of clarity or blind intuition produced mass subliterature. Nor had I explored how the chain of command and persuasion, economic and political interests, could obtain such results.

I told myself—and it was right to do so—that what I cared about were the effects on the readers. Mass media fiction, as opposed to art, leaves hardly any space for interpretation by the audience. With less leeway for participation, the passive consumer was restricted to certain foregone avenues and conclusions. So the reader I had in mind was not a real person who, with all his or her contradictions, must deal with that vision, accommodate it, modify it, fight it, succumb to it. My reader was, in a way, an idealization, an objective possibility that could be deduced or was implicit in the text itself.

A sociology of art, an examination of culture as an interplay between real readers and real producers, was not then, and is not now, my main intention. But the *Mampato* case gives us an opportunity, if not to answer questions about how such processes work in reality, at least to ask them and, by so doing, to note some of the limitations under which the previous essays in this book were originally created. By observing a mass media production for children unfolding in particularly vivid historical circumstances, we can not only enrich the conclusions we have already reached but clarify some of the issues which have been, so far, left out of our perspective.

Mampato, accompanied by Ogú, has journeyed into the far future in order to visit his girlfriend Rena, who typifies everything a young lady should be according to upper-class Chilean standards: white-skinned, blond, green eyes, slim, wearing the latest fashions. She and the other inhabitants of her land are peaceful, beautiful tele-paths who are technically very advanced (because here "all minds think in a united way") without having lost their naturalness and charm. Unfortunately, they are unable to defend themselves against their neighbors, "malign beings" out to "dominate the earth." Ferjus, the tyrant of that other country, can read minds, just like Rena. She, however, does not abuse this power ("It's not nice to invade private thoughts without asking permission"), while he uses it to subject and destroy his victims.

Each of these countries seems to be, in different ways, a recog-nizable metaphor for Chile. If Rena's land has the same topography (high mountains, cultivated valleys, the same sort of trees and birds), the despot's has the right shape. He reigns over a mammoth tree, as elongated and slender as Chile, its different floors or regions interconnected by elevators. If Rena's country is the utopia Chile might someday become (or, with its bucolic tranquility, what it supposedly once was), the realm of Ferjus projects the more contemporary and infernal image of a house ferociously divided against itself. Those responsible for such a sorry state of affairs are clearly "foreigners." Disciples of Ferjus, they are yellow-skinned usurpers of power who have many of the physical characteristics normally associated with villains: Dracula teeth, advanced prognathism, small heads on overmuscular bodies. To these features, which—as usual—seem to caricature the working class, may be added two which are typically Chilean: a certain Indian-like look; and helmets which are, in point of fact, the hard hats used by construction crews and identified with Allende's followers. Except for Prince Sicaliptus the First, the "stupid, cruel and lazy" son of Ferjus, there are no children or women among them.

These parasites have enslaved a hardworking, pacific, diverse-colored little (mutant?) people who, able of hand and nimble of wit, manufacture goods and till the land. They have done so with the help of spying rat-men, whose thoughts are so repugnant that Rena cannot even register them, and with the threat of the "Anthroposaurus," a prehistoric monster of colossal strength, with a hankering for slaves. Ferjus does not, however, need to call often on such extraordinary allies, for he can count on his armed forces, a mutant race of warrior giants, a good but befuddled lot who, time and again, with their confused leader, Gor, save the tyrant whenever somebody questions his authority.

Mampato leads the little people and their families in a protracted, desperate struggle for freedom. Time is running out. Previously, Ferjus had two kinds of weapons: primitive spears that he first used to conquer the tree, and more modern hand-held paralyzers which the little people have been producing against their will. Now he is forcing them to build an immense paralyzer with which to subjugate Rena's civilization and, eventually, the entire planet. Mampato's plan is to trick Ferjus. The little people will supposedly agree to his plan, while giving themselves time to plan a mutiny. Mampato is found out, taken prisoner, and is able to escape the tree only when one of the peaceful little mutants decides to use a gun to free his friend, overcoming his own disgust at the use of violence.

Outlaws (babes?) in the woods, they discuss the strategy.

"Those who have not accepted the rule of Ferjus are many. . . . But [Ferjus is] very powerful. The only thing we know how to do is work."

"That's it," exclaims Mampato. "That will be our weapon."

In the next episode, one of the most surprising events in the history of mass media comics occurs. In none of the subliterature we have examined would such an incident be possible. In fact, I can't remember a strike ever having been shown favorably in children's mass fiction. And yet, it is a general strike that brings the tree to a standstill. The "yellow" men yawn and complain. "There are no slaves to milk the cows. Nobody is collecting fruit. The elevators aren't working." It is this last factor that is decisive, both in the strip and, as we shall see, in Chile itself. All vertical communication in such a long country has been cut off.

The rat-men offer a truce, a dialogue, though their intentions are to spy on the patriots. "Peace and friendship," they murmur, brandishing a dirty white banner. They offer the little people their assistance but would like to keep some of their slaves. They are given the boot.

Ferjus then sends the giant Gor on a surprise attack. He is to exterminate those who head the insurrection. But he's beaten by Ogú. As he's retreating, he's captured by a Zorko, a vegetable mutant that "surrounds and devours its victims." The rebels decide to help their enemy, and they set him free. Before he departs, shamefaced, he's taught a lesson in good manners by Mampato. "Gor, the mutants have saved your life. Remember that you are one of them. In spite of that, you serve the tyrants who have enslaved your people. Now you may leave."

As the titan withdraws, he looks at his ex-adversaries tenderly. It is clear that, during the future confrontation, he will line up with them.

We interrupt this story to bring the reader a special announcement. The issue that carried this heartwarming reconciliation went on sale at newsstands around the country on September 5, 1973. Before the next Wednesday's adventure appeared, the Chilean armed forces—on Tuesday the 11th of September to be precise—had staged one of the bloodiest coups in the history of Latin America.

Meanwhile, back in the forty-first century, our friends have fallen into a trap Ferjus sets for them. He has given the Anthroposaurus the go-ahead signal, and that beast is about to cannibalize Mampato and company. Fortunately, Gor and the other giants have had a change of heart and turn on their former masters. "We are also slaves and have been used against the other mutants."

Without military support, Ferjus and his last comrades take refuge at the top of the magnificent tree. They swear that they shall "overcome them, enslaving them in worse conditions than before." (Once again, a word from our sponsors: I have used the translation "we shall overcome," which has a progressive and activist coloring, to render "los *venceremos*," which was the key phrase of the left in Chile, the one slogan publicly identified with the Allende regime from 1970 to 1973.)

The little people repudiate emigration as an alternative and decide to fight. "This is our land and we'll fight for it. The yellow race has come to enslave us and must go." While the enemy is alive, "there will be danger." An ingenious solution is arrived at: The tree has been "mined by the tunnels that the rat-men have burrowed." The mutants begin to "weaken the roots of the giant tree. Ferjus and his cronies will have to surrender."

But Ferjus won't get the chance. A devastating tempest knocks the tree down, extirpating it. Even though not intended by the good mutants, and not directly shown, the yellow race and the rat-men die. It is nature itself that has impersonally meted out justice. The brutality of this ending is somewhat mitigated by the fact that there were no women or children involved. Ferjus has, in a way, chosen the crazy path of self-elimination, punished by his own evil.

Now, "the tempest is over and the sun shines." Mampato says good-bye, while the little people, perched on the shoulders of the repentant giants or on the exposed roots of the tree, listen. "Mutant friends! The tyranny is at an end. You shall never more be slaves. Now you must all work together: the little people, the giants, the peasants and the cat-men. All the mutants laboring united will obtain a prosperous, free, and happy future!"

The end.

The end? Not quite.

We have just read a comic that, between May 1973 and October of that same year, week after week, has been telling the story of how an oppressor has been overthrown by an industrious and peace-loving populace. To those who reject the possibility that infantile literature can have political implications, the fact that the very story people were reading in a magazine was also being enacted in the streets may be no more than a surprising coincidence. But it is not enough to point an awed finger as if it were a "That's Incredible" situation. The parallels between the story and the history in which it was produced are simply too striking to be dismissed.

Allende was not ousted in a week. It took the ruling class almost three years of social mobilization, coupled with an economic block-ade from abroad and sabotage from within, plus many errors and divisions inside the Popular Unity parties, to recover the executive branch. When the military finally intervened, it was because major shifts had already taken place in that society. Allende had lost all the potential allies that he needed in order to carry out his program and liberate his land, allies on whose tolerance, at the very least, he counted when he began his period in office. From any point of view—economic, political, ideological—the working class, which was the main motor of the revolution, had become increasingly, dramat-ically isolated; the middle classes, the Christian Democrats, the Christians, in short all those forces necessary to create a national front for such a transformation and preserve the democratic process, had gone over to the other side.

To achieve these ends, those who controlled the media and the cultural machinery in Chile waged a campaign in which Allende was portrayed as if he were Ferjus, and the Chilean people as if they were the mutinous mutants.

Nobody attempts a coup d'état in the name of foreign companies that desire their mines and factories back, large industrialists who have lost their banks and monopolies, or a feudal aristocracy that has watched illiterate and impoverished peasants taking over its land. A coup d'état is always carried out in the name of morality, freedom, and the fatherland, eternal values undermined by corrup-tion and international communist conspiracies.[1] The crusade of ethi-cal surgery that will be painstakingly executed declares itself at the service of the "silent" people, the little folks, the peaceful and humble inhabitants of all social sectors who yearn for the "good old times" when they could work together without the artificial hatred imported from abroad by "aliens." An elected government, which jailed and tortured nobody, which stimulated total freedom of the press, which obeyed all judicial orders even when most of them were decreed by judges defending private interests and twisting the meaning of the law; a government which staged all scheduled elections and won most of them, was labeled illegitimate, unjust, and vindictive—in other words, a dictatorship.

The owners of Chile's economy, the perennial owners of its institutions, scrambled back into power by projecting the image of a noble country and a pure race besieged by malignant anti-Chileans bent upon taking over the world in conjunction with satanic international forces. These antipatriotic villains combined primitivism and modernity, stupid brutality with devious calculations. Public opinion was constantly being reminded of the terrors that the future held; the tremendous monster inside the working class which, once unleashed, would provoke a bloodbath and the end of civilization. This primeval force, which had been waiting in the darkness of the land and of the heart for an opportunity to attack an innocent population, could be defeated only by a miraculous intervention of the army, the navy, and the air force, the sole institutions left with the ability to safeguard the nation's continuity and identity.

The only way to deal with cancer is to cut, doctor, cut deep, and never mind the patient's screams. Allende's downfall, when it came, was seen by many not as a counterrevolution which would abolish democracy, not as the result of "destabilization" cooked up by Kissinger, but as the consequence of his own blind obstinacy or of tragic forces unchained from beyond, from the "very nature of things."

The adventures of Mampato in the forty-first century must be read in the context of this ideological war, whose presuppositions and thrust it shares. The comic strip does not portray the truth of what happened in Chile in those months but rather the version that the Chilean ruling class would have given, and gave, of those events. Mampato is the dream, the self-justifying, idealized way, the best possible acount they could have presented to their children, and to themselves, of the destruction of democracy in their land. Their own actions cannot appear under a more favorable light, nor advertise more honorable and disinterested objectives.

But *Mampato* is special not only because it is the scenario for the aspirations and the fears of a class that is reconquering power with the most drastic means at its disposal, but because it lets its protagonists use exactly the same tactics, and in the same order, as those that were actually used against Allende. Even more startlingly, *Mampato* often anticipated the stages of the uprising against Chile's leader. We can even summarize the strategy for both sequences with the same words, although we must adopt an uncomfortably neutral and dispassionate posture to do so.

A government that has a transitory monopoly on military strength has to be deposed. Insubordination begins weakly and doubtfully at first. Passive civil disobedience is followed by appeals to the authorities to mend their ways. Negotiations with the government allow time for the revolt to spread. Next come partial confrontations which the government can surmount due to the loyalty of the military. A strike paralyzes the country with the transport workers in the forefront. The government's call for a truce is rejected. Finally, after invocations of unity, liberty, and the fatherland, the armed forces break with their superiors and go over to the other side. The insurrection is successful, and those who caused the problem have not only disappeared but their very roots have been eradicated. The head of state's efforts to avert that outcome are useless: Each week finds him more alone, abandoned. He believes himself more powerful than he is, threatens everybody with an untapped, monumental force he has kept in reserve until now, accuses his armed forces of betrayal, takes refuge in a last sanctuary, refuses to surrender, and is wiped out with his faithful followers by a whirlwind of sudden violence.

We have just listened to the story of Ferjus; it is also the story of Allende.

Once a young reader, or an older one, has identified the two, at a subconscious, involuntary level, he is ready to interpret from the point of view of the plotters what is happening in his everyday life in those months, the prolonged and bitter struggle to oust Allende.

That sort of identification is furthered by a series of hints and overt parallelisms: the word "Venceremos" in the overlord's mouth; the speeches given by Mampato (almost verbatim renditions of many antisocialist slogans of the day); the description of the presidential guard in terms that remind us of the caricature of the Popular Unity partisans in the Chilean right-wing press. We could go on and on, showing how an element in one structure has dynamic counterparts in the other.[2] But such an exercise, for those unfamiliar with the details of Chilean history, is a boring and, moreover, useless undertaking. To note that when, in an early October issue, Ferjus calls his giants "traitors" and retires to his treetop, he reminds us of Allende going to die in La Moneda, the presidential palace, ordering the women to leave, and transmitting a defiant message, we are not really adding essential data. Once the good little mutants are surreptitiously identified as the people of Chile, and the yellow-skinned parasites discharge the role of evil foreigners who have come to enslave them, all the other equivalents either fall into place, or are incessantly adjusted so that they will.

These similarities between corresponding structures are not so surprising. After all, Chile itself was being modeled by the same forces that were generating the magazine. The reader's first basic and vague intuition that the rebels are good and the government bad will be increasingly confirmed by an ongoing struggle in the streets, the barracks, and the banks. Chilean reality was being changed, managed, driven, manipulated—and children's literature was a zone of that reality—by a class that also, of course, accompanied its actions and interventions with a social consciousness, an indispensable, almost automatic set of ways of interpreting and understanding what is being done. If we can assert that Chilean history causes Mampato, we can also announce the reverse: Allende's downfall was orchestrated by countless acts such as the writing of this scenario. Story and history overlap and mutually reinforce each other.

These observations have some bearing on the discussion of the genesis of the Mampato adventures. It is tempting to surmise that we are in the presence of a juicy and full-fledged conspiracy to brainwash children and make a bloody putsch look like a patriotic endeavor. The arguments for such a view are persuasive. *Mampato* was brought out by the Lord Cochrane Company, the same enterprise that published *El Mercurio*, the most important newspaper in Chile. Since its foundation in the nineteenth century, *El Mercurio* had not only defended the ruling class's foreign and domestic interests but had always been the ideological counselor behind all Chile's governments, an "organic intellectual" in Gramscian terms if there ever was one. Let us add that Lord Cochrane is owned by the Edwards family, perhaps the most powerful oligopoly in Chile, connected to many multinationals. (Agustín Edwards was even international vice-president of Pepsi-Cola for some years.) *El Mercurio* not only received funds from the CIA during the Allende period, but its media blitz against the left was, it has been stated, directed by North American propaganda experts, specialists in graphic design and disinformation.[3] What could be more natural than to cover all the bases by inventing a fable that would win the minds of the children?

Such suspicions are further enhanced by a strange incident. In late July, instead of continuing Mampato's adventures in the future, the readers were suddenly presented with a single-issue, self-contained episode involving Ogú in prehistoric times (supposedly due to "numerous solicitations"). It had nothing to do with current events. Such a bizarre and unprecedented interruption could always be attributed to technical difficulties or delays. However, there is another, more sensible interpretation for this lull. A few days before the issue was scheduled to come out, the Chilean cardinal, Raúl Silva Henríquez, called for national reconciliation and a dialogue between the Christian Democrats and the left to avoid civil war. The effort did not succeed, but there were rumors that a hefty sector of the opposition would enter a national-unity government. Under these circumstances, the publishers of Mampato's sortie against tyranny may have wanted to wait before committing themselves further to a strategy that might have to be modified.

Although this theory of a conspiracy is attractive, I feel it to be flawed. It is not just that we have no way of proving or disproving it, no way of researching the subject at the North American or the Chilean end, or even of listening to what we must conjecture would be the heated denials of Themo Lobos, the man who has written and drawn these adventures. This is not to say that I would be astonished to find out someday that it all was part of a preconceived campaign. I've long ceased to wonder at what the human mind—especially when the body is cornered, the life-style emperiled—can concoct. So many actions—among them a number that could be said to have no immediately verifiable political resonances—have turned out to come from conscious and rational planning, that this children's story might well be one of them. But such an explanation is, ultimately, no explanation at all.[4] It is too easy and reductive, almost intellectually slothful, to suggest that each ideological action, each cultural creation, each set of new ideas and emotions comes from some entity—Machiavellian, all-powerful, and calculating—which programs our lives down to their last detail. It is true that some planning is always involved, particularly if we are dealing with the mass media, which spring from a complex chain of production, but this does not necessarily mean overt and unremitting control over the contents of its products. It is nearer the truth if we consider stories such as *Mampato* as the automatic answer by artists, already equipped with mechanisms of expression and set interpretations of the world, to new conflicts that they are living along with their readers, by which means they work out their dilemmas and make them comprehensible to others. Indeed, the purported freedom to create stories without "interference" from above is essential to the survival of such a system. The less the author feels himself a pawn in a strategy he does not control, the better his performance will be. The more his relationship to unbridled power is cloaked and velveted, the easier it will be for him to develop his ideas and characters without restraint. And meet the deadlines.

The person who conceived these episodes of *Mampato* was not that different from millions of other Chileans. They all were confronted by an intolerably tense situation, a day-by-day instability of emotions, painful and confusing contradictions which did not seem to permit the usual outlets. At such moments, many tend to fall back on the most traditional, reassuring, and therefore dominant solutions. There is comfort in conservation. Someone who works in the media has at his disposal means with which such reactions (in many senses of the word) can be objectified and communicated to others. What the creator of *Mampato* did with his fiction and his imagination others were doing in a myriad of different ways. His creation was inserted in a mesh of dread and hope which by innumerable channels, simultaneously, was germinating in Chilean society. He might have been copying reality, as when he translated the October 1972 truckers' strike against Allende into the elevator-operator strike of the mutants against Ferjus, or he might have been anticipating what was going to happen, as when he predicted, the week before the government was crushed, the change in sides of the armed forces.

What is difficult and perhaps futile to estimate is the intentionality of the author. He may or may not have been aware of his work as a political instrument for altering the state of mind of his audience. The final effect of his words and drawings does not depend on his consciousness of what he is doing.

We can illustrate this by studying two other *Mampato* adventures published in 1973. Both were of normal length, that is, half the Ferjus episode. The first extended from January to March, and recounted the capture of Ogú's tribe. A "red monkey-man," who is more "civilized and cruel" than Mampato's friend, has taken over Ogú's magic stick, the instrument and symbol of his power. Even though Mampato scolds him ("Forget your stupid superstition and remember that it is your obligation to liberate your people"), Ogú feels helpless, unable to reconquer his birthright. He has lost faith in his own capacity to "overcome" an adversary. As he wanders through the jungle, lamenting his loss, his son, disobeying his father's injunctions, secretly trails him. When the boy is finally captured and is about to be devoured by (that's right, here we go again) a gigantic primeval serpent, Ogú leaps into the fray and is victorious. "You don't need your magic stick," Mampato tells Ogú. "If I'm this strong without it," counters the caveman, "imagine what I'll do now that I have it back." (You don't need to imagine. Just ask the Chilean people.) Mampato comments, "Nothing is too difficult if you love your children."

This episode appeared during the summer of 1973, in the midst of the parliamentary elections that the right wing was confident of winning. They hoped to dominate the new Congress and, from there, impeach the President: a comfortable way of avoiding the embarrassment of a military takeover. In the previous months the country had been shaken by turmoil, with heavy student mobilization against the government. The story seems to be saying that it does not matter if the country has been occupied by "red" barbarians, who have usurped the executive, the very instrument with which power had been wielded up to that instant. Youngsters, by going out onto the streets to protest, are showing the way. There's no need to be downcast. Soon we'll have our "instrument" back.

However, the next episode, from March to May, is filled with panic. Because Allende did not lose the election. On the contrary, gainsaying the trend—in Chile, as in so many other countries—whereby the government voting percentage invariably declines in its first congressional test, the left took forty-five percent of the parliamentary vote, up more than nine percent from the presidential totals of 1970. This popular backing of Allende's policies—although the economy was in a deep crisis—engendered an atmosphere of despondency among his opponents. It is this climate that prevails in Mampato's odyssey in Atlantis, of all places. A volcano is about to erupt, while other minor cataclysms beleaguer the natives, and all that Mampato and some other inhabitants can think of is escape. A story of this sort, where the hero is defeated by natural catastrophes and hounded by the fear of apocalypse, is uncommon, not to say nonexistent, in children's mass literature, where some kind of triumph is always depicted.

Clearly, the Atlantis episode was suddenly substituted for the Ferjus story, whose advent had already been glowingly announced in the last Red Ape Man number. Coming next week: Mampato against Ferjus, villain of the forty-first century. . . . In other words, the editors had planned, as their post-election issue, a struggle against a dictator in the year 4000. Having reconquered a tribe in the far past, Mampato and Ogú would now assault a tyranny of the future.

Instead, we get a story which howls that everything is lost. Paradise is about to be ravaged by fire. It is better to abandon the sinking ship and emigrate. We seem to be confirming the conspiracy theory.

But there is a slight problem. This episode corresponds to the mood but not to the interests or the intentions of the Chilean ruling class. I do not think it is correct to understand the Atlantis story as a mere attempt to adjust the reader's experience to prevalent beliefs. Instead, we must explore it, just as with any other aesthetic phenomenon, as a symptom of a contemporary crisis, a mirror for problems that are inscribed or reflected unconsciously in its structure. This is another sort of function, which goes beyond simple instrumentality.

All these examples, and particularly the last one, make it seem plausible that the man who was writing the script and drawing the characters, rather than being caught up in a conspiracy, was caught up in the mood of the times, fluctuating according to the social winds and undercurrents. More than part of a plan, his stories seem to have been part of a larger collective effort in imagining, foreclosing, even exorcising the future. In this lies, precisely, the strength of the dominant system. It enables each person to react to different situations, to adapt their thoughts and views in certain safe, preordained, sanitized directions. Nobody is commanding that they think or feel or interpret in this way.

Control over each idea and emotion is not required, because powerful political and economic interests hold sway over a more crucial link, or bottleneck, of the process of communication: They can select the messages, retain those that coincide with their positions, and prevent and discard those that are critical or doubtful.[5] One only has to imagine what would happen if the story of Ferjus were to appear in Chile today. It would be relatively incoherent, and might not fit as snugly as it did in 1973. There is, for instance, no truckers' strike against Pinochet (at least not yet), and the president's thugs are far from being construction workers. But in spite of certain inconsistencies, most of the population would deem it an attack on the current dictatorship. That is exactly why it would never be published. The owners of the magazine, or the people they have put in charge of it, would see to that. When a product deviates beyond a tolerable frontier, when it jars the existing web of beliefs and cannot be rewritten or accommodated, only then does the real power, the real ownership pattern, emerge from the shadows.

This sort of intervention, however, tends to be unnecessary. The less visible and purposeful it is, the more successful. If self-censorship does not do the trick, the genre itself, its techniques, perceptions, practices, and traditions oversee and influence the producer, keep him within limits. Let us not forget that, in general, these stories do not betray a direct, causal relationship with society. To go against the grain is political; to flow with it is entertainment. That is how the cards are stacked.

This reminds us that we could, after all, treat Mampato as we have treated Donald Duck or the Lone Ranger: We could watch the variations on a model which we have already established. Mampato and Ogú, for instance, continue in the tracks of the heroes we have examined. One of them represents the child-as-savage, the dominated social and psychological zones of life, while the other is the child-as-adult, acting out the predominant values with total responsibility, both of them working together to re-establish an order that has been menaced by chaos and "injustice." Or we could observe that Rena's people, like Babar's, have solved the tension between civilization and wilderness, between city and country, between science and the simple life, by embodying a *Reader's Digest* utopia where modern technology coexists with natural virtue. These, and so many other structures, would be found in most other mass media products for children and for adults in the Western world.

Because these formulations are disguised, or mediated, one needs considerable intellectual stamina and some mischievous malice, as this book proves, to disentangle their political genesis, unmasking the different stages in the manufacture of consciousness, the routes by which true problems are given false solutions. These forms of fiction cannot but exhibit themselves as fun, denying (and indeed erasing) any links to more serious issues or interests. What is fascinating about *Mampato* is that, along with the role of strategic defender of the status quo which it shares with other comics, it has been forced by history to assume a different role—a tactical one. This new function, in which infantile literature becomes instrumentalized in a political confrontation, is added to its previous and simultaneous existence as a guardian of "eternal" values and procedures, the very guidelines and storylines that the consumer has a taste for, has been led to expect. When a crisis of such dimensions as the Chilean one shakes the foundations of society, threatens to overturn and revolutionize prevailing conditions of power and property, the media tend to abandon their "neutrality." They divest themselves of the autonomy they normally need to operate without becoming suspect. At times such as these, the connection between culture and society becomes more manifest and can be laid bare. In this case, the permanent manipulation that has always been the invisible law behind *Mampato* is more effortlessly revealed, because the magazine itself has drifted—we cannot tell whether on purpose— into the arena of everyday conflict.

Our analysis of *Mampato* has an advantage over our preceding explorations: It has zeroed in on the specific, giddy moment in which a whole chain of mass-art production has been forced to adapt dynamically and change according to pressing challenges and requirements. This alteration under the stress of history is not unique. What Mampato performs with such urgent transparency is repeated constantly, almost mechanically, but on a different scale, in a different, slower rhythm, by other mass media products around the world. Each of them has been flexibly produced in a situation as solid, material, and full of uncertainties as the one that gave birth to Mampato, but because they were not responses to emergencies, their intricate, immediate relationship with society is not so easily uncovered. As if they were orphans set loose in the universe, nephews without a father, their origins have been lost, and it is an arduous, thankless, often impossible task to pinpoint and reconstruct the source from which they arose.

It is enough to understand, as we have done, I hope, the ways in which they link up with trends in society and forces in history, their inception in the prevalent ideological and cultural models. Our analysis of *Mampato,* however, affords us a vision of some of the richness we may be losing by not being able to ground these products in daily circumstances, where they could acquire added significance; and where, indeed, burrowing into the hidden turmoil of a period of social gestation, we might see how critical elements are dealt with as they emerge, and are answered by a system in unceasing evolution. Who does not dream of a "natural history" of cultural forms?

But just because the parenthood of Mampato's 1973 adventures is unquestionable, just because we have found out who his father really is (or is it only his stepfather?), does not mean that such an enterprise is, in itself, devoid of methodological risks. Even if we could operate in a similar fashion for each work we have studied, we would still have many pitfalls to hurdle. To prove, for instance, that the offensive of Mampato and his mutants is parallel to that of Allende's rivals, one must have established beforehand a periodization, stages in the attack, and a framework for the comprehension of Chile's recent history. Have we then discovered in the work only what we had already surreptitiously analyzed into it? Have we disintered only those structures that we wanted revealed in the first place?

Indeed, there are many who would not only reject my premises as absurd (children's literature has nothing to do with social issues, unless it is propaganda and intentional), but would also refuse to agree with the way in which I have dissected the struggles of the year 1973. A different viewpoint on that society might yield other results. Such an approach, an observer would assert, is not exclusive to *Mampato*. Indeed, it may be insinuated that it pervades the rest of the book: Mass fiction of this sort can be denounced as limiting people's capacity for understanding the world and transforming it, because the author has decided, before he began to write, that there was such an entity as a dominant system, and a manner in which it functioned and persuasively victimized its members. The conclusions of such a study would therefore be suspect, because they derive from a construction, an ideological position that leads the critic to detect, perhaps even to reconstruct, in the works he is researching a similar architectural configuration.

These sort of accusations hold enough truth to worry me. I feel that my observations on children's literature and on the childlike aspects of adult mass media production reveal the essence of their ultimate effects; but I also believe that I have not gone far enough into the complexities of the incestuous association between culture and society, nor have I taken sufficiently into account the fact that those who scrutinize these matters are themselves a product of what they are studying, occupy a mobile place both in history and in the field of knowledge. It is outside the range of this book—and, indeed, far from my current interests—to engage in an exploration of the sociology of culture, that elusive, all-encompassing scientist's apprentice. But that does not mean that I am unable to recognize that these methodological questions have implications for my conclusions and, in a perplexing manner, limit their impact.

I am also troubled by another aspect of this debate. By stating that the works I am studying are inimical to the freedom and humanity of those who read them, I am probably scaring off the very people I would like to reach. Although it is important to deepen the discussion with those who would concur with my belief that the present economic and political structures generate a culturally repressive situation, I would prefer to journey, as I stated in the first chapter, beyond the circle of the preconvinced and the already initiated. But, of course, to those who devour mass media products with all the innocence available to them, plucking specimens from the tree of fun, my reinterpretations of their reality from a radically diverse perspective will seem not only a disgusting and biased exercise but a threatening one. The only answer to this is that I am a historical subject, as much a product of history as Mampato or Babar or the *Reader's Digest* is. As much as the readers or nonreaders of these pages. As much as an author who would read these works from a supposedly neutral point of view, purely as archetypes, myths, entertainment, or psychoanalytical manifestations.

To recognize this condition, and make it part of the perspective from which we seek to comprehend our circumstances, to be wary of our own preconceptions and correct ourselves, is vital. There can be no retreat, however, from holding a position. For me, the only way in which it becomes possible to open the closed shutters of reality, the only way to break the idols and the icons and unlock their secrets, is to bring to them a view which is, in a sense, alien and blasphemous. To the general feeling of being an outsider, a rebel against the status quo, I add my coming from a continent which is in itself outside the mainstream of events. To be politically committed may affect the outcome of research, but it is also an instrument with which the surface placidity of things can be disrupted, whereby the object can reveal its innards, its skeleton, its truth.

There is, I think, no other way to advance our knowledge.

The case of *Mampato* shows us a breed of readers who lived history as it was sketched in a story, readers who acted as if reality were identical to what they were imagining through adventures in a faraway century. They were being subtly told that the death of Chilean democracy, the massacre of thousands, the denationalization of the economy, the assassination of the President, was in fact an epic struggle for justice and freedom. They did not even realize that they were being indoctrinated; because, just like millions all over the world who consume other mass media messages of less obvious origins, they cannot entertain the notion that their innocence, and that of their characters, is profoundly fraudulent.

If they were willing to risk the destruction of that innocence, they might be able to see that it is Mampato who helped plan the coup, Ogú who is pulling the trigger, Rena who is cleaning and absolving us all.

It would change them beyond their softest dreams.

But that, of course, would be another story.

Or do I mean another history?

SIX

CONCLUSION

> *"Ponce de León couldn't find the fountain of youth in Florida, so Walt Disney created it ten years ago. My congratulations on Walt Disney World's Tencentennial."*
>
> —Bob Hope

> *"If I could be someone else, I'd like to be Mickey Mouse because he never does anything wrong and he's loved by everyone."*
>
> —Mike Douglas

CHILDHOOD—or a certain perception of it—has dominated this book.

This should not strike us as strange. Many of the works we have looked at were originally meant for youngsters, even though afterwards their elders were included in that cheerful category of children-of-all-ages. Of course, along with this we have noted a tendency to infantilize the adult reader, to diminish the most complex dilemmas to simplified and simpleminded formulas. In fact, most of what we have been examining appears generally childish, in the specific sense that it uses its self-proclaimed innocence as a way of whitewashing—or is it rosewashing—the world.

It's no accident that this infantile core emerges time and again in these essays dealing with some of the major successes of mass media culture. It has been constantly observed that the cultural industry, tailored to answer the simultaneous needs of immense groups of people, levels off its messages at the so-called lowest common denominator, creating only that which everybody can understand effortlessly. This common denominator (as has also been pointed out frequently) is based on a construct of—what else?—the median, quintessential North American common man, who has undergone secular canonization as the universal measure for humanity. What has not been so clearly stated is this: When that man is reduced to his average, shaved of his adult faculties and conflicting experiences, handed solutions that suckle and comfort him, robbed of his future, what is left is a babe, a dwindled, decreased human being.

Perhaps it is inevitable that the consumer should be treated as an infant, helpless and demanding, in societies such as ours. As a member of a democratic system, he has the right to vote and the even more important right and obligation to consume; but at the same time he is not really participating in the determination of his future or that of the world. People can be treated as children because they do not, in effect, control their own destiny. Even if they feel themselves to be utterly free, they are objectively vulnerable and dependent, passive in a world commandeered by others, a world where the messages they swallow have originated in other people's minds.

Logically, the childishness of the media might be seen as having its source in this particular structure. Such an explanation, though interesting, is insufficient, for the procedure by which the spectator is dwarfed to an infantile status has another component. It is accompanied by a strategy intent on enhancing and rewarding this reduction. It cannot be a coincidence that Disney, the superheroes, and the *Digest* all propose to their readers, in one way or another, a rejuvenation of the tired adult world, the possibility of conserving some form of innocence as one grows up. Not only the characters, but those who absorb them, are offered a fountain of eternal youth, Ponce de León in a pill. This is not the idea that prevails, let us note, in the world of Babar. There the children are miniature adults who must be kept in their places and helped to tread, without nostalgia, the road to maturity with the least possible pain. This may be due in part to the fact that Babar was not intended to be a standardized weekly or monthly production on the assembly line. But the real reason seems to lie elsewhere. The adult-as-spoiled-child of Donald Duck, or the innocent-in-the-body-of-the-infinite-adult in Superman, or the reader-as-Adam-with-all-the-knowledge-of-Faust in the *Digest*—all complement and answer the needs of a subservient and passive consumer. They are also, significantly, all products of the United States of America, whose global pre-eminence—or should I say "coming of age"—has coincided with this century's technological leap in mass communication and left the U.S. in a very special position to use its media art to engender its most lasting and popular symbols. It is not simply a question of American economic power and know-how or the control of production and distribution by American multinationals. There is something else as well. The history of America, and the very particular sort of empire it became, seems to have allowed the process of the infantilization of the adult to be accompanied by images or intimations of innocence which were uniquely powerful and all its own. It may well be that such American images were reinforced by the magical, fairy-tale, ubiquitous quality of the media themselves, which could instantaneously transmit dreams and beliefs. The mass media added a new frontier, an unlimited, nonviolent one, to the prior unrelenting expansion of physical boundaries over a vast territory which could not be defended forever by its native inhabitants. Communication is a "peaceful" way of extending, reaching out to those planetary outposts where military interventions previously had been the preferred way of ensuring free trade.

America has been interpreted, time and again, as the domain of innocence. In a sense, a more extraordinary feat than changing thirteen colonies into a global empire in less than two centuries is that the U.S. managed to do it without its people losing their basic intuition that they were good, clean, and wholesome. Its citizens never recognized themselves as an empire, never felt bound by the responsibility (or the moral corruption) that comes with the exercise of so much power. Unlike the Spanish, the French, and the English, they did not create permanent institutions with a set of rules, regulations, and doctrines to deal with their possessions, and, because it was more a question of the marketplace than an occupation of territory, did not feel the need to do so. It was enough if trade was regulated and armed might was respected. The Americans wanted (and if William Appleman Williams is right, were almost doomed to want) the spoils of empire, but were not ready to assume the excruciating dilemmas that went with the knowledge of what they were imposing upon others. They desired the power which can only come from being large, aggressive, and overbearing; but simultaneously only felt comfortable if other people assented to the image they had of themselves as naive, frolicsome, unable to harm a mouse. Unlimited frontiers, abundance and plenty, the feeling of being reborn at every crossroads, led to the belief that growth and power need not relinquish, let alone destroy, innocence. Whatever obstructed or contradicted this vision was painted over by a curious sort of memory that reshaped the recent and receding past into myth as it moved. Conflicts could be cleaned up—by the brain if not by the body—before they became part of the future.

Americans felt themselves to be new and young, a country as recent as dawn, created by a break with the tyrannical past and the errors of yesteryear, by a revolutionary war that became a struggle for democracy, liberty, and a Bill of Rights. Along with this, of course, they, like all imperial peoples, upheld the concept of themselves as superior to, and certainly different from, the rest of humanity. Americans nurtured the belief that they were the last best hope for man, the saviors, the City on the Hill. But their dream of converting the heathen to the "true" way of life had a peculiar color to it, because they were inspired by the paradoxical certainty that they presented an example anyone could imitate as long as the whole world was turned into a marketplace. Deep inside, they believed alien cultures and lands were, or could be, identical to them. All those foreigners had to do was consume their products and they would become their exact mirror and equivalent.

If later on North Americans conceived of themselves as a "melting pot," they were animated from the beginning by the notion that the world could, in fact, be melted. Everybody and anybody could be renewed just as the United States had been. America imposed its experience of its own growth from anonymity in the wilderness onto the rest of humanity. If the world is a global village and we are all a family joined by tubes, wires, and voices; and moreover, if everybody is substantially an innocent, an unfinished, incomplete being waiting to unfold; then we can all evolve towards the same adulthood. We can become North Americans, unseparated by culture, interests, religions, creeds, races, ages. To become one, all we have to do is consume and dream the good dream.

It is this combination of infantilism and expansiveness, permitting Americans to view themselves as untainted children and the world as redeemable in their image, which may be the hidden fountain of much of America's mass media popularity. I am not denying the importance of production, ownership, art techniques, talent, marketing practices, the use of simpleminded success formulas. I only think it's also true that, due to its own self-image, its historic development and what it learned about humankind during that development, America was able to project a universal category—childhood—onto alien cultures that were subjected politically and economically, and to seek in them infantile echoes, the yearning for redemption, innocence, and eternal life that, to one degree or another, are part of the constitution of all human beings. American mass culture appealed to the child the audience would like to be, the child they remembered, the child they still felt themselves at times to be.

There may, in fact, be more than an economic, psychological, and social basis for this sort of success. In spite of resistance from national cultures and diverse subcultures which have rejected homogenization, in spite of overwhelming elite and intellectual criticism of these works of fiction, the infantilization that seems to be such an essential centerpiece of mass media culture may be grounded in a certain form of human nature that goes beyond historical circumstances. The way in which American mass culture reaches out to people may touch upon mechanisms embedded in our innermost being.

We are the only species, according to Stephen Jay Gould, that possesses neoteny.[1] Homo sapiens carries the features of the child into adult life. By doing so, it retains the evolutionary trend of primates, which led to our development. Other species change their faces radically, while humans conserve an amount of juvenility in them during their whole life-span. Gould notes that Mickey Mouse follows this law of nature in his own evolution on the drawing table. He began his career in the late 1920s as a mischievous rascal with snoutlike, disreputable, elongated adult features; but as he "became increasingly well behaved over the years, his appearance became more youthful. Measurements of three stages in his development revealed a larger relative head size, larger eyes, and an enlarged cranium—all traits of juvenility." Mickey was accepted in society, became an adult, an ambassador, a symbol to one and all, a logos in the sky, and did so in the measure that he visually progressed—or, to be accurate, retrogressed—into childhood characteristics. Obviously, this was not something decided by anybody in particular. As Gould points out, it was a process that took fifty years. The draftsmen themselves were probably unaware of it.

Mickey does nothing more than go the way of all North American mass culture. He joins power and infantilization, expands his influence and at the same time retain (or regains) ingenuousness, lords it over everybody, and lets an innocent smile disarm all criticism. The famous mouse, like the mass culture into which he was born, automatically reconciles the adult and the child by appealing to a biological attribute in us, the fact that humans are instinctually conditioned to protect their young and are prepared by nature to react well to anything that resembles juvenility. The mass media, as we have defined them, may use and abuse this sense of inner or moral neoteny of the species, if I can venture such bizarre terms, to ensure their development and domination. It may be that just as our faces carry the traits of a certain youthfulness forever, so our minds and hearts also, in whatever culture, may open up to that which addresses our most tender feelings for our progeny and for the future. Social domination can create the need, but it could be that we are ultimately manipulated because we accept with all credulity that story or situation which keeps and guards, burning beyond death, the child inside.

Did I write that? The child burning inside?

But what of another sort of child? The real child, at home, at school, in the streets, in bed waiting for a story, waking up in the morning ready for another story? What about him and her and them?

This book has been filled with childhood, but not with children.

It has tried to determine the adult values and hidden interests that shape and infect fiction for young readers. It has also explored the infantilization that the mass media seem to radiate onto adults. It has searched for the reasons why these forms are pernicious and why they are popular.

But it has not answered the basic question, a question that lingers.

Not: What is the relationship between ideology and entertainment? Not: How do empire and childhood go together? Not: What is the secret history of these forms?

Another question.

At the end of the *Diary of a Madman,* Gogol's protagonist screams, as his last warning to mankind and the audience, "Save the children."

That is the basic question.

How do we save the children?

It is a question that cannot be postponed, and yet I would have liked to avoid it. The opening of practical, immediate issues that have no easy answers threatens to spoil the unity of this book, and I've always been obsessed with the need for coherence, confident that each loose end may be fit into an overview that will dispel problems and present a context for gratifying explanations. Faced with such an omnipotent and tentacular adversary, there is no little comfort in the act of denunciation and analysis, the feeling that, by disclosing all these secrets, we have at least dealt the enemy a stunning intellectual blow.

But reality—may the *Reader's Digest* forgive me—is not a puzzle which carries with it the guarantee, before we buy it, that every last piece we need to complete our picture is in the box. There can be no certainty that once we have performed all the jigsaw operations the final product will look anything like the sunny panorama on the cover.

After I have written the essays, after the reader has read them, we are still left with the messy, sticky, hauntingly unconvincable world—the real one. We lift our eyes from the words upon words and the children are still there.

Quite frankly, I do not know what to do with them.

Just because I am able to dissect these works, just because I am persuaded that they are detrimental to our well-being, just because I have spent years trying to put them in a framework which makes their origins comprehensible, does not mean that I am any closer than other readers may be to solving the bewildering problems posed by their very existence.

It is good to admit this confusion. I have the right to be, the need to be, perplexed. This is not a superbook, a Junior Woodchucks

Manual, full of hints on how to do this or that. I refuse to consider my readers, or for that matter my children, as if they had to be saved by the sort of heroic act of wisdom on my part or that of their parents which would cast us in the role of the *Reader's Digest* or the Lone Ranger. Our young ones are at this very moment assimilating fiction which, under its pert and smiling guise, turns them into competitors, teaches them to see domination as the only alternative to subjection. They are learning sex roles; perverse and deformed visions of history; how to grow up, adapt, and succeed in the world as it presently is. They are learning not to ask questions.

The solution is neither to retire from the world, nor to prohibit those reading or viewing activities. I have never (I hope I haven't ever) forbidden any sort of cultural wares in our house. My children buy, and will probably continue to buy if they feel like it, the very same dreams that I have so vigorously denounced. In one sense, this is mere realism. What else can they do? Turn their backs on what are the prevalent channels for reality in these times? Feel isolated from what is popular, from the ways in which society has enacted its conflicts, the destruction of inner fears, the feelings of love, the survival of nightmares? Are they to transform themselves into little geniuses, critical at every step, uneasy with their own emotions and friends, unable to speak the language with which their peers communicate? Are they to be so critical of society that they will be unable to live within its limits and limitations? Are they to parrot views that have not sprung from their own experience, that are simply repeated to make their elders feel more comfortable, less corrupted by the world?

Are they to live their lives or ours?

We cannot treat the children, or the adults that were once children and are still dealt with by the media as if they were underage, as if they had been cannibalized, eaten up, devoured by the fiction they enjoy. The mere act of entering into contact with all these visions has not made them, has not made any of us, suspect forever or contaminated beyond relief.

People are never "lost," as the mass media would have us believe.

I once proclaimed—it was at the Russell Tribunal on Latin America in Rome and I was trying to impart the reasons why I thought the Chilean people had the means to defend their culture—that if the black magic of the television screen or the comic book is everywhere, invading every outlet of reality, there also persisted the white magic of people, waves made out of the capacity of thousands to renovate, rebel, criticize. Such a statement smacks today of oversimplification. The enemy is inside, and we find it hard to distinguish him from some of our innermost thoughts and nurturings. We have been produced by the same world that produced the *Digest*, Babar, Superman, Mampato, and Donald Duck. We have grown accustomed to the way in which they whisper to us, dawning in our eyes as a second nature does, a second and secondary humanity of which we only become aware when we try to change it. But that does not mean that my initial, oversimplified statement holds no value. Because people *are* everywhere, this is also true, and there is in them a decency, a humanness that is always on the verge of getting out of hand, a dangerous addiction to humor and sanity and—if I can rescue this word—common sense. There is in men and women a deep refusal to be manipulated. We have in ourselves intimations of another humanity, and from it we can build, we have been building since there has been memory.

We do not have to wait for tomorrow to launch this small, modest crusade.

Of course, if far-reaching and radical modifications were to occur in society and in art, the media as we know them now would be unrecognizable. More democratic societies would automatically limit or perhaps even cancel the sway that these pseudo-imaginings have upon us. People would not only be better able to control the sources of the power that generates what is being served to them and their children as entertainment, but also would find that the experience of being in command of their own existence shows up the dominant myths, makes them foreign and alien instead of familiar and comforting. If such a change in the social situation were accompanied, or anticipated, by changes in the ways of making art, there would also exist an alternative vision, created by teams and individuals in an elite or by millions elaborating their own participatory, multiple, plural counterimages. People who are aware of their identity, or have come to learn it in the process of growing out of the colors and habits defined for them by others, do not have to escape their grim circumstances through dreams; like that woman from the slums, they can dream reality.

But let us insist that such long-range alterations, such a blueprint for the future, the practicality and availability of which will depend on the real choices each person must make, do not have to be waited for. It is precisely in the prolonged, confused, stuttering attempt to reach that other humanity that we discover the means, the platform, the vision, the strength by which we can differentiate ourselves from what we have been assured we are by those who seek to control our beliefs and emotions.

In a sense, every action we take each day can be of assistance on the long road towards the transformation of those dominant messages. The very way in which we live our lives, in which we judge, or love, or pardon, or understand, or stand up for what we believe in, the ways in which we try to model our own private worlds, can introduce, for the receptive child and anybody else, in the damnable middle of our web of tangled visions, a different, defiant point of view. This sort of influence may encourage more independence than directing solemn attention, through intellectual arguments, to each trick or pitfall in mass media culture. The very popularity, the very innocence that such entertainment has fostered, representing itself as a fun-filled and secluded oasis, far from the everyday swamps of boredom, makes all raids seem a form of proselytizing or propaganda. This does not mean that we must renounce our right to read along with our children. Anybody can break into the closed bunkers and place the seeds of doubt, laughter, justice, rage. We can return to the accumulated treasures of our species, the artistic wonders that stir mysteries and crack conformism. And just in case anybody is suggesting that I am against the use of reason, certain structures can be gently pointed out; they can be countered; they can be brought into the open and discussed.

But above all, and without blushing, without sounding like one of the products I have been analyzing, I say we must have faith in our children. They have to be able—with the challenge of our assistance, with our respect for the pain it entails, with our own fuzzy limits between what is true and what is false, with the mutual patience that comes from building together a future for which no insurance policy can be bought—stubbornly to reinterpret reality.

We have told many stories in this book.

Most of them have not been to our liking.

Maybe there is time, before we finish, for one more. It comes from the Greeks and advises us, thousands of years after it was first conceived, on how to slay monsters.

Because the dominant media and their fictions are somewhat like the Medusa that Perseus had to destroy. The Medusa had once been a wondrous maiden, but the gods had made her so hideous that she could turn into stone anyone who looked her in the face.

To kill her, remember, you must not look her in the eyes. She will convince you to chain yourself to her body, convert your heart to rock and your mind to sand. But also remember that you cannot be rid of her if you are not prepared to see her, to guide the sword hand with the eyes. If you live outside her scope and the influence of her overwhelming enchantment and horror, of "the loveliness like a shadow" that Shelley gave her in his verse, you will certainly fail.

You cannot kill her if you look; and if you do not look, you will not kill her.

Perseus solved this riddle by watching the monster's reflection in the shield that Athena, the goddess of wisdom, had conferred on him. Then he cut off the Gorgon's head.

We also have shields which can be used as mirrors.

Reflect the head in the mirror; accept and understand it; cut it off. Carry it with you all your life, because even after death the Medusa can still exercise that frightening power. Your actions and the art you enjoy can be mirrors; your children, your loves, your friends, your causes are mirrors which allow you to see the head obliquely, with your back turned, fully within the hissing breath, advancing crablike so as not to be destroyed.

I hope, in fact, that this book could be used as one of our mirrors, a fragment of glass to help us on our way.

But this is not the only story.

For what is a tale in a book like this one without children, without descendants? . . . Many years later, decades later, the great-grand-son of Perseus was born. His name was Hercules. One of his specialities seems to have been slaughtering monsters.

The second of the twelve tasks he was commanded to perform was to kill the Hydra, a colossal serpent with nine heads, the middle one of which was immortal.

It was deemed impossible.

Each time he clubbed one of the heads, two more grew in its place. Assisted, however, by his nephew Iolaus (I hope the Disney corporation is satisfied that we have somehow managed to smuggle a nephew into this legend), he was able to burn all the heads but one with a red-hot sword. That final, immortal one was cut off and buried under a rock.

So this is a story in which we use our mirrors today and in which our children's children draw their swords tomorrow.

It is a story that should alarm us. The struggle that is offered is almost endless, and not easy. Heads multiply and bloom forth. To attack them is to help them gain strength. Even after they have been cut off, they continue to harden people and make them weary. And there is something in the monster that will not die, that will threaten underfoot no matter how deeply it is buried.

But listen. Listen closely.

Is there any place in that story where it is said that the heads of the monster are infinite? Is there any place where it says that the monster is invincible?

NOTES

Chapter 2: Of Elephants and Ducks

1. See Maurice Sendak's Introduction to *Babar's Anniversary Album,* by Jean and Laurent de Brunhoff (New York: Random House, 1981). The back cover also has a short introductory note by A. A. Milne.

2. A view of the world as having been written, as a sort of scripture, in Michel Foucault, *The Order of Things* (New York: Pantheon Books, 1971). The impact of books (and other means of communication) on nations and tribes that still live in an oral stage of history, in—among others—the section "The World Turned Upside Down," in Edmund Carpenter's *Oh, What a Blow that Phantom Gave Me!* (New York: Holt, Rinehart & Winston, 1972).

3. All the quotations, up till now, have been taken from that first book, *Babar the Elephant* (New York: Random House, 1937). I have preferred this form of reference in order not to burden the text with footnotes. I'll use the same method for each book.

4. Stith Thompson, *Motif Index of Folk Literature* (Bloomington: Indiana University Press, 1955), 6 vols., and Marc Soriano, *Les Contes de Perrault: culture savante et traditions populaires* (Paris: Gallimard, 1968).

5. Bruno Bettelheim, *The Uses of Enchantment: The Meaning and Importance of Fairy Tales* (New York: Vintage Books, 1977), especially the introduction, "The Struggle for Meaning," pp. 3–19.

6. Richard Schickel's *The Disney Version: The Life, Times, Art and Commerce of Walt Disney* (New York: Simon & Schuster, 1968), gives us a brilliant analysis of this general attitude. After having examined the way in which Disney adapted folklore and infantile books, a process which he calls "disneyfication," Schickel notes how such conduct is connected to a vision of foreign lands: "He came always as a conqueror, never as a servant. It is a trait, as many have observed, that many Americans share when they venture into foreign lands hoping to do good but equipped only with knowhow instead of sympathy and respect for alien traditions" (p. 277).

7. See David Kunzle's introduction to Ariel Dorfman and Armand Mattelart, *How to Read Donald Duck: Imperialist Ideology in the Disney Comic* (London: International General, 1975).

8. See Marcia Blitz's, *Donald Duck* (New York: Harmony Books, 1979).

9. "The myth, therefore, does not give meaning to an object which before the myth lacked it; on the contrary, it takes as its point of departure the signs which compose social reality and *superimposes* upon them a second meaning. . . . This second, 'superimposed' meaning is presented in the myth as the only one and makes the other disappear or, if you will, 'hides' it." Eliseo Verón, *Conducta, estructura y comunicación* (Buenos Aires: Jorge Alvárez, 1967), p. 26.

10. Roland Barthes, *Writing Degree Zero* (New York: Hill & Wang, 1977).

11. It is interesting to observe that in Disney's film adaptation of *Bambi* the mother's death is accepted, closely following Felix Salten's original book. But this circumstance, which could be due to its production in the midst of the Nazi menace and may represent a belated expression of the psychic defenselessness of the thirties, is ignored as soon as the story of the young deer is transcribed into comic strips. The period preceding the tragedy is depicted there as if the happiness that was taken from Bambi in the movie could be joyfully resurrected later.

12. Schickel, *The Disney Version.*

13. Statements by Disney to *Parade*, "How Disney Sells Happiness," March 26, 1972; quoted by Michael R. Real, *Mass-Mediated Culture* (Englewood Cliffs, N.J.: Prentice-Hall, 1977).

14. I consulted this comic strip in Chile in 1970. It was taken from the magazine *Disneylandia* #430.

15. Magazine *Disneylandia* #432, published in Chile. (In Mike Barrier's bibliography, the North American equivalent is *Donald Duck* #9, published in 1965.)

16. Wolfgang Kayser, "Origen y crisis de la novela moderna," *Mapocho*, año II, t. III, n. 3, vol. 9. pp. 58–80.

17. Gaston Bachelard, *El aire y los sueños: Ensayo sobre la imaginación del movimiento* (Mexico City: Fondo de Cultura, 1958).

18. See Ian Watt, "Robinson Crusoe as a Myth," in *Eighteenth Century English Literature* (New York: Oxford University Press, 1959), pp. 158–79.

19. See Marx's famous description in his first book of *Capital*.

20. The reader should consult the extraordinary essay *Calibán* by the Cuban Roberto Fernández Retamar, Cuadernos de Arte y Sociedad (Havana: Editorial Arte y Literatura, 1979).

21. The most remarkable examples are Jorge de Montemayor's *La Diana*; Shakespeare's pastoral comedies; Lope de Vega's dramas; Sannazaro's *Arcadia*; and Honoré d'Urfé's *Astrée*.

22. See Donald Bogle, *Toms, Coons, Mulattoes, Mamies and Bucks* (New York: Viking Press, 1973).

23. Bettelheim, *Uses of Enchantment*, especially p. 57.

24. Dorfman and Mattelart, *How to Read Donald Duck*.

25. "The sexless sexiness." The phrase was coined by James Agee, criticizing Disney's *Victory Through Air Power* in *The Nation*. Quoted by Schickel, *The Disney Version*, p. 275.

26. Bettina Hürliman, *Three Centuries of Children's Books in Europe* (Cleveland: World Publishing Co., 1968), p. 181.

27. Basil Davidson, *The Search for a New Society: Which Way Africa?* (New York: Penguin Books, 1964), and by the same author, "What's Wrong with Africa?," in *International Socialist Journal* (Milan), 1, n. 4 (August 1964).

28. Davidson, *Search for a New Society*, p. 482.

29. "From the newly constituted League of Nations they accepted the duty of governing them [the African countries] as a 'sacred trust of civilization' until such time as they were able to stand on their own feet in the arduous conditions of the modern world." Roland Oliver and J. D. Fage, eds., *A Short History of Africa* (New York: Penguin Books, 1962), p. 210.

30. W. W. Rostow, *The Stages of Economic Growth: A Non-Communist Manifesto* (London: Cambridge University Press, 1960).

31. See Lincoln Gordon's comments in the anthology, *Latin American Issues, Essays and Comments*, Albert O. Hirschman (New York; The Twentieth Century Fund, 1961), p. 66.

32. At any rate, the prophet Gordon did not abandon his language resonant with family connections. As U.S. ambassador in Brasil he watched, not to use another word, the destruction of democracy in that country in 1964. The name of the American operation? "Brother Sam." Things remain, as usual, all in the family. In fact, from October 1980 to April 1982, he was a member of the CIA's Senior Review Panel. As of April 1982, he was made a National Intelligence Officer at the National Intelligence Council.

33. Geoffrey Barraclough, "The Haves and Have-Nots," *New York Review of Books*, May 13, 1977, quoted in Orlando Letelier and Michael Moffitt, *The International Economic Order, Part I* (Washington: Transnational Institute, 1977).

34. If interested in this situation, consult Samir Amin, "Growth Is Not Development," *Development Forum* (April 1973).

35. See Paulo Freire's *Pedagogy of the Oppressed* (New York: Herder & Herder, 1972).

36. The best analysis I have found on *Disneyland* is in Michael R. Real, *Mass-Mediated Culture*, in his chapter "The Disney Universe: Morality Play," pp. 46–89.

37. *Babar's Castle*, 1962.

38. Frantz Fanon, *Black Skin, White Masks* (New York: Grove Press, 1967), p. 18.

39. Posthumously published in 1940, first in England and only afterwards in France.

40. *Babar et le Professeur Grifaton* (1956), *Babar and the Professor* (1957).

41. See Louis A. Pérez, Jr., "Underdevelopment and Dependency: The Colonial Concept of Tourism," in *Communication and Class Struggle,* vol. 1: *Capitalism, Imperialism,* edited by Armand Mattelart and Seth Sieglaub (New York: International General, 1979), pp. 339–45.

42. Let us notice that this name is similar to the French *barbare*: the elephant as a quasi or incomplete barbarian, a barbarian who lacks the letter *r*.

43. Hürliman, *Three Centuries of Children's Books,* p. 198, on the figure of the Old Lady.

44. See Sendak's already mentioned "Homage to Babar on His 50th Birthday" and the "Picture Story" which accompanies it by Laurent de Brunhoff.

45. *Les Vacances de Zephir,* 1937. Originally translated into English as *Zephir's Holidays,* its title was later changed, perhaps for commercial reasons, to *Babar and Zephir.*

46. *Babar and His Children,* 1937.

47. It is my guess that such a method is already influenced by Sunday-paper serialization, but I have no way of finding out if this is true.

48. Alec Ellis, *A History of Children's Reading and Literature* (Elmsford, N.Y.: Pergamon Press, 1968).

49. Dallas Smythe, "Time, Market and Space Factors in Communication Economics," *Journalism Quarterly* (Winter 1962).

50. *Babar's Mystery,* 1978.

51. *Babar and the Wully-Wully,* 1975.

52. *Babar Loses His Crown* (1967), *Babar's Visit to Bird Island* (1952), and *Babar Visits Another Planet* (1972).

53. *Babar Learns to Cook* (1978) and *Babar and the Ghost* (1981).

54. Martha Wolfenstein, "French Parents Take Their Children to the Park," in *Childhood in Contemporary Cultures,* ed. Margaret Mead and Martha Wolfenstein (Chicago: University of Chicago Press, 1955), pp. 115–16.

55. Published in *Revista Disneylandia* #434 in 1970 in Chile.

56. See Albert Cook's *The Dark Voyage and the Golden Mean* (New York: W. W. Norton, 1966).

57. *How to Read Donald Duck,* p. 35.

58. Les Daniels, *Comix: A History of Comic Books in America* (New York: Outerbridge & Dienstfrey, 1971).

Chapter 3: The Lone Ranger's Last Ride

1. Quoted from a publication by the agency which produced the Lone Ranger for radio in the fifties, called *The Lone Ranger: Standards and*

Background, parts of which are reproduced in an unpublished doctoral dissertation of David Wilson Parker, "A Descriptive Analysis of the Lone Ranger as a Form of Popular Art" (Northwestern University, 1956), p. 212.

2. Parker, "Descriptive Analysis of the Lone Ranger," p. 213.

3. *Ibid.,* p. 200.

4. Jenni Calder, *There Must Be a Lone Ranger: The Myth and Reality of the American Wild West* (London: Abacus, 1974), especially Chapter 5, "Home on the Range."

5. James Ridgeway, *The Politics of Ecology* (New York: E. P. Dutton, 1971), p. 41.

6. See Barbara Ward, *The Home of Man* (New York: W. W. Norton, 1976).

7. Ridgeway, *Politics of Ecology,* pp. 15–16.

8. Laurent de Brunhoff, *Babar and the Wully-Wully* (New York: Random House, 1975).

9. See the aforementioned book by Calder, and also Will Wright's *Six-Guns and Society: A Structural Study of the Western* (Berkeley: University of California Press, 1975).

10. See William Appleman Williams, *Empire as a Way of Life* (New York: Oxford University Press, 1980).

11. Fran Striker, *The Lone Ranger in Wild Horse Valley* (New York: Grosset & Dunlap, 1950), p. 9.

12. *El Llanero Solitario: Historia de un Rural de Texas* (Barcelona: Editorial Fher, 1967), pp. 48–49. I have been unable to find—even in the Library of Congress—the original English-language version of this book.

13. Striker, *The Lone Ranger in Wild Horse Valley,* p. 19.

14. Lukacs discovers in this absence of an active subject the reasons why, in society, "an illusion can be fostered that the 'laws of the economy' can solve the system's crisis just as they led to them." *Historia y Conciencia de Clase* (Mexico City: Grijalbo, 1969), p. 256; *History and Class Consciousness* (Cambridge, Mass.: MIT Press, 1971).

15. Umberto Eco, *Socialismo y Consolación* (Barcelona: Ediciones Tusquets, 1970).

16. Parker, "Descriptive Analysis of the Lone Ranger," p. 137.

17. John T. Galloway, *The Gospel According to Superman* (Philadelphia: A. J. Holman, 1973). The first quote is from p. 93, the second from pp. 54–55.

18. R. Barthes, *Mythologies* (New York: Hill & Wang, 1972).

19. The creator of the Lone Ranger thus anticipates the Comics Code of the fifties. Eco, *Apocalípticos e Integrados ante una Sociedad de Masas* (Barcelona: Lumen, 1968), notes something similar in Batman, Green Arrow, and Superman. It is a trend which slowly asserted itself, in any case, because it was not definite at the beginning. According to Martin Williams, in *A Smithsonian Book of Comic-Book Comics,* ed. Michael Barrier and

Martin Williams (New York: Smithsonian Institution Press and Harry N. Abrams, 1982), Batman in his first adventures killed the criminals without handing them over to the police.

20. *El Llanero Solitario,* p. 33.

21. *Ibid.,* p. 29.

22. *The Legend of the Lone Ranger Storybook* (New York: Random House, 1981).

23. The agency, *The Origin and Development of the Lone Ranger,* quoted in Parker, "Descriptive Analysis of the Lone Ranger," p. 135.

24. Quoted in Parker, "Descriptive Analysis."

25. Fran Striker, *The Lone Ranger* (New York: Grosset & Dunlap, 1936), p. 2.

26. Fran Striker, *The Lone Ranger in Wild Horse Valley,* p. 101.

27. Calder, *There Must Be a Lone Ranger,* p. 188.

28. Wright, *Six-Guns and Society.*

29. Otto Rank, *The Myth of the Birth of the Hero and Other Essays,* ed. Philip Freund (New York: Vintage Books, 1959).

30. Mary E. Bickle, *George W. Trendle: An Authorized Biography* (New York: Exposition Press, 1971).

31. See "Dissociation in a Hero: Superman and the Divided Self," in Arthur Asa Berger, *The Comic-Stripped American* (New York: Walker & Co., 1973).

32. E. Nelson Bridewell, in his Introduction to *Superman: From the Thirties to the Seventies* (New York: Crown Publishers, 1971), p. 10.

33. John G. Cawelti, *The Six-Gun Mystique* (Bowling Green, Ohio: Bowling Green Press, 1971). Also, for the relationship established between private and public law, André Bazin, *What Is Cinema?* (Berkeley: University of California Press, 1971).

34. See Oscar Masotta's *La historieta en el mundo moderno* (Buenos Aires: Paidós, 1970), pp. 89–91.

35. It is as if Gramsci had had the Lone Ranger in mind when he wrote: "The State is conceived, of course, as an organism which belongs to a group, and destined to create conditions favorable for that group's greatest expansion; but this development and expansion are conceived and presented as the driving force behind a universal expansion, a development of all 'national' energies; in other words the governing group concretely aligns itself with the general interests of subordinate groups and the life of the State is conceived as a continuous formation and surmounting of the unstable balances (unstable in terms of the law) between the interests of the fundamental group and those of the subordinate groups, balances in which the interests of the dominant group predominate, but only to a certain point, i.e., not as far as their petty economic-corporate interests would like."

Antonio Gramsci, *The Modern Prince and Other Writings* (New York: International Publishers, 1957), p. 170.

36. James Steranko, *History of Comics* (Reading, Pa.: Supergraphics, 1970). It is interesting to note that it was also in 1932 that Jerry Siegel conceived Superman as a character, although it was only in 1938 that he could appear, not as a *comic strip* but in a *comic book*. See his interview given to John Kobler, "Up, Up and Aw-a-y! The Rise of Superman, Inc.," in *The Saturday Evening Post,* June 21, 1941.

37. The phrase belongs to Alfred Kazin, in *On Native Grounds* (New York: Harcourt Brace Jovanovich, 1970; 1st ed. 1942), p. 366.

38. Gramsci relates the detective novel and the popular dime novels of the day to nineteenth-century man's increasing alienation in his rat-race routines: "In other words, with the excessive precariousness of existence, joined to the conviction that no individual defence can be presented against that precariousness. . . . That is why people aspire to a 'beautiful' and interesting adventure based on individual initiative, marking a difference with the 'ugly' and degrading adventure which others impose upon us." Antonio Gramsci, *Cultura y Literatura* (Madrid: Ediciones Peninsula, 1967).

39. This was Hoover's attitude at the beginning of the depression. "Economic depression . . . cannot be cured by legislative action or executive pronouncement. Economic wounds must be healed by the action of the cells of the economic body—the producers and consumers themselves." Quoted in Frederick Lewis Allen, *Since Yesterday, 1929–1939* (New York: Bantam Books, 1965), p. 29.

40. Karl Polanyi, *The Great Transformation* (Boston: Beacon Press, 1965).

41. Paul Sweezy, *The Theory of Capitalist Development* (New York: Oxford University Press, 1942), p. 317.

42. Frederick Lewis Allen, *The Big Change: America Transforms Itself, 1900–1950* (New York: Harper & Brothers, 1952), p. 150.

43. Ernest Mandel, *Iniciación a la teoría económica marxista*, 2nd ed. (Bogotá: La Oveja Negra, 1971), p. 74.

44. See the subchapter "From Little Caesar to Citizen Kane," in Richard H. Pell, *Radical Visions and American Dreams: Culture and Social Thought in the Depression Years* (New York: Harper & Row, 1974).

45. Trendle, according to Bickle's book, was an enthusiast of Horatio Alger.

46. Jeremy Tunstall, *The Media Are American* (New York: Columbia University Press, 1977), p. 84.

47. Allen, *Since Yesterday*, p. 34.

48. It is worth insisting that this trait is not exclusive to the Lone Ranger. In Trendle's radio series *Sergeant Preston of the Yukon,* the dog Yukon King is just like Silver. The sergeant says to his savage dog, after having rescued him from the wild steppes: "I'll teach you to respect good men and to hate evil ones. Your instinct will show you the difference. . . . I'll

show you how to practice self-control and how best to use your great strength" (Bickle, *George W. Trendle,* p. 137). So when these natural beings save their masters over and over again, they do it in the name of their instincts, which have, of course, been previously socialized as something positive.

49. One of the Ranger's objectives, according to the agency, was to "teach Americanism around the world" (quoted in Parker, "Descriptive Analysis," p. 210.) And in another publication, "Teaching Democracy Through Adventure Stories," they suggest that "in many senses, the Lone Ranger has taught the real meaning of the word Democracy" (quoted in Parker, p. 185).

50. In the anthology *Superman: From the Thirties to the Seventies,* p. 49.

51. Les Daniels, *Comix,* p. 2.

52. This is not the sole change. In general, a comparison of this abbreviated version (*Babar's Anniversary Album* [New York: Random House, 1981]) with the original (*The Travels of Babar* [New York: Random House, 1938]) shows that the newest one tends to sweeten Babar up, discarding episodes of violence or betrayal. A whale that abandons them on a rock in the middle of the sea in the original book does not appear in such a cruel light in the anniversary volume. The death of the King of the Elephants or the threats of the rhinoceroses against Arthur have also been omitted.

53. "What makes the apparent contradictions [between the characters in Superman] work cohesively, is Superman's sense of humor, which was to be emphasised more and more as his career progressed." Les Daniels, *Comix,* p. 12.

54. Donald F. Glut and Jim Hamon, *The Greatest Television Heroes* (Garden City, N.Y.: Doubleday, 1975), p. 34. Also Jules Feiffer, *The Great Comic Book Heroes* (New York: Dial Press, 1965).

55. See especially the chapter "Groups and Techniques: The Professional Plot," in the aforementioned book.

56. Godfrey Hodgson, *America in Our Time* (New York: Vintage Books, 1976), p. 15.

57. Alan Wolfe, *America's Impasse: The Rise and Fall of the Politics of Growth* (New York: Pantheon, 1981).

58. Jonathan Schell, *The Time of Illusion* (New York: Alfred A. Knopf, 1976).

59. Marcus Raskin, "The Kennedy Hawks Assume Power from the Eisenhower Vultures," in *The Pentagon Watchers (Students Report on the National Security State),* ed. Leonard S. Rodberg and Derek Shearer (Garden City, N.Y.: Doubleday, 1970), p. 72.

60. Hodgson, *America in Our Time,* p. 494.

61. Even in a western like the Lone Ranger, this is true. In one of the episodes studied, "The Crystal Ball," our hero is faced with beings who

seem omniscient, because they have the ability to foretell the places where crime will strike. But the Ranger's capacity for generating ideas is greater than his rivals'. A trick traps them and shows them up. The representative of the common man can enjoy the power that science gives without its defects or dangers.

62. Engels-Marx, *La Sagrada Familia* (The Holy Family) (Mexico City: Grijalbo, 1967), p. 267.

63. Quoted in Parker, "Descriptive Analysis," p. 175. It is also interesting to note, according to a poll mentioned by the same author (p. 202), that black kids tend to identify more with Tonto than with the Ranger.

64. Bickle, *George W. Trendle*, p. 124.

Chapter 4: The Infantilization of the Adult Reader

1. "Articles manuscripts are returned to the *Digest* editors with every fact isolated, noted, underlined, and approved or disapproved." James P. Wood, *Of Lasting Interest: The Story of Reader's Digest* (Garden City, N.Y.: Doubleday, 1967), p. 85.

2. *Ibid.*, pp. 213–14.

3. *Ibid.*, p. 215.

4. *Ibid.*, p. 15.

5. See Panofsky's ideas about "compartmentalization" during the Renaissance.

6. Wood, *Of Lasting Interest*, p. 20.

7. See Balibar's ideas on feudalism in Louis Althusser, *For Marx* (New York: Schocken Books, 1979).

8. Hyram Hayden, *The Counter-Renaissance* (New York: Grove Press, 1964).

9. I cannot refrain from letting loose here a literary allusion: it is like a democratic parody of the infinite and artistocratic Library of Babel of which Jorge Luis Borges speaks in his *Ficciones* (New York: Grove Press, 1962).

10. Wood, *Of Lasting Interest*, p. 138.

11. "The transformation of the *Reader's Digest* into something more than a digest began in the early thirties." John Bainbridge, *Little Wonder, or The Reader's Digest and How it Grew* (New York: Reynal & Hitchcock, 1946), p. 54.

12. Wood, as faithful an apologist for the *Digest* you can find, believes that this constitutes "a two-way communication": "Here a man or a woman can participate in the creation of the magazine. He can talk about himself and

can tell someone besides his wife, husband or neighbors of the funniest thing in the world that he just saw or heard or did."

13. Something similar happens with the author. In the last years, and this is one of the only alterations that can be observed, and may be due to DeWitt Wallace's retirement, there has been a trend towards including a wider variety of writers in the magazine, some of whom are not that typical: Ray Bradbury, Jorge Amado, Woody Allen. But just as those lives that comfort us are selected, or the aspects in those lives that confirm that comfort, so it is that out of the multiplicity of the writers' works, only those that flow along with the *Digest*'s philosophy have been chosen. Amado appears in his more picturesque side ("Bahía My Love," May 1981), Bradbury with a story that proves that "if I depend on my own effort, I'll be successful" ("The Magic Slippers," September 1981), and Woody Allen gives his incomparable humor without a contemporary barb being visible ("A Sandwich According to Woody Allen," May 1981).

14. Schickel (*The Disney Version*, pp. 283–94) makes a critical examination of the way in which Disney reduced animal lives to his own fantasy.

15. Samuel A. Schreiner, Jr., *The Condensed World of the Reader's Digest* (New York: Stein & Day, 1977), p. 71.

16. *Ibid.*, p. 72.

17. Bainbridge, *Little Wonder*, p. 3.

18. Schreiner, *Condensed World of the Reader's Digest*.

19. *Ibid.*, pp. 196–97.

20. According to Schreiner, Max Eastman initiated this policy in his July 1943 article, "We Must Face the Facts about Russia."

21. Bainbridge, *Little Wonder*. And he adds: "The article contains nothing that cannot be grasped readily by a high-school student of average ability. There are no hard words. There are no difficult ideas."

22. Wood, *Of Lasting Interest*, p. 266. The same author quotes Mary Martin: "The *Reader's Digest* is more like a personal friend than an impersonal product of paper and ink . . . a friend bringing new interests, exciting discoveries and refreshing mental experience into all our lives."

23. A phrase from "Love and Adventures of Goethe," April 1980. The *Digest* adds, about Faust, maybe in order not to cause disquiet among its readers on such subjects as knowledge and its limits: "Just as in life, [*Faust*] has blurry passages and its meaning is not always clear. 'They ask me what *Faust* deals with. As if I knew!' the author used to protest."

24. "The secret stream" is the title of an article on nature in the April 1980 number. "Father and son had shared a place whose enchantment they wished could last forever" is the subtitle.

Chapter 5: The Innocents March into History
. . . and Overthrow a Government

1. For that ideological offensive, see the anthology *Cultura y Comunicación de Masas: Materiales de la discusión chilena, 1970–1973*, ed. M. A. Garretón and H. Valdés (Barcelona: Laia, 1975). Also, F. Castillo, J. Larraín, and R. Echeverría, "Etapas y perspectivas de la lucha ideológica en Chile," *Cuadernos de la Realidad Nacional*, no. 13 (July 1972), Santiago, Universidad Católica de Chile, pp. 114–52. For the year 1973, some of my journalistic articles, collected later in *Ensayos Quemados in Chile: Inocencia y Neo-colonialismo*, analyzed this offensive, especially looking at the main right-wing newspaper *El Mercurio*'s version of the events.

2. Just one further example will do. Incipient forms of popular power had emerged in Chile, among them, the *cordones industriales*, which were groupings of workers, on a regional basis, surrounding the Santiago metropolitan area. The left threatened to unleash the workers, and the right feared that this was not an idle threat. The Anthroposaurus, a hidden terror about to attack, is just that fear made specific.

3. See Fred S. Landis, *Psychological Warfare and Media Operations in Chile, 1970–1973*, mimeo (Washington, 1975). For *El Mercurio* and the Chilean oligopoly, see Ricardo Lagos, *La concentración del poder económico* (Santiago, 1969). Also Peter Schenkel, "La estructura de poder de los medios de comunicación en cinco países latinoamericanos," in *Comunicación y Cambio Social*, ed. Peter Schenkel and Marco Ordóñez (Quito: ILDES-CEPAL, 1975), pp. 13–56.

4. On the limits of the "conspiracy" theory in the mass media, and the way in which manipulation works, see Herb Schiller's masterful *The Mind Managers* (Boston: Beacon Press, 1973).

5. A recent study of the work of Eugène Sue shows how popular works by an author are not allowed to change their meaning and thrust: "If the bourgeoisie has not produced more true (*véritables*) popular novels, it is not only because, in order to be authentic, such literature must come from the people, but because, when works of this nature do appear, *the whole system gears into motion to prevent its dissemination and to paralyze its action*" (René Guise, Marcel Graner, Liliane Durand-Dessert, "Des *Mystères de Paris* aux *Mystères du Peuple*," in *Europe* [Paris], March–April 1977, p. 167; my italics, my translation from the French).

Conclusion

1. See "A Biological Homage to Mickey Mouse" in Stephen Jay Gould, *The Panda's Thumb: More Reflections on Natural History* (New York: W. W. Norton, 1980).

ACKNOWLEDGMENTS

All books are brought into being by more persons than the author. This is particularly so in this case. To rewrite previous material, while in exile, in a complicated financial situation, is not—as I have said in the first chapter—easy. Rather than enumerate all those who helped me, either with small suggestions or big company when things became difficult, I wish to single out the three persons who were essential in helping me to finish the book. One, of course, is my wife, María Angélica, who is such a part of my process of creation that she should be listed as a co-author in everything I do. The second is my friend and agent, Tom Colchie, who gave me support and enthusiasm when I most needed it. And finally, there is my editor, Tom Engelhardt, who worked over the manuscript with a painstaking care I had never before encountered, forcing me by his obstinately intelligent remarks to clarify issues, sharpen ideas, rewrite long paragraphs and—no mean task—bridge the communication gap between two cultures and two languages.

FOR THE BEST IN PAPERBACKS, LOOK FOR THE

In every corner of the world, on every subject under the sun, Penguin represents quality and variety—the very best in publishing today.

For complete information about books available from Penguin—including Puffins, Penguin Classics, and Arkana—and how to order them, write to us at the appropriate address below. Please note that for copyright reasons the selection of books varies from country to country.

In the United Kingdom: Please write to *Dept. JC, Penguin Books Ltd, FREEPOST, West Drayton, Middlesex UB7 0BR*.

If you have any difficulty in obtaining a title, please send your order with the correct money, plus ten percent for postage and packaging, to *P.O. Box No. 11, West Drayton, Middlesex UB7 0BR*

In the United States: Please write to *Consumer Sales, Penguin USA, P.O. Box 999, Dept. 17109, Bergenfield, New Jersey 07621-0120.* VISA and MasterCard holders call 1-800-253-6476 to order all Penguin titles

In Canada: Please write to *Penguin Books Canada Ltd, 10 Alcorn Avenue, Suite 300, Toronto, Ontario M4V 3B2*

In Australia: Please write to *Penguin Books Australia Ltd, P.O. Box 257, Ringwood, Victoria 3134*

In New Zealand: Please write to *Penguin Books (NZ) Ltd, Private Bag 102902, North Shore Mail Centre, Auckland 10*

In India: Please write to *Penguin Books India Pvt Ltd, 706 Eros Apartments, 56 Nehru Place, New Delhi 110 019*

In the Netherlands: Please write to *Penguin Books Netherlands bv, Postbus 3507, NL-1001 AH Amsterdam*

In Germany: Please write to *Penguin Books Deutschland GmbH, Metzlerstrasse 26, 60594 Frankfurt am Main*

In Spain: Please write to *Penguin Books S. A., Bravo Murillo 19, 1° B, 28015 Madrid*

In Italy: Please write to *Penguin Italia s.r.l., Via Felice Casati 20, I-20124 Milano*

In France: Please write to *Penguin France S. A., 17 rue Lejeune, F–31000 Toulouse*

In Japan: Please write to *Penguin Books Japan, Ishikiribashi Building, 2–5–4, Suido, Bunkyo-ku, Tokyo 112*

In Greece: Please write to *Penguin Hellas Ltd, Dimocritou 3, GR–106 71 Athens*

In South Africa: Please write to *Longman Penguin Southern Africa (Pty) Ltd, Private Bag X08, Bertsham 2013*